notes from LITTLE LAKES

BY MEL ELLIS

notes from LITTLE LAKES

BY MEL ELLIS

The story of a family and fifteen acres.

Illustrated by Suzanne Ellis
Edited by Ted J. Rulseh

The Cabin Bookshelf

1234 Hickory Drive • Waukesha, WI 53186

NOTES FROM LITTLE LAKES
by Mel Ellis
edited by Ted J. Rulseh.
Foreword by Don Johnson.

Notes from Little Lakes
© 1996 by Mel Ellis

The Cabin Bookshelf
1234 Hickory Drive
Waukesha, WI 53186

Cover painting and illustrations
© 1996 by Suzanne Ellis, Madison, Wisconsin.

Text and cover design © 1996 by Tamara L. Cook,
TLC Graphics, Madison, WI

Publisher's Cataloging in Publication
    (Prepared by Quality Books, Inc.)

Ellis, Mel, 1912–1984
    Notes from Little Lakes/by Mel Ellis; with foreword by Don
    Johnson; illustrated by Suzanne Ellis; edited by Ted J. Rulseh.
        p. cm.
    ISBN 0-9653381-0-X
    1. Natural history — Wisconsin. 2. Human ecology. 3. Nature.
    I. Title.
QH105.W6E55 1996   508.775
                                          QBI96-40209

Library of Congress Catalog Card Number: 96-85950

TABLE OF CONTENTS

FOREWORD

By Don L. Johnson

For a legion of old friends and fans of Mel Ellis, this book invites fond reunions at a familiar place. Others, visiting Little Lakes for the first time, are about to take an unforgettable journey with an extraordinary guide. For nearly three decades, Mel shared his Little Lakes retreat with his readers. Wielding words like brush strokes from a master's palette, he was able to draw us into his surroundings until, in the mind's eye, we each could see the old white frame house on the hill, the flowers, the trees, the ponds, the paths. We could hear the birdsong and the chuckling of the creek.

Just as deftly, he introduced us to his family, the Rebel Queen and the Little Rebels, as well as fellow travelers of all shapes and sizes. Dogs and ducks, geese and gulls, rabbits and raccoons, woodchucks and chipmunks were included in a legion of characters met at Little Lakes. And each acquired a pet name. Not even Bumpy, the truck, escaped that treatment.

Mel performed his magic not with great panoramas of words, but rather with wondrously descriptive glimpses. In time, those bits were seen to fit together like pieces of a puzzle. And it was in that way, too, that Mel's own vision widened. Although he was a skilled and widely traveled outdoorsman, it was not until he settled at Little Lakes that he truly paused to smell the flowers. During the ensuing years of wonder and discovery, his appreciation and understanding of all life grew. And so, then, did the power of his words.

"I have experienced nature as a deep, deep, significant feeling that I'm part of the earth," he wrote. "An owl at night or a coyote howling or a bright running stream are all part of me and I am part of them. We're all part of each other."

Although he described himself as "a simple man of endless inquiry," he sometimes seemed filled with contradictions. He suffered his share of human frailties, yet he was as tough as rawhide. His sense of humor ranged from quiet quips to practical jokes. He could be angry and irreverent one moment, prayerful and poetic the next. And, although he often shared deep feelings with his readers, he remained in many ways a very private person.

"Privacy is one of the most precious and expensive things in the world," he lamented as a subdivision drew close to his hideaway.

For years, Mel and I worked for different, and sometimes competing, newspapers. Still, we were always friends. When our trails crossed, we would stop to sip a convivial cup, puff our pipes and share our views of the world. I thought I knew him well, but there were things he never mentioned.

I was aware, for example, that he had been a radio operator/gunner on heavy bombers during World War II. (It was, after all, "our war," and we'd traded stories, some funny, some grim.) However, it was not until I read his obituary that I learned that he had been awarded the Distinguished Flying Cross, five Air Medals and the Legion of Merit.

Clearly, it would be futile to try to fit the full measure of such a man into the space I have here. You will find that instead in Mel's own words. This is simply the introduction.

Melvin Richard Ellis was born on a farm in Dodge County, Wisconsin, on February 21, 1912. His parents, Fay and Paula (Hinkes) Ellis, had two other sons and two daughters. Early on, the Ellis boys learned outdoor skills from their father, who hunted and trapped to supplement his income as a salesman.

Mel attended elementary and high school in Juneau, then enrolled in the University of Notre Dame. He graduated with a degree in journalism in 1933. It was a hard time, for the country was still in the depths of the Great Depression. He knocked around the country, working at whatever jobs he could find, including stints as dishwasher, stevedore and garbage collector, before getting jobs on newspapers in Sheboygan, Wisconsin, and Rockford, Illinois.

He enlisted in the U.S. Army Air Corps soon after war broke out in December 1941, and he was among the first to be shipped to England to begin bombardment of occupied Europe and Hitler's Germany. He received his discharge in August 1945, married Bernice Schumacher and moved to Milwaukee to edit a publication called *Sports Review*.

He joined the staff of *The Milwaukee Journal* in 1948 and soon was teamed with the legendary outdoor writer Gordon MacQuarrie. Together, they set a new standard for newspaper outdoor coverage, a standard Mel helped maintain after MacQuarrie died in 1956.

Meanwhile, Mel had moved his growing family to an old, frame house in Waukesha County. It overlooked fifteen acres of partly wooded land not far from the Fox River. Although only thirty-five minutes from Milwaukee, the land was off the beaten path and not visible from the road. Among its attributes were flowing springs.

Mel saw the possibilities at once, but, as he often observed later, he did not then envision the amount of time, treasure and toil it would take to make the dream a reality. There were trees and flowers to be planted, ponds to be dug, rocks to be laid, trails to be made. It was to become a longtime family project and a true labor of love. Soon, the place had a name, and, early in 1957, *Journal* readers were treated to a column introducing them to Little Lakes.

Mel's "Notes From Little Lakes" was an immediate success, and it gained a large and devoted following during the next five years. However, he stopped writing the column soon after Bernice, the Rebel Queen, died in August 1962. He retired from *The Journal* the following year.

Before leaving the paper, he had firmly established himself as a freelance writer. He was an associate editor for *Field & Stream* magazine, and his byline had appeared in dozens of other national publications. For a time, however, deadlines and other demands of writing seemed to overwhelm him. By nature a disciplined writer, he tried to keep a schedule. He would be up before dawn, seated in his favorite chair, a large writing tablet on his lap. However, the words came hard. During that period, his four daughters were his mainstays.

Much to the delight of *Journal* subscribers, dispatches from Little Lakes reappeared early in 1965. They introduced a new Rebel Queen, the former Gwendolyn Krebs, and a fifth Rebel, Gwen's eleven-year-old daughter. Gwen, a widow, had read Mel's work and had sent him an appreciative letter. In that letter, he recognized the sentiments of a soulmate who would share his trials and dreams. And that she was.

Mel remained a contributor to the Sunday *Journal* for several more years, and also wrote syndicated articles for the Associated Press, but books began making increasing demands on his time and talents. His first book was a chronicle of the years he had shared with a German short-haired pointer named Rainey. Mel called the story "A Strange Love Affair," but the publishers, Holt, Rinehart and Winston, changed the title to "Run, Rainey, Run." Released in 1967, the book was a runaway success, and it soundly established Mel as a book author.

Thereafter, he averaged about one book per year. Several won awards and national acclaim. "Wild Goose, Brother Goose" (1969) became a Reader's Digest Condensed Book selection and a Disney movie; "Flight of the White Wolf" (1970) was also adapted for a Disney film.

Meanwhile, things at Little Lakes were flourishing and flowering, the payoff for the drudgery and dreams of earlier years. And Mel had matured as a true philosopher of nature, a man who would observe that "the mouse who steals my corn is as much a part of the purpose as an Aristotle or an Einstein."

In a dispatch from Canada in 1959, he had instructed his daughters: "Put your roots down now — deep. Then, if you must leave, there will always be some part of the rich country you are part of clinging to your memories." And he had heeded his own advice, thrusting his own roots ever deeper at Little Lakes.

In 1979, twenty-five years after his arrival there, he exulted that he had lived in one place long enough to be shaded by a tree he had planted as a sapling. "I know how lucky I am," he declared.

The trees and flowers, paths and ponds, remained a source of inspiration and strength, even after severe respiratory disease confined his ramblings to trail rides on Phantom, his electric tractor. When I last visited, he was keenly aware that his time was short. Nonetheless, he was still writing, still reveling in small discoveries. He died on September 1, 1984, at age 72.

Today, with Gwen as their guardian, the charms of Little Lakes remain. They are much as Mel left them, still hidden from the main roads. However, you can find them here, too, as readers always have, in the enduring words of Mel Ellis, a true poet of the land.

Don L. Johnson, retired outdoor editor of The Milwaukee Sentinel, *now lives in Menomonie, Wisconsin. He is an author, freelance writer, and Editor at Large for* Wisconsin Outdoor Journal *magazine.*

BOOK ONE

Introduction

"Notes From Little Lakes" by Mel Ellis debuted with no fanfare in The Milwaukee Journal *on Sunday, February 3, 1957. The first entry ran a mere three paragraphs, tucked into a corner of the Men's and Recreation Section. Other early installments were just as brief, but readers soon took notice, and "Little Lakes" evolved to a full-length column.*

Many readers in and around Milwaukee imagined Little Lakes as a hideaway somewhere in the Northwoods. They soon learned, to their surprise, that the property lay almost within sight of the city's smokestacks, just outside the Village of Big Bend in southern Waukesha County.

Each Sunday in "Notes From Little Lakes," Ellis reported on the changing of the seasons, the comings and goings of all manner of birds and wildlife, the antics of his daughters, known as the Rebels, and the joys and travails of nurturing fifteen acres of trees, wildflowers and spring-fed ponds.

Even when afield on hunting and fishing trips to northern Wisconsin, Canada or some faraway land, Ellis submitted "Little Lakes" columns, sometimes in the form of open letters to the Rebels and his wife Bernice, the Rebel Queen. Those columns, as well as any, showed the writer's deep love for his home acres and his family.

"Little Lakes" told of a simpler time when fish and game laws were less restrictive and land development was regulated far less closely than is the case today. That is why Ellis could alter the course of the stream on his property, called Watercress Creek, and dig, enlarge and deepen his ponds with little restriction. For similar reasons, the Rebels were able to keep two Canada geese behind wire, and take in abandoned or injured creatures — raccoons, woodchucks, seagulls, squirrels, chipmunks — to raise as pets.

At the same time, the absence of modern environmental standards led to one of the family's greatest sorrows. As Dutch elm disease swept across Wisconsin, it soon infested some of the more than one hundred fifty mature elms that shaded Little Lakes. The law at the time required the spraying of the elms with DDT in an effort to kill the beetles that carried the Dutch elm disease fungus.

The long-term effects of DDT had not yet been discovered, but Ellis and his family knew the poison would take its toll on the birds they had attracted in abundance. With deep misgivings, Ellis ordered the spraying in hopes of rescuing his beloved elms. Birds, frogs, snakes and other small creatures suffered greatly, and the ultimate failure of the treatment only made the losses more painful.

The death of the elms was not the only disappointment at Little Lakes, but Ellis looked upon failures and setbacks as a part of the natural order. To Ellis, nature was capricious, always out of balance, often cruel, its creatures ever at war among themselves. Birds fought for nest sites, small animals were ever on watch for predators, and even trees and plants battled, one species choking out another in the struggle for sunlight.

"Nature," Ellis wrote, "is not a kindly old lady but a tough old hag with poison ivy in her hair."

Still, Ellis appreciated the profound beauty he saw all around him, beauty that only increased in proportion to his efforts.

At the time he introduced "Notes From Little Lakes," Ellis already had one Sunday Journal column, "Mel's Mixed Bag," covering the hunting and fishing scene. "Little Lakes" endured much longer. In an important way, it marked the start of Ellis' transition from rod-and-gun writer to observer and chronicler of the natural world.

As the story of Little Lakes begins, Rebel No. 1 (Sharon) is fourteen years old, Rebel No. 2 (Suzanne) is ten, and Rebel No. 3 (Debbie) is six.

"The Rebel Queen," Ellis wrote, "won't tell her age."

The entries in this section are arranged mostly in chronological order to capture the daily ebb and flow of life at Little Lakes.

~ T.J.R.

chapter one

THIS PLACE CALLED LITTLE LAKES

WINTER

Crystalline waters

It is doubtful the water from the springs that form the ponds here at Little Lakes, our home place, has any special healthful ingredients. Once, however, many years ago, these bubbling blue-green springs had something of a fountain of youth reputation, and a half million dollars was spent to pipe the sparkling flow to Chicago so visitors to the 1893 world's fair might slake their thirst. Chicagoans evidently did not like the water, and little wonder. It had to travel through eighty-seven miles of pipe before it arrived. The project was a stupendous undertaking for the 1890s. Labor was imported and the pipeline was laid in ditches dug with pick and shovel. The company went broke, and now nothing remains except the bricked-in spring and pieces of pipe in which bullheads hide when the sun lights up the depths of the crystalline waters.

Risk for comfort

We can't decide whether the juncos that visit the bird-feeding station are smart or, like some people, willing to take a reasonable risk for a measure of comfort. During extremes of cold, they fly behind the coniferous shrubs banked up around the house and huddle next to the foundation where heat from the building prevents the earth from freezing. The various sparrows, chickadees, starlings and cardinals all perch in the higher spruce, out of reach of cats, weasels, dogs and other prowling predators.

※ ※ ※

A ring-necked duck visited Blue Pool, which does not freeze. After feeding, it left. Next morning, a flock of ring-necks, perhaps on invitation, scouted the area but apparently were fearful of alighting.

Though spawning season is months away, bluegills are already coloring. Squirrels are mating. Ten tame mallard hens are flirting with the three emerald-headed drakes.

One warm day, thirty-two degrees, is enough to put holes in the ice of Fish Pond and Clear Pool. Spring water comes from the ground at forty-eight degrees and melts a hole through the ice.

☙ ☙ ☙

Two months ago, we rerouted the creek that feeds Blue Pool. Now we are breaking our backs hauling in rocks to keep the banks from eroding. The new stream looks barren, but under each rock and among the roots exposed along the sides of the creek bed, thousands of snails and freshwater shrimp have already established homes.

Fireplace monument

At least one Indian brave has a fire lighted over his grave almost nightly during the summer here at Little Lakes. The springs that furnish water for the ponds once attracted various Indian tribes, and peaceful powwows and councils of war were held hereabouts. When the foundation for the outdoor fireplace was being dug, the skeleton of an Indian was uncovered. Size indicated it was a brave. We put the bones back carefully, and now the fireplace of fieldstone is a monument of sorts. There are mounds of various sizes and shapes in the vicinity.

Water power

Water was the big news this week, gallons and gallons of water sweeping across frozen ground, boiling at the bends in the creek, and uprooting large rafts of watercress that finally jammed the Blue Pool outlet. The water came at night. It went up an inch a minute, broke over the banks and went roaring off to the mill pond. At 11 p.m., with the Rebel Queen holding the flashlight, I waded into the flood with a crowbar to clear the pipe. The crowbar was yanked from my grasp and swept through the outlet when the debris collected there suddenly blew through like the cork from a champagne bottle.

Wild blood

Wonder what the law would say if we turned loose one of our tame mallard hens so the wild mallard drake on Blue Pool might marry up with it. The tame mallards are in a pen on top of the hill. The wild drake has come to live in the open waters of Blue Pool, and the Rebels have been feeding it. By turning free a hen or two, we'd get some new wild blood in our mallard flock with the hatching of youngsters in the late spring. There is a law, of course, about restraining any but mallards twice removed from the wild stage. But how to interpret it? The hen surely comes from domestic stock. Therefore, the youngsters would be half wild and half tame.

SPRING

Just five minutes

Five minutes is all I sat, just five minutes. Below, two small trout swam lazily along the clear stream between the bright-green, moss-covered rocks. One cedar waxwing tilted an inquiring bright eye. A cardinal whistled that this was his domain. Sunlight through a tree separation set the dogwood afire. Drops of water, one to the second, tripped off an ice ledge to tick off time in the creek current. Nothing was different, but in a mere five minutes, I came away with a quiet heart.

Little Lakes Refuge

Somebody shot the mallard who has been keeping a solitary watch on Blue Pool. The duck was in good health when we took the Rebels to church last Sunday, but two hours later, there was only a pool of blood on the shore where it had been sitting.

Later on, we found the wild drake on the shore. One leg was dangling and there was blood on its feathers just below a wing. The duck could fly, so we could not catch it to administer first aid. Still later, we found a Canada goose among the cattails. It permitted us to approach within ten feet. We surmise it was also shot and wounded.

The Rebels carried food to both birds, and each time they went near the pool, they came away in tears. Sometimes it is pretty difficult to explain that all people are not lawless, that ninety-nine percent are good and warm-hearted.

Monday the goose was gone. It either crawled back into the rushes and died or found the strength to go on. The mallard surprised us all. Though its one leg is hanging by a thread, it is taking food and looks as though it might survive. I wanted to shoot it and put it out of its suffering, but the Rebels would not hear of it. Now the Rebels are printing refuge signs, convinced that there are no people who would violate a refuge. Such faith!

Angry possum

An opossum who resides in the hollow at the base of a big basswood tree has the dogs frothing. When they are turned loose, they head for the possum's home and take turns trying to wedge their heads through the narrow opening. The growling is something to hear. The possum bristles and backs away with a fine show of teeth. One of these days, one of the beagles is going to get its head through and its growls will surely change to howls, because this is one possum who apparently has no intention of playing dead.

Mourning doves are paired and on the road getting gravel each morning. They will be nesting very shortly. Last year, practically every nesting dove on the place lost its first brood because of bad weather.

Starlings are tough little customers. They have even driven a pair of gray squirrels out of a hollow tree. This is the first year we have noticed starlings using the martin house. We hope the martins are tougher than the squirrels when they return from their southern sojourn to take possession.

Always at war

The marsh, trees, creek and pools, and even the air, are battlegrounds these days as birds, animals and insects war for mates, nesting sites and hunting grounds. Skirmishes begin at dawn and, except on cold or windy days, a fight of one kind or another is going on throughout the day. Red-winged blackbirds, which have staked out territories, are continually repelling invaders. Starlings war on every bird that comes within diving distance of their nest sites. Even the sweet-sounding and seemingly peaceful song sparrow fights for its particular patch of sumac, grassy bank or willow brush. We have never seen the mourning doves fight, which isn't to say they do not. They are building nests now.

Even the tame mallards were quarreling, but that is over. One drake ended up with one hen, another has a harem of three, and the third drake has five wives. That seems to be the division. How it got so lopsided is more than we can understand.

Within days, the teal and ring-necked ducks will be back on Fish Pond. Then there will be some battles royal as pairing takes place or as pairs fight off intruders. Northerns are fighting the current of the creek to get into spawning areas. As soon as the weather warms, bluegills will be fighting each other and the black bass will be rushing anything that swims by. The kingfisher is occasionally called upon to sound its war whoop and fly an intruder from its section of water. Even the spiders are outlining private hunting preserves with webs. Watching the wars, it occurs to us that life was not meant to be easy.

Scrambling for food

The scramble at the bird-feeding station on the day after the big snow was something. Blackbirds, grackles and even doves and robins competed with scores of smaller birds and just about every squirrel on the place. The arrival of migrants has increased the feathered population probably tenfold, and a water pail of grain does not last long.

Bashful goldfish

Ever wonder why you can't see fish in perfectly clear water? Usually it is because a fish can hide in bottom vegetation so sparse it seems nearly transparent. A two-pound, fiery red goldfish had lived in Clear Pool for two years and had been sighted only three times, even though the pool is so clear that a dime is visible on the bottom. Recently, we put in two more two-pounders. Now, with two to give it confidence, the lonesome one shows itself on sunny days.

Endangered elms

We are worried about Dutch elm disease. There are numerous elms at Little Lakes, and some are towering veterans with huge trunks. A state forester looked the trees over last fall and found the elm tree beetle present in numbers, though there was no evidence of disease.

Tons of stone

Well, the creek that was rerouted to provide fresh water to all parts of Blue Pool finally has been stoned in. The Rebels, the Rebel Queen and I moved twenty-five tons of rock to build a wall on each side of the creek to a height of three feet. All told, we wore out thirteen pairs of gloves handling the fieldstone.

Visiting ring-necks

Ring-necked ducks moved onto Fish Pond Monday. One flock of eight and a trio consisting of two hens and a drake immediately found enough food to keep them popping beneath the surface. When the dogs frightened them off the pond, we immediately salted the bottom with shelled corn. The ducks returned shortly after the dogs were kenneled and will probably stay now until about the middle of April.

Reaping rewards

Now is the time to reap the rewards at Little Lakes. It is the time, too, for discovering mistakes and planning to profit by them. Now is the time to read the book. Did the water iris planted last spring survive, and will there be purple blooms along the shores of Fish Pond this spring?

Did the birds leave enough millet seed for a crop? Will the white water lilies and the yellow spatterdock planted last May shade the home of the bass and the bluegill? How did the five hundred cedars survive the drought of last summer? Will some of the brown trees turn green again? How about the five hundred spruce planted last April? What percentage will live? How about the wild rice? The smartweed? The weeping willows? The duck potato? The multiflora rose? Which of these found the soil, the angle of sun, the percentage of shade, the temperature and the depth of water suited to growth?

A year is a long time to wait to find out, but it is worth it when duck potato catches in one corner and lifts white flowers over blue water, or when a birch goes shooting skyward and whitens into maturity, or when the islands are surrounded by white water lilies.

The outlaw Silver

Silver, a Muscovy duck, has turned outlaw. He killed a tame mallard hen and his life hung in the balance while the humans at Little Lakes debated his fate. If I could have had my way (a rare occurrence), he would have ended up in the oven. But the death penalty is rarely invoked these days at Little Lakes. Starlings, grackles, English sparrows and weasels can thank three soft-hearted Rebels that sterner measures aren't taken.

After he killed the mallard, we turned Silver out of the spacious duck pen to roam the premises. The second day out, mother heard the youngest Rebel weeping. She went out to discover Silver had chased the Rebel into the car and would not let her out. Next day, Silver put Rebel No. 2 up a tree. Third day, Silver left Fish Pond, crossed over to the mill pond and went visiting the fair female ducks next door. A drake ran Silver back into the water, and mother and Rebel No. 2 finally had to bring him home in the trunk of the car.

Fourth day, he led the two Labradors and the short-haired pointer on a half-hour chase from one end of Fish Pond to the other. So, there was nothing left but to put Silver into solitary confinement, back where the prickly ash forms a thorny fence.

Green submarines

Bluegills in Clear Pool are learning to eat commercially prepared fish food in pellet form. At first, the fish spat out the pellets. Gradually, they learned to eat. Several feet down, hundreds of minnows swarm like mosquito clouds to eat any pellets that get past the bluegills. While the minnows are swarming frantically about to get their fill, bass swimming tight to the bottom come in like green submarines.

They surround the minnows. Suddenly, one of the bass darts into the cloud of little fish. The action is almost too swift to see. The minnows dart away from the bass right into the open jaws of other bass in the circle. When a bass drives a minnow into the bottom vegetation, it stands "on its head," waiting. The moment the minnow so much as moves a fin, the bass dives in. The hunter always comes up with a mouthful of grass and, sometimes, the minnow. Somehow, the bass separates the minnow from the grass in its mouth, then spits the grass out, swallows the minnow and starts hunting again.

What is this Little Lakes?

People sometimes ask us, "What is this Little Lakes?" And they have an idea that it is in the North Country among towering pines where sometimes the coyote howls or an otter comes to play. So then we tell them it is so close to Milwaukee that we can see the haze from the city's smoke. Southwest, we say, southwest of Milwaukee, and though it is not in the glacial kettles, it is just on the edge. It is where the Fox River, the one that flows through Waukesha, makes two fishhook bends before straightening a little to run through lush pasturage on its way to Waterford.

It is a white house on a hill and a long slope of grass that runs down to a welter of springs feeding five ponds, three of which belong to us and two to neighbors. It is giant elm trees more than a hundred years old. It is spruce groves and Norway and white pine and practically every tree native to Wisconsin, along with wild and tame flowers of many colors.

Then they say, "But how can you have such beautiful things so close to the city?"

We tell them there are many, many places within sight of Milwaukee that have blue waters and tall trees where even deer come to visit. And though we have no deer at Little Lakes, we are privileged to be host to all the smaller wild things that come to hide in the cedar and spruce groves, to dig in the gravel knolls, to hide in the tall grass that surrounds the spring-fed ponds.

And we tell them there are many, many places just outside Milwaukee where the wildflowers grow. They grow at Little Lakes, too, and we help them by keeping ahead of the bulldozers where a new road is going through and bringing the plants to our place. If ninety percent of the flowers cannot stand the shock of being rooted up from their native places, then ten percent can, so we are gradually surrounding ourselves with as much of a variety as soil and terrain will accommodate.

They ask about the ponds, and we say they were dug. Machines gouged out pockets where the springs were. We stood and saw the water bubble up and, when each pond had filled, we watched the silt settle.

About the fish, they ask, "How did they come?" Well, we bought them and put them in the ponds.

"Well, it sounds sort of like heaven," they say. "Is it?"

No, it is not. It is a place of small successes and some monumental failures. It is a place of sweat and calluses, some profanities, some accidents and sometimes so much love it overflows in tears.

It is surely a little like your backyard, like the city park you visit, only perhaps there is more of it and it is some wilder. It is a place like your home, with all the good things and all the sad things and all the little everyday happenings which, added up, accumulate into living. It is a place where children live, and where children live life necessarily renews itself, and every day seems to have at least one warm smile, no matter how badly the day otherwise went.

Life at Little Lakes starts out every morning just as your life does with kids to get off to school. Then there are dishes to wash, beds to be made, dusting to be done. But then, sometimes things start jumping, especially if we have a special project in progress.

Take last Saturday. Where a new pool is being dug, the cable broke on the backhoe. A fifteen-ton truck was axle-deep in a spring hole, a concrete truck slid off the dike into the spruce trees, and concrete being poured into forms on the bank of the new pool bulged up and filled the drainpipe. In the house, a flushed toilet was plugged, so soon the living room was swimming and it was raining in the basement.

Rebel No. 3 fell headfirst off a retaining wall and cracked her head.

A piece of stone being moved across water punctured the deck of the boat. The plug to the big tank that stores water from Fish Pond was lost and a geyser was gouging a cave into the soil. Coffee was forgotten on the stove, and it turned to syrup. Meatloaf in the oven became a burnt crisp. Mabel, a hen, wouldn't sit on her eggs.

But by evening, most problems were solved and the bass who has a nest in Clear Pool was watching hundreds of newly hatched fish hardly bigger than a pin head. So we slipped a dishcloth beneath the swarming newborn fish and lifted it because we do not want bass in Clear Pool. We hurried the bass kids over to Fish Pond.

Flies were hatching and a few fish were dimpling Blue Pool. Birds were slipping in among the spruce to roost and, shortly, the kids were catching a mild sort of hell for not brushing their teeth. Then night and the stars and only mother and me and the sound of a big truck grunting up a grade.

Requiem for Rosy?

Rosy van Etta is a noisy mallard hen who bites the kids and is too lazy to build her own nest. Instead, she piles eggs in nests belonging to the other hens. One of Rosy's sisters now has twenty-two eggs to incubate. Another has sixteen. Rosy reminds us of the cowbird, which lays its eggs in other birds' nests to avoid the responsibilities of parenthood. Except that the cowbird goes scotfree, whereas Rosy van Etta is sealing her fate. When butchering time arrives in fall, Rosy is going to wind up in the freezer.

☀ ☀ ☀

Just thinking: There is no doubt animals and birds learn to recognize friends. The mallard hen lets Rebels No. 2 and 3 fondle the ducklings. If I even go near them, the hen hisses and then attacks. Chipmunks, mourning doves and cottontails permit the children to come close, but flee from adults.

☀ ☀ ☀

A child's prayer for rain because the trees or vegetables she planted are wilting becomes more than lip service when the rain comes and the lettuce turns green and the dry twigs sprout leaves.

☀ ☀ ☀

This will be the last week for the apple, plum and cherry blossoms. It will be the last week for the violets that purple the green cover and for the marsh marigolds at the mouth of the creek. But the week will bring other flowers to take their place.

Bees at work

Bees have commandeered the shagbark hickory alongside the garden. Through a triangular wedge near the bottom of the trunk, they come in steady procession each sunny day to add to their store of wild, dark amber honey. Their honey is safe. The tree is too beautiful and healthy to cut and, even if it weren't, watching the bees at work is worth more than their hidden riches.

SUMMER

Casualties

Death has been a frequent visitor these last weeks. Martins, which must feed on the wing, found no insects in the air and starved. Grackles have lost families in Blue Pool and Clear Pool. Mourning doves have again been struck down by some disease, and youngsters often never get on the wing. Something has also taken its toll of ducklings, always within two days after hatching.

Mostly, these deaths are normal casualties suffered every spring by birds in their struggle for survival. So, nature compensates. Mourning doves nest as often as five times in a single season. Robins who lose their youngsters are right back at egg laying shortly after the tragedy occurs. Wrens move from house to house and often raise three broods. Mallards who have lost their young start laying in new nests.

⁂ ⁂ ⁂

Been counting our rewards again: Spatterdock planted at some expense and considerable labor has yellow flowers around the islands on Fish Pond. Duck potato is coming up in profusion after a slow start following a late planting last spring. White water lily plants are showing pads, but no flowers. Smartweed is not showing. Neither is wild rice. The purple water iris planted last year is blooming along the shores of Fish Pond.

The work of many

As Little Lakes becomes more beautiful with each succeeding year, it is easy to forget that many people are responsible. Most of us are inclined to view only our own handiwork, forgetting that generations have preceded us and that even their mistakes are responsible for our successes. It is easy, especially at Little Lakes, to forget how someone planted and nurtured the thirty-foot blue spruce and the groves of white and Norway pine and spruce. I find that I am inclined to look with pride on the stones I sweated into wall formations, but forget those my predecessors juggled into place.

After the failed attempt to pipe the spring water to Chicago, the Washicheck brothers made the next improvements. Both men had a passion for water. With shovels, they opened new bubblers and then, using wheelbarrows and muscle, began creating the first ponds. One brother is dead, but Jerry Washicheck still lives on the shores of one of those ponds.

Next came Emil Noehre, a retired sausage maker from Milwaukee with such a green thumb as few men possess. He planted and nursed thousands of conifers and brought in hundreds of deciduous trees from surrounding forests. Rock gardens, shrubs, flower beds and grape arbors turned the rolling country green and beautiful. My Rebel tribe came next to build more ponds, plant more trees, and improve on what other men and nature had already made beautiful.

Little Lakes dogs

The five dogs who get their board and room by working only during fall and early winter have a rigid caste system in their little canine community. Sergeant, the squat and lumbering little beagle, is the clown, and the others do not take him too seriously. Captain, the red, fine-boned beagle who shares quarters with Sergeant, is an aloof creature. He bothers no one and, except for some little needling from his room-mate, is left strictly alone.

Bucko, a four-year-old yellow Labrador, by the sheer power and abandon that typifies youth, has become the boss dog. But his high position provides him with little satisfaction, because the two dogs who are his seniors sometimes seem to laugh at his threats. When he tries to make an issue of something, they turn away as though to say: "Aw, go bark up a tree!"

The two old dogs, Rainey, a German shorthaired pointer, and Ace, a black Labrador, have no desire to usurp Bucko's position. They have carried hundreds more birds than he has, and they are happy to leave things be, to hunt a little, eat a little and sleep a lot. Only occasionally do Rainey and Ace show their irritation at Bucko's blustering. They growl and shove, but then, remembering the many battles that brought them nothing but grief during times even before Bucko was born, they turn away when the big yellow dog offers to fight.

So, like Don Quixote, Bucko is a battler of windmills. The big dogs will not fight back, and though the little beagles will give him what for what, the canine code will not permit his laying a tooth on such mites as Sergeant and Captain. So the big yellow Lab hollers at every squirrel, rabbit or chipmunk that goes by. He shouts to the high elms that he is top dog, that he is boss. And the wise old dogs sleep even during the uproar and the little guys just laugh.

Menacing minnows

Bluegills in Clear Pool, no matter how vigilant, are having trouble keeping minnows from devouring their spawn. Hundreds of minnows swim in circles around each nest. While the bluegill is chasing out one gang, another gang darts in and feasts.

☘ ☘ ☘

At least one bass in Fish Pond discovered it does not pay to be a pig. We found this fellow wallowing helplessly among shore grass. He measured nineteen inches and was choking to death on an eleven-inch bass he'd captured. The eleven-incher's tail was still protruding from the nineteen-incher's mouth.

Mysterious friend

Well, the Rebels have discovered what ate the heads off the little dead ducklings laid alongside the fence for burial in the Little Lakes pet cemetery. They were, of course, quite perturbed to think that their home grounds harbored a creature who lived on duckling heads, until they discovered what it was. Mink and weasel were ruled out because there were no tracks in the moist earth where the dead ducklings lay. In fact, there were no tracks at all, and it almost seemed as though some mysterious creature had swooped right out of the sky to snatch the heads.

How right they were! It was a night creature who moves on silent wings and daytimes haunts the dark hollow of a big, dead tree. It was a creature who makes weird, melancholy whimperings in the night, a creature of large, yellow eyes and a swivel head that it can rotate like a balloon on a string. Savage as all these characteristics sound, the creature turned out to be a quite tiny, harmless bundle of feathers who, when discovered, became an immediate friend of the whole family. We even gave it a name: Screechy, the owl!

Out of balance

Mostly we permit nature to rule our roost, hoping she will keep things in balance. Instead of tender, young rabbit, we eat beef stew. Pan-fried squirrel usually turns out to be porkchops. Turtle soup has a habit of coming out of a can.

But sometimes things get out of hand, like last week. Rabbits got all the beet tops, and of all the greens, none pleases our palate like new tops mixed with crisp fried bacon. A snapping turtle got into the ducklings on Fish Pond and we had to kill one badly mangled youngster. Shortly, the robins will take all the cherries. The chipmunks and birds will get the strawberries. Then, in a little while, when the tomatoes redden, there will be ragged craters left by hungry wildlings.

It is not always what nature's creatures do to us, but to each other. The grackles are a menace to the mourning doves, and we are tempted to collect fledglings to feed to the big bass. Blue jays, too, make regular raids on the nests of other songbirds. And the green herons and the kingfishers work the shores of the pond all day eating fish.

Wild things are perpetually at war. We have no wish to terminate that war, whether directed against us or lesser creatures. It is only when the odds become overwhelming in favor of one or another species that we are tempted to step in and arbitrarily settle things.

Some see it all

Many have looked at Little Lakes, but few have seen it. For some, the trees might as well be wearing dollar bills instead of leaves, since they cannot think except in terms of cash value. Others see only the work — pools to be stoned in, grass to be mowed, gardens to be weeded, thistles to be cut — and at least they get some satisfaction from knowing they do not have to do it.

Still others see a park, as pictured on a postcard, in large green and flowered patterns. All detail escapes them. Fishermen, of course, see the fish. Swimmers see the swimming place. Flower lovers see the flowers and bird lovers see the birds.

Then sometimes comes one who sees it all, and this one appreciates the struggle nature is making to reclaim a small portion of what man has deprived her of. This one sees the birch tree that is going to survive and the birch tree that is going to die; the ferns that need shade and the ferns that need more water; the fence that could and will hold more wild grapes.

This one knows that soon more kingfishers will live along Fish Pond because there will be more trees for them to dive from, and that more and more ducks will be stopping off because the duck potato is flourishing. This one sees the "weeds" but almost instinctively knows that in plant life succession, more desirable species will replace them if given but half a chance.

Do not tell me how some see these things without ever having had any technical training. Perhaps it is because all their lives they have not only looked at the world around them, but seen it, too.

Jackie the pigeon

Most beloved of all the creatures at Little Lakes is a white pigeon crippled from birth. Its beak grows like a fingernail and must be trimmed. Its wings are rigid and it cannot fly. The children call the bird Jackie. It lives in a small wire enclosure and is visited by the other pigeons. The children provide it such comforts and foods as normal pigeons rarely receive.

❊ ❊ ❊

Saw the first wild flock of nine mallards swing over Fish Pond. Teal are feathered and will be on the wing any day. Bluegills are still spawning, and there will be some late breeders right through August. A pair of seagulls, Sail and Soar, are starting to feather out. We are keeping a photographic sequence of their growing up.

Dragon patrol

These are the days of the dragons. On parchment wings, they patrol the ponds in squadrons seeking to zoom down on their prey with incredible agility. No man-made air vehicle can duplicate their maneuvers. They hover, fly backwards and come to an abrupt standstill while in speeding flight. Mostly, they prey on such flies as are the householder's enemy. Sometimes, inadvertently or on purpose, they try to close with an inch-long horsefly or even a tiny tree frog. Having more than they can handle, they break off and look for smaller prey.

Mellow moment

Corn is in the milk. Cucumbers are green against the hot ground. Apples are reddening. Grapes are becoming tinged with purple. Chestnuts have swollen into spiky nut clusters. Squirrels are opening the walnuts. Hickory nuts are as large as they will get and need only to ripen. Currants, raspberries and blackberries are about done, and birds are finishing off what's left. There are warm, fertile odors where backwaters meet black soil. This is the full, mellow moment of summer, the lazy interlude before autumn with its crisp nights and sharp, sparkling days.

Teeming ponds

Watercress is two feet high and blossoming, and muskrats are gorging themselves on the plant stems. Wild rice that failed to show in spring is coming up in isolated islands of green where coontail did not choke it out. Blue Pool, seven months old now, is settling down. It will grow through a succession of plant changes until the cold water group of flora dominates.

Red-winged blackbirds are flocking. Grackles gather in loud groups at the edge of the water to eat. Young martins are on the wing. Always we hear the cardinals calling, but rarely do we see them. Wrens are winding up work on their second brood and probably will sail right along to hatch out a third gang. Two pairs of cedar waxwings, which we suspect have nested somewhere in the hedge where prickly ash rises into thick chokecherry trees right at the edge of a spruce grove, have not been seen for a long time.

Pet status

Just a year ago, a dozen pigeons came to Little Lakes. They were destined to die in order that a young Labrador retriever might learn his lessons. Six did die before our three Rebels intervened. The remaining six, only one of which was female, took up residence in boxes nailed to the walls of the duck pen. The female, an immature bird on arrival, eventually got around to laying eggs, and now there are Comanche, Snowball, Flash, Apache, Picadilly, Tumbleweed, Ringtail, Dawn and Tattoo, plus three youngsters not yet named. Young of the single female now are mating. The pigeon colony is bound to outgrow its present quarters. What I am wondering is: When will the Rebels quit naming each new arrival, thus giving it pet status? If they do not stop, I will never acquire any pigeons for training the dogs.

Poachers strike

Sometimes we at Little Lakes become discouraged, not with nature but with people. Twice now this summer and last, the green sunfish and bluegills we were hand-feeding were stolen. The fish, residents of Clear Pool, were so tame they accepted bread from the lips of the children while they were swimming. Our purpose in feeding these fish was to determine how much weight we could put on a panfish by artificial feeding. Twice we almost brought the experiment to a successful conclusion — almost, but not quite. The young men who took the fish must have had great sport.

Gluttonous gulls

Even an abundance of food during all their lives fails to stifle the seagulls' instinct to fight for every scrap of fish in sight and to gorge until fish tails are protruding from their beaks and they topple over backward from the weight of the meal.

Sail and Soar, the pair of baby gulls living next to the duck pen at Little Lakes, are no exception. All their lives they have had all they can eat three times a day. Still they fight as though each piece of fish is the first they ever had and is likely to be the last. They gorge until they cannot cram down another morsel, and then, with bulging eyes and crops, they watch the piece that is left, so the moment digestion makes room for more, they can grab it.

It is part of their heritage. For centuries, the seagull's life has been one of feast and famine. When the silvery schools of little fishes are running and the big fishes are slashing through them, there are plenty of leftovers. When the tide is kind, the pickings are good. When the wind blows toward shore for days on end, there is food the length of the beach. When the fish boats are out and entrails are being pitched overboard, the feast is on. When picnickers swarm the beaches in summer, there is at least some food.

But in between are the days of famine. Winter days on the Great Lakes, when no boats are spewing garbage in their wakes, are hard days. Then, when the ice stretches almost from shore to shore and blizzards blow for days on end, the gulls hunker on the ice and are hungry. Even during the sunny days on the island rookeries, there is so much competition that many starve. So perhaps that is why there is bred into every gull the constant drive to crowd every digestible scrap of food down its gullet before some other gull gets it.

As for Sail and Soar, they are eating about twenty bluegills a day now. If they increase their food demands, it is going to take a good fisherman to keep them supplied. Though only about six weeks old, they are as different as children of the same family sometimes are. One is a loud-mouthed, belligerent cuss. The other is complacent and almost polite.

March of the turtles

From among the flowers in the sunken garden, along the southern slopes of the gravel knolls, where the soil is hard-baked from the sun at the edge of the sweet corn patch, in a score of places, hundreds of tiny turtles are working their way out of the caves in which they were born and heading for water.

One painted turtle nest at Little Lakes had a premature opening Tuesday. Nearly ten weeks ago, the Rebels saw the mother turtle deposit her eggs in a little cave she had dug. They boxed in the area, sinking the sides of the prison into the earth so the tiny turtles might be captured after birth.

Finally, the suspense was too much. So we dug into the nest, took out a single egg and opened it. The little turtle, about the size of a quarter, would have broken out of the egg within a few days. It was alive, but its shell was soft, and the little egg-breaking spear that all unborn turtles grow on the ends of their noses was not completely formed. We covered the nest again so that the remaining seven eggs may hatch in their own good time.

Painted turtles, often called mud turtles, deposit their eggs in the earth in June or July. If cold weather catches the kids in the cave, they stay there, existing on what is left of the egg yolk all through the winter, and emerge in spring. That is why, when the sun of the first summery days warms the earth, there are already tiny turtles hunting food in the waters of the state.

AUTUMN

The busiest airport

No airport in the world handles as much traffic as a single fieldstone that is part of a retaining wall along the outside entrance to the basement. Within a minute, a hundred landings and take-offs are negotiated, and collisions are rare. Yet, there is no tower to provide landing instructions or give clearance to approaching or departing fliers. So, perhaps, the honey bees — for those are the fliers — have built-in radar systems.

Occasionally, there is a collision. When it happens, the fliers just pick themselves up and continue on. Though the bees come in head-high to a human, I have stood in their flight path for as long as a half-hour without having a flier so much as brush a wing against me. The children run through the flight pattern continually. Chipmunks climb across the stone landing field. The dogs often are in the way. To date, no one has been stung, nor have the bees done anything except mind their own business. Fortunately for us, they cannot read minds, because if they had an inkling what we have planned for the honey they must have stored in the stone wall, I am sure we would be the objects of an all-out assault.

We have found another colony of wild honey bees, not one hundred feet away, about thirty feet up in a big basswood tree. The second colony apparently has five times the population of the first, but we are not planning to raid it. Being attacked on the ground is one thing. Hanging from a limb and fighting off bees is quite another.

Wild in the sky

A wild clamor at three o'clock the other morning brought us from bed to the window. The moon had whitened the world outside, but there was nothing to see except a rabbit in the sunken garden. Then, from the sky, high above the trees, a wild mallard quacked, and the penned flock clamored back in unison. The wild one wanted to come down, I presume, and I am sure the penned mallards wanted only to be free to join the wild one in sky.

Autumn mist

Mist is on the meadow each morning. Water of the pools is warmer than the air, and only the tops of the trees and the knoll show above the ground fog. Birds refuse to fly. Cedar waxwings and blue jays wait among the spruce. Teal stay down on Watercress Creek. Green herons sit on snags alongside Blue Pool. The sun is high and bright before the mist melts. Then there is the mill pond, sparkling now in the sun. Blue Pool looks black because it is still in the shadows. Clear Pool reflects the light and looks silvery. Fish Pond is a patchwork of dark and light because of the weed beds. Bright yellow daisy-type flowers nod on seven-foot stems. The Fish Pond dike is red with sumac. Purple gentians in large, tall bouquets cast reflections in the water.

Mouse menagerie

Something mysterious had been happening in the garage. A half-dozen times we caught the two youngest Rebels coming from there with guilty looks on their faces. So, we spied on them and discovered that in the vermin-proof room in which duck and dog food and seeds are kept, they had gathered a mouse menagerie. The youngsters were spreading corn and sprawling on their stomachs to watch while the mice came within inches of their noses to nibble at the kernels. We learned, then, that they were also feeding mice in the duck pen and the kennels. Having heard us say some uncomplimentary things about mice, they kept their secret lest we spread poisoned wheat or put out traps. The climax came this week when we caught the youngest in the living room with a young mouse. Mouse and Rebel went scooting out the door, for mother was mad. So we have compromised. All mice in the garage and in the dog kennel must go. But the mice in the duck pen may live and even be fed.

Well fed

Chipmunks, perhaps a hundred or more, live under all the buildings and in stone walls, hollow trees and old drains everywhere at Little Lakes. Right now, they are striped bundles of energy as they hurry along regular routes to empty their bulging cheeks in underground caches. One got into a barrel that had cracked corn at the bottom and was not discovered until it had been there for at least three days. When turned loose, it staggered as though intoxicated. Its eyes were nearly closed. Crawling through the wire pen that houses Jackie, the crippled pigeon, the chipmunk lowered its head into Jackie's water and drank until its sides were bulging. After resting, it staggered away, resolved, perhaps, never again to try to hog a whole barrel of feed.

※ ※ ※

Muskrats are nearly as frantic as the chipmunks. They are working around the clock on new burrows, thatching roofs of new houses and eating, eating, eating. Brook trout, too, are in a frenzy. They are honeymooning. Males clear the bottom of debris by twisting, turning and whipping their tails about. Then they wait beside the nest for a female. Eggs are then covered with gravel and the trout go their separate ways.

※ ※ ※

If fish eat more in fall to fatten up for the winter months ahead, we have never seen any evidence of it at Little Lakes. Bluegills feed lazily. Black bass are more wary than ever.

Let them go

Brule, Wis.
Bernice Ellis
On Little Lakes

Dear Bernice:

You will just have to tell those kids to let those chipmunks go. When you told me on the phone last night that the six-year-old had to go to the doctor for a tetanus booster shot because another chipmunk bit her, I figured it was

time to call a halt to some of this stuff. Anyway, if they do not let the chip-
munks go pretty soon so they can store up some food for the weeks below
ground before and after hibernation, we will have to keep them all winter.
And I can just see you with chipmunks running all over your basement.

Say, I forgot to tell you when I left: That watercress is good now — the
new stuff that has taken hold where the new pond is. Eat that first and let
the old beds go until they freshen up some. Bring Ace into the house once in
awhile so he doesn't feel too bad about being left behind, and tell Rebel No.
2 to run those beagles so they do not get too fat. Take it easy now. I'll put up
the rest of the storm windows when I get back.

Love,
Mel

Carpet of leaves

Rain is beating leaves to the earth this morning. The once-green
lawn is covered with a carpet of reds, yellows and browns. Some hardy
flowers still bloom but, down off the hill, frost has blackened the
daisies, wilted the purple gentians. The leaves will be used. Some will
blanket flower beds against the cold. Some will go into a pit. When
spring comes, potato seedlings will be put beneath this bed of leaves
and then, without further attention, will produce a crop of spuds in
fall. Most of the leaves will be mulched, however, to become fertilizer
for the lawn.

What about the duck?

A strange duck is visiting the tame mallards on the hill. It must have
flown into the wire enclosure. It looks like a wild mallard except that
it is smaller and much darker than a mallard. It is not, however, a black
duck. The Rebels want to keep it. I told them that if it is wild, it does
not belong to them, but to all the people of the state. They argue that
if a duck wants to stay, it certainly is privileged to. They ask, "Doesn't
the duck have anything to say about it?"

Hello from on high

It is disconcerting to lift an elbow from a warm bed on a frosty
morning and see a big black crow peering intently through the bedroom window. And it is infinitely more disconcerting to be strolling
through the spruce grove that surrounds Blue Pool and have a voice
from the sky shout: "Hello!" But we at Little Lakes are not the only
ones who have been startled by the crow who can talk. We have it from

a usually reliable citizen of Big Bend that the crow sat in an apple tree one afternoon and told the village gossip to "Shut up!" One of the crow's favorite hangouts is in the trees bordering Jerry Washicheck's pond. Both Mrs. Washicheck and Jerry are able to get the crow talking. Our No. 2 Rebel did a little sleuthing for us and her report follows:

"The crow's name is Caw Caw. He belongs to Dale Schram, who is nine or ten years old. He was taken from a nest when young and it took him about six months to learn to talk. He can say, 'Hello, Joe' and 'How are ya?' and 'I'm fine.' He gargles and it sounds like water running from a bottle. He eats meat and he steals clothespins from the line and hides them. He follows Dale to school. He flies all over the village but comes home nights. He is a beautiful bird. Why do people say a crow is all bad? I think he is beautiful. I wish I had a pet crow."

Slinging mud

Mudslinging is an art. Not the verbal kind of mudslinging in which one neighbor tries to bury another under a pile of dirt, but the kind that has been going on out here these past days. Anybody can sling mud with a shovel and slap it into a reasonably accurate mold, but it takes years of training and experience to throw mud around with a twenty-ton machine that handles a ton bucket hung at the end of a long steel line. Some men become so expert at the latter type of mud-slinging that they can flick a fly off a fence post with the huge bucket.

Charlie Deback, 64-year-old dragline operator and our neighbor, is one of these. He has been digging pools at Little Lakes. At one point in the operation, he repeatedly dropped the bucket within an inch of a signpost in the water of one pool and dredged in front of it without ever moving the post. Another time, while balancing the big machine on a twelve-foot dike that shook and shivered as though made of jelly, he cut a trench as sharply as though sliced down with a sharp spade.

The battles of birds

The dispositions of birds are not as beautiful as their songs or their feathers. Even the seed eaters, the so-called songbirds, are greedy and belligerent, and feathers sometimes fly around the three feeding stations outside my window. The battles are not always between birds of different species. Cardinals fight cardinals. Blue jays battle blue jays. What is more, fighting to stuff their crops with suet and seed is not enough. They carry off the food and cache it. In one day, nuthatches hauled away a pound of suet and stored it piece by piece beneath the bark of trees.

Silver, the Muscovy duck, has turned outlaw.

Only the unpretentious English sparrows seem to get along. In spite of what you may have read or heard, the sparrows rarely quarrel, but sit around chirping in peaceful flocks. But let one of the "important," gaudy birds find a feeding station occupied and the war begins. Until a storm comes. Then, when the wind is howling and snow is piling up beneath the feeding stations, all birds forget their differences in the face of a common threat to life.

Then they feed side by side and roost in the same tree. Then, because they have a common foe, their own grievances, one with the other, lose significance, and they live in a peaceful community, a peaceful world, until the storm ends. Not much different from the people of nations, races, religions.

Beautiful walls

Within the year, the Little Lakes Redevelopment Association (that's us) has erected three stone walls having a total weight of sixty-seven tons. Our stone walls can hardly be called works of art, simply because we are not masters of the craft.

The fieldstone walls offered the greatest challenge, but they are the most beautiful, too. The infinite variety of stones permits the builder to give every fieldstone wall its own character. One wall may give the illusion of being a massive, indestructible fortress. Another can flow away in lines that blend right into the surrounding terrain and its flora. The fieldstone walls take many shapes, and on their faces color and grain can be combined in an endless number of designs.

Our walls are strictly utilitarian. They have been built to keep water from wandering. One such wall has thirty-five tons of stone. It holds in Watercress Creek. The other walls are of lannon stone. One bulwarks Fish Pond. The other sweeps around Clear Pool. These are beautiful, but hardly artistic. Even though they are not works of art, we feel like architects building homes for freshwater shrimp, many varieties of caddis worms that each year hatch into flies, not to mention frogs, snakes, crickets, spiders and ants — whole cities populated with creatures.

Our walls contain no mortar, but depend for their stability on one stone fitting precisely and squarely on top of the other. This process increases our admiration for the old-timers who built fieldstone houses like the one a few miles southwest of us and the fireplaces that still decorate many homes in Wisconsin. But even for amateur wall builders like me, there is quite some satisfaction in seeing these stone structures rise out of the earth and flow along. What is more, there is no better way of melting down a middle.

chapter two

NEW POOL, NEW REBEL

WINTER

Tamer in winter?

An animal's resistance to cold seems to be in direct ratio to its food consumption. If you cut down on the dogs' diets, especially their portions of cod-liver oil concentrate and table fats such as grease, they are not out in the yard barking to be turned loose. Instead, they are curled in their kennels, trying to ration body heat so they can stay warm.

All except hibernating creatures need food daily, not to keep from starving, but to keep from freezing to death. Even a few cold days following a heavy snow that has covered their food seem to take the life right out of animals and birds. The children argue that the birds and animals are tamer in winter. It is, of course, only that the wildlings are less wary because they are incapable of putting forth the extra effort that saved them from predators during warmer months. Rabbits sit tighter, birds permit humans to approach closer and squirrels stay at the feeding stations even when threatened by hawks.

The physical degeneration of animals and birds unable to get enough to eat during cold spells is surprisingly swift. Rabbits almost literally fade away. Pheasants freeze in their night nests. Sparrows topple from their perches. At Little Lakes, we see the warning signs within a matter of days. Juncos huddle against the house foundation for warmth. Cardinals sit wing to wing with blue jays at the feeding tray. Plenty of suet and sunflower seeds, which are rich in oil, help at once.

Prisoners of habitat

All creatures are prisoners of habitat. Never has this been illustrated more dramatically than during the recent sub-zero weather that strangled the ponds, leaving only two tiny pools of open water. One goldeneye and a pair of mallard hens, fugitives from the pen on the hill, were driven by the ice off their usual rather extensive watery domain into the little pools. Here they must remain or perish.

Most people are prisoners of habitat, too, mostly because we wish it to be that way. We stay where the food is best, the chair is the most comfortable, the bed is the warmest. Lines of least resistance are always most comfortable to follow. Fortunately for us, some people have believed that some things were more important than a comfortable cave. So they left the cave and eventually lived in houses. They left comfortable houses and came to this country to live in huts. They left the huts to cross the country in wagons. Lesser animals than man leave their homes only when these homes are too cold, the food is all gone or a threat to their lives is ever present.

Christening

Since we have no champagne, we are thinking of breaking a bottle of spring water over the new twenty-four-ton lannon stone wall now completed.

⚜ ⚜ ⚜

Now that the water is coming up over the ice along the sides of the new dikes on Fish Pond, we have been carting frozen earth to raise the two tiny islands so they will not be drowned.

⚜ ⚜ ⚜

The other day we watched sparrows trying to drink beads of ice from a spruce bough. The little birds tried again and again to drink the translucent but solid drops.

Not so lonely

All of us at Little Lakes had been feeling sorry for the single golden-eye on Blue Pool, because we figured she was lonely. The duck shares the pool with two mallard hens and, lately, four tame ducks. Being a diver, the goldeneye has nothing in common with these larger puddlers. So, we were pleased to see and hear five goldeneyes come whistling out of a snow-filled sky to set for a spell with the lonely one.

There were three drakes and two hens in the flock, so things were nicely paired off, since the duck in residence is a female. But there was no bobbing of heads, no friendly talk. Instead, the female in residence dived. Coming up beneath the intruders, she got herself a bill full of feathers. She kept up these tactics until the visiting five were jumpy as a drop of water on a hot skillet.

From my hiding place among the spruce, I watched for twenty minutes before going to the house for a cup of coffee. It was snowing hard when I came back to the pool. The female still had not made friends. Members of the flock were still rising two and three feet off the water each time she jabbed them from below. Finally, they left. The goldeneye hen slithered up onto a skirt of ice along the shore and preened.

Striking red

Already there are signs of spring. Each day the cardinals look more crimson than yesterday. They are more brilliant than fire or a sunset or a ripe cherry. Sometimes when the sun shines on a cock cardinal as he perches on a spruce bough against a patch of snow, the effect is startling. The hundreds of spruce around Blue Pool belong to the cardinals. Here the birds flit like flakes of fire. The pool rarely freezes, and it is so blue it is almost black under cloudy skies. When cardinals fly across the pool, their reflections make sparks in the water.

↝ ↝ ↝

For the second time, I saw a cottontail swimming. The rabbit had several holes and a building to run under, but when the dogs came up, it entered the water where Watercress Creek widens upon joining the mill pond. It swam across easily and swiftly. Sergeant spotted it and jumped into the water. He was the most surprised dog I have ever seen. Perhaps he thought the water would be as warm as in summer. Anyway, he turned back and scrambled ashore. The rabbit swam about thirty feet, climbed out onto the snow-covered bank and made good time in getting into the bullrushes.

↝ ↝ ↝

This is surely the most beautiful winter we have spent at Little Lakes. Each day lately, the hundreds of spruce and pine trees get fresh blankets of white snow. Then when the sun shines, the place glitters.

Much to do

Winter is no time of waiting out here. Frozen chunks of peat moss are hacked from Fish Pond dike and brought into the basement to cover bulbs so the plants will have a start of growth when spring comes. Fences are being strung around pens that will house pheasants, quail, mallards, Canada geese, and whatever crippled wildlings the Rebels pick up during their jaunts around the premises.

Twenty-one yards of sand have been hauled in and shoveled down the hill onto the beach of Clear Pool. All the trees less than thirty feet tall have had their winter trimming so they will grow straight up toward the sky. Weeping willow limbs are soaking in water in the darkroom. Soon they will be sprouting so that when they are planted in spring they will grow at once.

Lannon stone has been laid around the sunken garden. At other flower beds, old fencing is coming down and more stone is taking its place. Boats must be scraped so they can be painted in spring.

Planning is a part of winter, too. Rough maps must be laid out and decisions made for spring planting locations for Norway pine, cedar and spruce trees. As soon as the frost leaves the ground, there will be multiflora rose, bittersweet, highbush cranberry, dogwood and many other shrubs to be planted.

The new pool, not yet finished, must be laid out on paper so that when the machinery comes back in spring to finish the job, the underwater drainpipe and the overflow pipe can be dropped in exactly their proper places. A score of other jobs must be done so they do not hold up the projects that can only be finished in spring.

SPRING

Nature fights back

Nature has a way of taking care of her own, and sometimes when people interfere, the Old Gal has a way of retaliating. Right now, she is slapping us around because we decided we could manage things better than she could.

It started a couple of years ago when we got good and mad at the muskrats because they were making some of the dikes look like sieves. So we embarked on what amounted to a muskrat eradication program. Then, last year, we decided that the fish weren't growing fast enough in Fish Pond. So, we spent a considerable sum on commercial fertilizer, but we did not pour in enough to cloud up the water, and the weed growth made a jungle of the pond. The fish grew, and there were no muskrats to poke holes through the dike, so we figured we were making progress. Still not satisfied, we decided to give the fish more water by bringing in a dragline and gouging out some more holes. To do that, we had to lower the water.

Well, to make a sad story short, Fish Pond froze before water levels were back to normal last November. All the weeds decomposed beneath the thick layer of ice. There were no muskrats to eat the vegetation and to keep holes in the ice open along the shorelines. So now, the fish we have been working so hard to grow are lying dead on the bottom of the pond and all our work has been for nothing. At least we fear they are all dead. Looking through holes chopped in the ice, we can see them on the bottom. It will be another three weeks before we know for sure how many we lost. But it appears three years of work have been wiped out at one crack, and we will have to start all over. And all because we figured we were smarter than nature.

Life without spring

Having lived briefly in California, Louisiana and Florida, I have nothing but sympathy for permanent residents of those states because they have no real spring and can't know the exhilaration a northerner experiences when the rivers break from their icy prisons, geese return, earthworms are red against a spadeful of garden soil, and the earth almost explodes with new, green life.

This rebirth is an annual experience so refreshing and exciting that any inconvenience caused by winter is small payment. In winter, activity is restricted and life is hazardous. Then, within a few weeks, the frosty grip is broken and the lean and hungry days are over. Last week, we trimmed the pencil-sized trunks of about five hundred cedars so they will shoot straight up. While we crawled from one tiny tree to the next, red-winged blackbirds and cardinals sang a symphony and mourning doves, already nesting, kept the beat.

Big flakes of snow were falling and, though the temperature was near forty, the ground turned white. So I went down to Blue Pool to watch the big flakes disappear into the water. I found three blue-green mallard eggs in the mud on shore, and they had been sucked of their contents. A muskrat had left an overland trail. Small northerns were trying to breast the current of Watercress Creek. Willow tips were furred, and the dogwood was as fiery red as the cock cardinals fighting each other for territory.

Two trout were dead in a backwater and examination showed swollen and infected gills. Fifty or more cedar waxwings whirled out of the spruce and speckled the bare branches of an alder clump. The white lawn was dotted with grackles who had just arrived. Chipmunks were stealing sunflower seeds from the bird feeders. And, in the maple trees, squirrels were hungrily licking sweet drops of sap that had bled from the trees and frozen into candy icicles.

On the way back toward the house, I saw bluegills in the half-open waters of Clear Pool. I exercised a little willpower and did not pick up the flyrod, but went back, instead, to trimming cedar trees.

Regal couple

Duke and Duchess have arrived, and if their automobile ride was hardly as dignified as befits such royal birds, the red carpet was surely out when they got to Little Lakes. Duke and Duchess are a pair of Canada geese. They were cut out of the flock on a mink ranch at New Holstein and, after being stuffed into sacks so they could not struggle and injure themselves, they made the bumpy ride to Little Lakes. We kept the windows open but, upon arrival, both were wet with saliva from the excitement. Duke, first out of the sack, set up a wild clamoring for his mate. When the Duchess came out, he immediately quieted down.

Once out of the sacks, the geese were all dignity again. There was no wild rushing against the wire as with pheasants or ducks held in captivity. They walked entirely around the pen, stretched their necks for a look at the ponds below the knoll, then drank deeply and began preening. After the geese were cleaned up, Rebels No. 1 and 2 went visiting. Watching from a window in the house, I surely expected the geese to panic, but they did not. They watched the Rebels, but permitted them to approach within a few feet before the Duke hissed a warning.

Next morning, they seemed somewhat at home, but still alert. Just a movement of a curtain in the house two hundred feet away brought Duke to his feet. He sees everything from a falling leaf to the pigeons turning somersaults in the air above. A barrel made comfortable with straw is waiting for eggs from the Duchess. We hope she lays them so that in summer there will be goslings.

Onyx in cotton

Clear Pool is never more startling than after a heavy snow. Black by contrast, it is held between snowy hills like a huge onyx in a box of white cotton. Watercress Creek comes out from under the bridge like a writhing black snake of water.

Copperking

These mornings the shimmering feathers of Copperking catch the morning sun as he lifts to the tips of his toes and screams and flaps his wings. Three honey-colored hens, his harem, come out from beneath the spruce trees laid in the pens. The dogs bark in a kennel nearby, and the Canada geese talk deep down in their long, graceful throats.

Pigeons coo, mallards gabble, cardinals whistle, and robins and a whole choir of birds sing to the new spring day about to bless Little Lakes.

Copperking is a Mongolian pheasant. Every color of the spectrum glistens from his feathers, but his trademark is his chestnut-colored throat. The pheasant rooster is a calm, quiet bird. He struts for the hens even when the kids have their noses through the wire.

Duke stays home

Perhaps even freedom sometimes comes with too high a price tag. Duke, the Canada goose, flew the coop. Once out, however, he discovered there was one thing he wanted even more than his freedom. It was his Duchess. The Duchess cannot fly. When she did not follow Duke over the wire, he came back and stayed as near her as the wire would permit. When the door was opened, he gladly returned to confinement. All that day, wild Canada geese were following the skyway route north. Duke cocked his head, eyed them and honked plaintively, but did not try to fly again.

Blizzard of waxwings

One sunny day last week, we were visited by a blizzard of birds. While I sat on a chair I have hauled down to Blue Pool, a hatch of tiny black flies formed a halo around my head. At once, a flock of fifty or more cedar waxwings positioned themselves in the low willow bushes. Then they made forays into the bouncing cloud of flies, almost knocking my hat off. Once in the fly cloud, a bird would fan the air with its wings to maintain position and pick the insects like berries from a bush.

Marooned

Being marooned on an island hardly bigger than a desk might have been good for a laugh, except that my waders were full of icy water. The boat broke away while I was rip-rapping the banks of one of the Fish Pond islands, and when I tried to follow an underwater ridge to shore, I was dunked and had to scramble back to safety. The Rebels were still in school. The Rebel Queen was taking a nap. The place was deserted. So, after whistling and shouting, I sat down to wait. It was more than an hour before I spotted the Rebel Queen walking along the top of the hill. I whooped and she came down and said maybe the island was a good place for me, because I surely couldn't get into any trouble out there.

New growth

Spring rains have dyed Little Lakes green. New grasses are sprouting — redtop in the bottoms, canary reed on the dikes, clover and blue-grass on the slopes. Cedar planted last year has lost its drab black-green color and is vivid. Norway pines are putting out candles. Hybrid poplar cuttings planted only a week ago are leafing. Trees and shrubs now going into the ground include lilac, highbush cranberry, blackhaw, multiflora rose, wayfaring trees, honeysuckle, dogwood, bittersweet, spruce, black locust, cedar, Norway pine, wild plum and black walnut.

Thirteen was unlucky for the wild mallard hen who hid that many eggs under a spruce near Blue Pool. A raccoon ate all of them. The coon missed another nest containing eight eggs. Everybody out here is hoping it will not come back.

Hard times

Cold weather is giving swallows and especially the martins trouble again. Almost every year, birds that feed on insects while flying starve about this time. It is incredible that they do not delay their migration until the insect supply is certain. But, if the scientists are right and the daily amount of light is responsible for the time of departure north, they do not have much choice in the matter. The bird cemetery in the garden has a lot of new graves. These are perilous times for songbirds. In their rush to get new homes built and eggs laid, they crash into all sorts of obstacles such as wires, cars and windows.

Museum pieces

The Rebels have a collection of animal skulls. They are simply intrigued by them. Why, we do not know. But any pile of bones has them sorting out parts to piece together the skeleton. Even dogs do not drag home as many as these little girls. There are a couple of skulls we cannot identify. The Rebels insist we haul them to the museum so they can be labeled.

Pee Wee

A world of humans must be a terrifying place for a baby woodchuck. The tiny chuck was accustomed to spending its days in a dark cave except for a short time it spent afield mornings and evenings to feed in the clover. Big hands coming down from giants to pick it off the ground must horrify the animal. So it is no wonder that Pee Wee bites. His teeth are long and sharp, but his jaws do not have, as yet, the power to inflict a dangerous wound. Within two months, however, Pee Wee will be able to bite right through a dog's paw or a human hand. The Rebels are having trouble getting acquainted with the baby woodchuck. So far it has been up to me to handle him.

⁂

Now is the time! The orchard is white and pink with cherry, pear, plum and apple blossoms. The lilacs are crowned with purple clusters. The leaves on the grapevines are unfolding. The ferns brought from Door County are uncurling. Violets and marsh marigolds are everywhere. Only the swamp ash, reluctant tree, still does not have leaves.

Umbrella for Goldie

I was not home but I heard that, on the stormy Saturday when the tornado warnings were out, mother was looking to herd the Rebels into the basement as the west darkened and rain pelted down. All except Rebel No. 2 stood ready to duck for the cellar. She was finally found in the duck pen holding an umbrella over Goldie, a mother duck whose eggs were hatching.

⁂

Survival of a species must be a tremendously important part of nature's plan. We have lost count of the number of eggs lost to predators by the three wild mallard hens. It is over fifty, and each duck had at least two nests destroyed. They are all trying again, however. Maybe they will make it this time.

⁂

The new pool, still unnamed, is fast filling with water. The clay from which it was dug will give it a green-blue cast and apparently the water will be clear. The pool will have a solid spruce hedge to the west, Norway pine and white spruce trees to the east, huge willows to the north and a large elm and basswood shading it on the south. One turtle has found its way to the pool.

Taps for a woodchuck

In a world of human suffering, the death of one tiny animal is of little more consequence than the quenching of the flame of a match. But when little girl voices sang taps at Pee Wee's funeral Tuesday, the pain was the same and as poignant as those more consequential sufferings that each must someday bear. Pee Wee was the baby woodchuck finally convinced by kindness to be kind. He died of internal injuries suffered in a fall from the top of his eight-foot cage, where he sometimes crawled to sit on a two-by-four.

SUMMER

Ghosts

Sometimes, it seems, ghosts visit these Indian burial grounds. Especially on new moon nights, when a mist lifts from the water and seeps up the banks of the ponds along the lawn, there are echoes from the past among the towering elms.

The children are the first to sense it. Then they wonder if the Indian buried beneath the outdoor fireplace is going to the springs for a drink, or standing on the hill watching the river for canoes, or searching the forests for his family. The dogs are uneasy, too, and they do not bark but howl mournfully and then act frightened and run into their kennels. It is more than just imagination for the kids and the dogs, because there is a sharp snapping, like no daytime sound, among the trees, and there are shadows, swift and silent, past the window.

So I go to quiet the dogs and the Rebels hang on to my jacket and press close while I explain that the sounds in the trees and the shadows are owls, and that the mist is not really campfire smoke, and that the Indian under the fireplace is not roaming. They know what I say is true, but they do not believe me because they do not want to. And sometimes I am not so sure myself that Indians long dead do not visit this place and gather in ghostly council.

Hungry plant

Weasels, mink, raccoons, dogs and the humans of Little Lakes are not the only ones who eat meat. Down among the bogs along the lip of Fish Pond, there is a hollow-stemmed plant that stands stiffly erect, now that it is blooming, and it, too, thrives on meat. It is the pitcher plant. It stands about a foot or fourteen inches above the earth and has a reddish, waxy bloom. The flower gets its name from the pitcherlike leaves coated on the inside with a honey-sweet substance that attracts insects. At the bottom of this death trap, there is a tiny well of water to drown insect visitors. In winter, the leaves stand green and strong and the pitchers are filled with ice until snow comes to cover them.

Midnight terror

Terror struck at midnight. A sleek, wet, long moving shadow, it came slithering out of the jungle of marsh grass that borders Watercress Creek. The night was partly overcast. A moon filtered just enough light through the clouds to give the water a misty sort of shine, to throw grotesque shadows where cattails stood.

Unable to sleep, I had come to a favorite spot beneath a weeping willow to listen. It isn't often we see night creatures. Mostly we hear them. But the long moving shadow, intent on something, passed close and paid me no heed. Near the edge of the water, it disappeared. It moved silently, and it crept so deftly not even the grass moved.

Then it struck, and all the wild mallard ducks and their kids exploded in every direction with great splashing and loud quacking. All fled, except one. The mink had managed to get its teeth into a half-grown youngster and drag it from a log into the water. In the water, the mink could not get enough footing to kill the duckling, but neither would it turn it loose. The three adult hens and the drake made such a racket that the entire village on the hill must have heard.

The three hens repeatedly returned to attack the mink. It submerged just enough to avoid their bills and flailing wings, but never relinquished its hold on the duckling. There was no way for me to get out to where the youngster was dying; it was really none of my business anyway.

It took a long time for the duckling to die, but as soon as it did, the little flotilla of mallards quieted down and swam off to another night spot. Then, within seconds, the frogs were croaking again, the mink crawled onto a log to dine and I went back to bed.

Longing for home

The Jungle, Nicaragua
The Rebel Gang
On Little Lakes

Dear Rebel Gang:

Are the tiger lilies blooming and have the berries ripened? Did the mulberries turn purple before the birds got them? Is the canary reed grass coming up as rank and green as we hoped when we were planting it? Will the cedars in the wet spot grow, or are they turning brown? And how about the new weeping willow trees? Did they root? Are they putting out branches?

This Nicaraguan jungle is a strange and exciting land, but I am no part of it. I belong where the thistles are heading out and the goldfinches are happy about it. My heart is always at home where only cattails grow their own little jungles and the water runs clear, sweet and cool. I wonder these hot, sultry nights how cool the breeze really is as it crosses the ponds and moves up the hill and ripples through the bedroom curtains. Have you had watermelon yet? Red, almost icy and juicy sweet? Is any sweet corn ripe? Have you had fresh beans from the garden? Are the tomatoes reddening?

They have strange fruits here. I prefer a dish of currants with sugar and cream. Or strawberries, warm right from the garden. Or an apple from the tree and, if it is a little green, then salted some. Here the coffee is good if the cook does not burn the beans while she is roasting them in an open pan. But coffee at home is better and iced tea in a tall glass better still, especially if sipped in the shade of the big elm that guards the house.

The fishing here is, of course, fantastic, though it is a brutal sport of muscle against muscle instead of a fine art of floating a fly so properly a trout is fooled. But I will be home soon, and then I will sit on the stone steps beneath the big oak and just look and just marvel at the blue-green coolness of the pool below.

My love, of course,
Mel

What had to be

The Jungle, Nicaragua
Bernice Ellis
On Little Lakes

Dear Bernice:

Rebel No. 2 was justified in killing the two creatures and she is not to fret. There are emergencies that can only be met with bloodshed. Thank God, they are rare. You write that she is very upset about the affair. I can understand that. She and the other two Rebs always did hate to see anything killed. They make me feel like a murderer every time I come home from a hunt.

So I am sure it took more courage for her to shoot and kill the squirrel and gopher than it might have to capture them alive and risk being bitten, and perhaps contracting some disease. I know this is contrary to the precepts of many religions and some social orders, but supposing the squirrel or the gopher, or both, had had rabies or tularemia. Suppose they had succeeded in their attacks on the small ducks or the sitting hens. Suppose the affliction would have spread to the dogs, to the Rebels themselves.

No, when the two intruders refused to retreat and there was no adult present to act for her in the emergency, she did precisely what she should

have done by taking the pellet gun and killing them both. Tell her that.
Assure her that she did the right thing. I'll be home soon.

The Old Man,
Mel

Basswoods buzzing

The basswoods are buzzing as thousands of bees collect honey from
their blossom clusters. The air from one end of Little Lakes to the other
is fragrant, but already the narrow, bladelike leaves from which tea can
be brewed are covering the grass. Shortly, the nutlike fruit of the tree
will make mowing difficult. Chipmunks do not mind the mess the
basswoods make. They collect and hoard the tiny round nuts for winter food.

⚜ ⚜ ⚜

There is a good crop of hickory nuts at Little Lakes this year, but not
a black walnut on any of the trees. Despite the drought, the springs are
running well, although Fish Pond is below its normal level.

Two worlds

Summer has laid a hot hand on the hills here. She has parched the
grass and it turns powdery underfoot. Stones cast up by the gophers are
white in the sun and hot to bare feet. Elm leaves are shriveling. Lilac
bushes are browning. Only June grass stands high and haughty, impervious to heat and mower blade alike.

But the bottoms are lush. Even now, water stands beneath the spruce.
Jewelweed is damp at noon from mist, which whitened the morning.
Wild cucumber and nightshade threaten to strangle small trees. Wild
rice stands tall. Duck potato casts arrows of shade at the water's edge.
Cattails rear brown spires from each cluster of green wands.

On the hill, even the gophers are finding it hard to get food. Along
the bottoms around the pools, there is food in abundance: frogs, snakes
and fish for the green and blue herons; mice and crickets for the
snakes; mosquitoes, flies and other insects for the frogs; birds for the
mink and crayfish for the coons; and so much greenery for the rabbits
that they can stuff themselves without moving.

As you stand on the hills, the bottoms appear an oasis of green. As
you stand in the little valley and look up, the hills are Sahara dunes.
Coming off the slopes, out of the sun into the shade, is like moving
from one world into another.

Which shall live?

Mice may be a national menace and annually consume many times their weight in food that humans have reserved for themselves, but if you are out this way, do not let the Rebels see you raise so much as a finger against these, their friends. Right now, they are waiting for a litter of white-footed mice from the pair they have in captivity. The first mouse in their catch-them-alive trap was a female. Subsequently, they caught five males in a row.

They kept the first male, but I voted to kill the rest of the mice, in keeping with rodent control programs advocated by wise men the world over. The Rebels' protest would have warmed the tiny heart of every living mouse. So, as a compromise, we carried each "unnecessary" mouse to the far end of the property. I suggested painting the tail of each mouse red to determine whether they were coming back to live high on the dogs' food and whatever they might steal from us. The Rebels would have no part of this. Paint, they said, might poison the mice.

This, of course, was not their real reason for not wanting the mouse tails painted red. I am sure they were afraid I would discover that the mice were coming back and that I would then invoke the death sentence. But the more important problem, as I see it, is what stand do I take officially as far as rodent control is concerned? Do I recognize the Rebels' live-and-let-live policy, or do I go along with the mouse eradication program as advocated by the wise men?

Be careful, because it is not that cut and dried, according to the Rebels. If a mouse may be killed, why not a squirrel? And, if a squirrel may be killed, why not a raccoon? And, if a raccoon, why not a dog, a horse, a man? You can get around that logic and so can I, but try leading a couple of Rebels around it.

New Pool

New Pool is finally finished — grading, seeding and all. It is clearer than Clear Pool and bluer than Blue Pool.

We dug nearly two hundred feet more waterway for Watercress Creek, using an ordinary sump pump to transfer water at three thousand gallons an hour from Clear Pool to Fish Pond. Green herons are all over the place, feeding on a tremendous hatch of bluegills and bass.

Beautiful in fall

Red sumac, yellow goldenrod, purple gentians, green-blue spruce, brown-eyed susans, blue grape clusters among bright green leaves, aquamarine waters, purple-black chokecherries, yellow basswood leaves, bright bronze sunflowers nodding beneath the weight of their own seeds, and lacy cobwebs putting a filmy haze over the colors now previewing fall. Little Lakes is never more beautiful than in fall. There are maples soon ready to take fire and birch that will turn into golden arrowheads. All the flowers are flamboyant. They are the last glory, the final flame before the drab days.

⁂

A foot-long northern and a three-pound smallmouth bass are whittling away at the thousands of tiny green sunfish and bluegills we are trying to raise in Clear Pool. Escapees from the net, they are the only mature fish in the pool. Now they spurn fishing lures and even live bait. If ever fishermen needed a concrete example of the way fish can be conditioned to avoid a hook, these two outlaws are providing it.

Welcome rain

This will go down in the history of Little Lakes as the Dry Summer. Though rain fell all around us, sometimes within seeing distance, rarely did it speckle our ponds. Often, thunderheads reared on the horizon and we stood waiting, watching, almost praying they would march across the sky and dump water on the brown grass, the withering garden, the thirsty trees.

Without water, the world is nothing. Without rain, Little Lakes languishes. Eventually, of course, the ponds would go dry, the slopes become barren, the trees become skeletons. So, when the rain finally came last Wednesday, it received the greeting it deserved. The children, who sleep upstairs, heard it on the roof. They got up and were laughing and running about, though it was still dark.

I switched on a yard light and the gleam on the puddles was more beautiful than a sunset. I could not sleep after that. On the way to work, I drove across the lawn, and it was soft beneath the tires. I stopped to measure the puddles, to see how clean the blue spruce, the stones by the creek, the planks of the bridge.

At the top of the slope, I stopped to look back at the dripping trees, the shiny puddles, the rivulets of running water. It was like quenching a thirst long denied. The drought was over. Now, if we can go into winter with enough additional rain to keep the ground moist, I believe nature will have no trouble getting things green next spring.

⁂

Rickey, the once-tame raccoon, still wanders the premises, though we never see him. There are only his tracks in the soft mud, the pincers of crayfish left along the shore, to tell of his passing.

Roof for thousands

Though we seldom pause to think that we are jarring someone's house with every step, the earth we walk on at Little Lakes serves as a roof to thousands of creatures. Along the grape arbor, fat yellow bumblebees have a door down to a home honeycombed with tunnels. Chipmunks have scores of warehouses and sleeping rooms connected by a maze of tunnels in and around the rock garden and the stone walls at the basement entrance.

Gussie, the woodchuck, has an elaborate underground palace. Ants and earthworms live by the millions underfoot. Crayfish tunnel long distances and build fancy chimneys of clay. Even the snakes, turtles and frogs will be going down soon to hibernate, and every dike and every shoreline of the four ponds has dark entrances where mink and muskrats move in and out of their homes.

The Rebels delight in seeing how close they can get to the bees without getting stung. On sunny days, they sprawl on their stomachs watching the front door to a chipmunk's home, or hunch over an ant heap trying to figure out what the scurrying is all about.

Sometimes we at Little Lakes disturb a subterranean home and get quite a surprise. One day, I was sucking silt from the newly dug section of Watercress Creek and the pounding of the pump startled a family of mink. I saw a big black mink scoot out of the creek and along the bank to disappear into the willows.

Sounds of migration

Nights are never silent now. A whole continent of birds is shifting south. We hear them. Kildeers calling all night. They sound lost; their call has such a plaintive, searching insistence. Night-herons. Eager to be down and requesting guttural clearance from others already roosting. Canada geese. Ancient passing sadness. Snow geese. Excited babbling. Widgeons. Swift sign of passing wings. Yellowlegs. Mellow fluting. Swan. Rare, distant clamor destined for death. And like nothing and then something, a twittering so thin and elusive it is perhaps no sound at all.

Peanut butter diet

Chicken soup, chicken ala king, roast chicken and chicken sandwiches are the order of the day, but Rebels No. 2 and 3 are on a cereal and peanut butter diet. Seems they are not up to eating Maude, Mabel and Marj, the last of the three hens who so faithfully sat on pheasant and duck eggs. It won't be long now and some of the mallards will have to be butchered. That, too, will be a sad time.

Trying to raise anything for meat at Little Lakes is a losing battle. Silver, the big and useless white Muscovy duck, has been gobbling corn for three years and will probably die of old age. Now, the Rebels want some pintails and wood ducks. Chances are, they will coax until they get them. But they had best never ask for rabbits. After all, we've got to save room for ourselves.

While standing on a ladder one dark midnight looking down where spotlights brightened Blue Pool, I saw what certainly looked like an underwater monster. The creature, all of eight feet long, flashed silvery and green in the light and swam underwater with almost incredible speed. Just as I thought I was losing my mind, I recognized the strange creature as a muskrat with a long trail of rushes heading to where it was building a home.

Day of rest

Here is a typical "day off from work" at Little Lakes:

4:30 a.m.   Up and off the three miles to Big Muskego Lake to shoot two ducks.

7:30 a.m.   Back for a breakfast of oatmeal, boiled eggs and toast.

8:00 a.m.   Pluck, singe and remove the entrails from the ducks.

8:30 a.m.   Plug in the pump that shoots water from Clear Pool to Fish Pond. Check the mink-feeding stations where traps will be set in November and bait them with duck entrails. Feed the bluegill fry in Clear Pool a ration of soaked and mashed pellets. Hack a new path through the impenetrable spruce to Watercress Creek. Watch brook trout on their spawning beds.

9:30 a.m.   Into boots and into the creek to cut a bushel of watercress. Sit in the sun chewing a mouthful of watercress and mint leaves. Haul the cress to the house for the women to clean and put in the crisper.

10:30 a.m.   Throw a new plank bridge across the tiny gully where water is overflowing from New Pool and washing itself a tiny river bed. Sit in the sun talking with Rebel No. 2 about getting muddy hands and sticktights on slacks.

11:30 a.m.   Take the five dogs and two Rebels for a walk around Fish Pond to see how much the cedar has been growing and to stand and watch a blue heron feeding on fish.

12 noon   Cheese and sausage sandwiches and peaches in cream, then onto the davenport in front of the television to watch the football game.

1:00 p.m.   Sound asleep.

1:30 p.m.   Rebel No. 3 howling in the kitchen because Rebel No. 2 has clouted her on the head in an argument about who is to get the dirty end of cleaning out the dog pen.

2:00 p.m.   Cup of hot black coffee to wake up, then to the easy chair next to Blue Pool to watch the fish feeding on a minor fly hatch. Cedar waxwings getting flies the fish miss; blue jays screaming among the willows.

3:00 p.m.   Run a hundred fifty feet of hog fencing from the duck pen to the dog pen so the dogs will not run off into the subdivision where a new home is going up.

4:00 p.m.   Back down to the pools to feed the fish, turn off the pump, test the lights and check the alarm wiring. Meanwhile, the Rebels feed the dogs, ducks, geese and other creatures.

5:00 p.m.   Jacksnipe, green-winged teal and watercress for supper.

6:00 p.m.   Read Saturday's paper and lecture Rebel No. 1 about scratching the car while backing it into the garage.

6:30 p.m.   With two Rebels, go to Blue Pool and climb the ladder to watch muskrats feeding under the spotlights. Chase a cat off the place and vow to clear the land of cats with a gun. Of course, the Rebels protest.

7:30 p.m.   Rebels do the dishes and homework while the Rebel Queen and I watch television.

9:30 p.m.   Snoring.

Another Rebel

Red leaves and brown chestnuts. Dew jewels on spider webs shining in a morning sun. Leaves for piling high and rolling in. Moon through

Rebel No. 4 has arrived at Little Lakes.

the bare and stretching arms of a naked tree. Apples so frozen they hurt your teeth. A midget owl's mourning. All these are nothing without people to appreciate them. So we are more than especially glad these days about how the brown oak leaves sound like spirit robes rustling in the night wind, because now there's another at Little Lakes who will someday see the red thornapples carpeting the ground.

You see, Rebel No. 4 came home this week. She is right in the Rebel groove by being the fourth female in a row and by coming along seven weeks ahead of schedule, and while her Old Man was away, hunting in South Dakota. This next week we will take her for a walk around the grounds. She will be so bundled there will be no part of her peeking out. But I will walk her around just so that, twenty years from now, I can tell her about it. And, this week, I will be wondering, will she be frightened of water and snakes? Will she, like the other Rebels, enjoy the dogs and crawl into the kennels and sleep with them? Will she get the feel of the earth and learn, as she grows to be a woman, that a blade of grass, a bird, a sunbeam, is important even as are atom bombs and presidents?

chapter three

AN ABUNDANCE OF ANIMALS

WINTER

Return of Rickey

Rickey the raccoon, released nearly two months ago, is back. But now he comes at night and not as a friend. He waits until the house lights are turned low and then he moves out of the trees, creeps along the Fish Pond shores and comes up the hill to where the pigeons, geese, ducks and pheasants live.

Signs indicate he climbs the mulberry tree, swings from a lower limb to the top of the pigeon house and then crawls through a hole in the building to make his nightly raids. To date, he has made off with eight of the twenty-one pigeons. The Rebels cannot bring themselves to set a steel trap for their former friend, but they are losing birds who have sat in their laps to eat corn.

The live trap on the place is not large enough to contain a raccoon. So now, we have boarded the holes so that only a pigeon can enter, and the Rebs are waiting to see if Rickey will look for dinner elsewhere.

⚹ ⚹ ⚹

These are not necessarily dreary days at Little Lakes. A fire crackles in the fireplace. On occasion, snow turns the spruce, pines and cedars white. Ice puts a shiny border on the ponds. There are pine cones to be picked and spruce boughs to be cut for Christmas decorations. Inevitably, the catalogs come out when the supper dishes are done, and Christmas lists grow. And, of course, the work goes on and the chores must be done. Now that the outdoor water system has been disconnected, there are pails of water to be lugged for the five dogs. The birds must be fed and watered and the fish continue to eat, even in winter. The traps are still out and must be tended, so there are muskrats to skin and stretch. The Rebs, of course, cannot wait for deep, deep snow. We tell them they will be almighty sick of the white stuff by spring, but they are happy for today and tomorrow, and next spring might as well be a thousand years away.

Chilling grip

Winter has clamped its icy vise on Little Lakes. All the pools except Blue Pool are frozen. Even the earth is unyielding and resounds to the careless ax. Pigeons fluff against the cold. Ducks refuse to run, but squat so their vulnerable legs and webs stay warm among feathers.

Dogs bark less and sleep more. Cardinals, blue jays, juncos, chickadees, squirrels and rabbits are on bird-feeder relief. Muskrats are only bubbles under the ice. Copperking the pheasant does not crow at dawn, but sulks under a roof of spruce boughs with his hens. Duke and Duchess, the Canada geese, spend lazy days tail-deep in a pile of leaves.

Fish lie deep down on the bottom. Stamp on the ice and they are darting shadows. The summer green of cedars has turned to bronze. The warm glow of life has left the willows, and they are almost waxen in their winter death. Sparrows bed close to the warm house. Night catches the kids with chores only half finished, so the flashlight moves about the yard in the darkness.

Water steams from the pail. It freezes where it spills. Frost crochets white lace. Sunrises and sunsets are red fire and purple smoke, and the short day in between is brittle and bright or biting and leaden. Ice pendants hang from the eaves.

⁂ ⁂ ⁂

Some western cutthroat trout in Blue Pool are such eager feeders that an occasional individual leaps from open water right out onto the ice and then dies there.

A blue-winged teal, looking like a pony among a herd of elephants, has joined the five mallards in Watercress Creek.

The Rebels and all of us are getting a little taste of what life was like before water came from a faucet. Pump trouble has us hauling milk cans of water up from Clear Pool.

Light in the window

There was a light in the window last night, and it was for Cynthia. No, she wasn't lost. How can a white-footed mouse get lost? They are at home anywhere. The light was put on in the garage, where Cynthia shares a small cage with a pile of corn and sunflower seeds, so she could see to drink the water that Rebel No. 2 had been tardy in taking to her. When we explained that a mouse does not need three one-hundred-watt bulbs in order to see to drink, Rebel No. 2 went out and flipped the switch.

Christmas prayer

Consider the following bit of sentiment as the Rebels' contribution during this holiday season:

Dear father, hear and bless
Thy beasts and singing birds;
And guard with tenderness
Small things that have no words.

Adjusting to winter

Cottontails learn to use reflected sunlight as a source of heat by hunching out of the wind on the south side of a pond so warmth is reflected from the ice around and the bank above. The ducks spend the nights with their feet in the water. Springs keep the water open, so they roost on willow roots just below the surface. The water temperature seldom goes below forty and is usually close to forty-five. Since the ducks' legs and webs are particularly vulnerable to cold, they like to keep them immersed.

Sweet music

Starlings, though considered a nuisance in a class with the English sparrow, make some of the sweetest winter music heard at Little Lakes. Six to a dozen congregate in the tops of the big basswoods, and they imitate many bird species with their whistling and chirping.

Feeding the livestock

Feeding animals and birds around the place can become expensive. Though it varies from season to season, we figure we've been shelling out sixty dollars a month just to keep the "livestock" alive.

The five dogs consume about twenty-five dollars' worth of food a month. Often, especially in winter, this cost is much higher. Ducks, geese and pheasants, kept mostly as pets, eat about five dollars' worth of food per month during the winter and, when their kids come, this cost goes way up. Wild birds, rabbits and squirrels get an additional fifteen dollars' worth of food through the winter. Fish get approximately fifteen dollars' worth in a month. This sixty dollars a month amounts to more than seven hundred dollars a year. We could do a lot with that, but once these feeding projects are started, it is pretty hard to convince the Rebels that this bird or that animal ought to be eliminated.

Of course, we do get some money back when we eat the fish and butcher the ducks, but it is nowhere near the cost of the operation. And now, the Rebels are hollering for a horse!

January thaw

The warm, almost springlike spell of weather wiped the ice from Blue Pool and brought renewed vigor to raccoons, opossums and even what muskrats are left after some intensive trapping. During cold spells, such as the eleven-day stretch of sub-zero weather in early December, coons stayed aloft, possums only rarely made their garbage routes, and even cottontails spent daytimes underground or beneath buildings. Now even the birds seem to be making up for lost time by eating more so they can fatten against the time when another sub-zero wave will restrict their food-gathering forays.

*   *   *

The mallards and the tiny teal are competing with the trout for floating food pellets. They swim right among the feeding fish and, once in awhile, the teal gets bounced right out of the water as a trout comes up under it.

*   *   *

The sunflowers we planted last year so the birds and especially the cardinals would have plenty of food have not a seed left. Long before winter set in, the birds had picked the bending heads clean. Even mice climbed the stalks to get in on the feast.

Winter carpet

We are reluctant to let the dogs out after a fresh snow. It is much the same as turning a herd of cattle onto a newly landscaped lawn. In minutes, the beautiful white carpet is as messed up with tracks as the kitchen linoleum is when the Rebels come home from school.

SPRING

Ice out

Blue Pool is clear of ice. The ice on Clear Pool is so honeycombed it is unsafe. Fish Pond has holes in the ice through which runoff water is swirling. New Pool is losing water right off the top of the ice, which is level with the spillway.

Spring is a feeling

Spring is a vagrant. It comes and goes, visiting some, but passing others by. There is no special day set aside for its arrival, nor does it come at the same time for all of us. Spring can come even in the middle of winter. Usually it comes suddenly, without preliminaries, on a sun shaft through an office window, on a soft south wind through bare trees at night. I may hear it in the honking of geese. You may hear it in the trickle of water. Spring is not necessarily gentle. Sometimes it cuts banked snow with a ragged edge and the sound of it is in the roaring water. Spring is not really a season. It is a feeling. It is a quickening of the pulse, a lifting of the head, a flaring of the nostrils. It is a laugh and a skip and a jump. It is gratitude for being alive and an overwhelming desire to live. When it comes, you will know.

⚜ ⚜ ⚜

Grosbeaks have left, but a cloud of cedar waxwings has blown in to take their place. Little northerns from the mill pond are banging their heads against the screen, trying to get into Blue Pool. Male red-winged blackbirds are moving in to stake their claims to nesting areas. Tufts of fur along the paths indicate cottontails are mating.

Winter's scars

Winter was wonderful. There always was ice for skating and sliding. Snow drifted high enough to present a challenge. Many times the spruce trees were white spires. More birds than ever before came to the feeding stations.

Snow piled so high in the kennel runs that the dogs could very nearly step out. The many days of below-zero weather made the house a warm, welcome refuge. It was a good winter in that it made some of the old-fashioned winters we and other middling to older folks are always talking about look mild.

But the day of reckoning is here. The damage the winter did is starting to show up. It looks as though the conifers were hard hit. They are turning brown. Big slices of sod thrown up by the snowplows line the roads. More damage will show up as the snow melts. Ice damage to earth dikes and islands may be considerable. When the frost leaves, the ground will probably be muddy for weeks, and wheels and feet will kill off grass.

The animals and birds came through all right, but only because of an intensive feeding program. The trout survived in good shape, but the warm-water fishes of Fish Pond probably suffered. There was evidence a month ago that they were freezing out. So now, we pay for the wonderful winter just ending.

Frozen fast

Two hen pheasants behind wire on the hill squatted in the slush during a recent thaw. When they tried to move out, they discovered their tails were frozen fast. They managed to extricate themselves without losing any tail feathers, but are waiting for another thaw to loosen the lumps of ice they are dragging around.

Muskrat's talent

Determination, or perhaps a primeval instinct to persevere and survive, is just about the only talent a muskrat has. Tear a hole in its house a hundred times and it will patch it a hundred times. This is admirable, and no one should complain unless, of course, the muskrat is determined to become a nuisance. This has happened out here. A muskrat, who last week was given a pat on the rear with a shovel so it would get down off the hill into one of the pools, is back living in the mallard and Canada goose house. It hunkers down behind a barrel during the day, and at night chews holes into the feed boxes and bags of corn, scattering grain over the floor. Though it has been routed a number of times, it crawls back through the fence and, from all indications, it will become a permanent member of the duck and goose flock.

Mallard nests

Wild mallards have been nesting about ten days, according to the number of eggs in nests we recently discovered. One hen has her home under a spruce tree exactly where a raccoon or an opossum raided it last year. Another put her nest under a dock that had been pulled from the water. We removed the dock and built a board shelter over the nest. It didn't bother the duck. The other mallard hen is nesting under an overturned boat on the shores of Fish Pond. The boat will have to be moved and another wooden shelter built. One mallard has built a nest right in the middle of the Rebel Queen's favorite flower garden. I think we will let her fight that out with the state Conservation Department and the federal Fish and Wildlife Service. The wardens might discover they have tackled a little more than they can handle if they tell the Rebel Queen she has no legal right to move that hen's eggs.

✻ ✻ ✻

Eight hooded mergansers landed on Clear Pool, lined up like soldiers and dived in formation into the clouds of small bluegills and green sunfish. They glutted themselves until they were hardly able to fly.

✻ ✻ ✻

It will not be long and the lawn will be purple with violets. Then, as every spring, the same decision will have to be made. Either the grass will have to grow for a while or it will have to be cut and the violets' blooms cut down, too.

Gussie and Ossie

Gussie the woodchuck and Ossie the white-footed mouse are central figures in the most recent controversies between the Rebels and the lady who is fighting a losing battle to keep them from turning our home into a zoo.

Gussie, recently out of hibernation, has a ravenous appetite. Greens are at a premium, so rosy red apples, carrots, endive and lettuce have been disappearing from the kitchen. Now, the Rebel Queen works on a food budget, which she takes pride in keeping balanced, and it does not include expensive, out-of-season greens for a woodchuck. Luckily for Gussie, the local grocery store supplied a big box of lettuce leaves. Perhaps it will last until there is clover on the hill.

The problem of Ossie being in the kitchen has not been solved. The mouse escaped its cage last fall; it was content to spend the winter in the basement and only recently moved upstairs. The lady says the mouse must go. The Rebels would settle for the mouse's freedom, but are up in arms when the talk turns to murder. Mesh on live traps is too large to contain Ossie, so the lady wants to set the standard mousetrap. Of course, Ossie and the entire controversy could go up in smoke if the mouse chews on the electric stove wires.

✻ ✻ ✻

Two wild cock pheasants have established crowing grounds and are collecting harems at opposite ends of the property.

Chipmunks galore

Chipmunks, though cute, are also cantankerous and sometimes downright murderous. They have tunneled into the stone foundation beneath the summer porch, and we wonder sometimes what holds the porch up. They've made a shambles out of the fieldstone wall around the sunken garden, burrowed into the lawn, cleaned the punk from the hollows of standing trees and even sneaked into the basement occasionally.

If food is short, they climb the blue spruce and eat mourning dove eggs and young. They will even tackle a blue jay nest and stand off the irate parents with bared teeth. The colony out here probably numbers somewhere between fifty and a hundred. They are everywhere: in and under the garage and dog kennels, in the duck and pheasant pens, in the bathhouse, in every fieldstone and lannon stone wall. I have been tempted to whittle the population to about half of what it is, but it would be like walking on wildflowers.

Cottontails may be scarce in many areas of Wisconsin, but there are plenty out here and more showing up every day. The doe rabbit sprawls on the grass in plain view, head high and ears forward. She is nursing her young. The best way to get a look at the young is to mark the exact spot where the doe has been lying. The youngsters will be in a fur-lined hole hardly larger around than an orange or grapefruit and only a few inches deep.

Ribbon of fluorescent red in the tip of a deep green cedar. Child's balloon? Candy wrapper? I moved closer. Unbelievably vivid. No living thing for sure. But it moved to a neighboring cedar. Tanager, scarlet as its name.

Renegade trout

I like to think I know a little bit about fishing, but one fourteen-inch rainbow trout has taken some of the conceit out of me. The trout, who gained access to a screened-off portion of Watercress Creek, defied my angling efforts for two weeks. I tried spearing and netting to no avail. The fish took refuge behind the boulders where the banks are undercut.

On Friday, the day before a shipment of fingerling trout was due to be put into the screened-off section of the creek, dad was in and suggested I put in a setline. It worked. The setline with six hooks loaded with angleworms had the fish flopping within a half-hour.

There still was, however, a small grass pickerel of perhaps eight inches. Mother did not seem concerned. "Such a little fish," she said, "will not eat very many trout."

So we put the fingerlings, measuring between two and three inches, into the creek. An hour later, we spotted and caught the little pickerel. It already had two small trout in its stomach and one, which it could not swallow, protruding from its throat.

The little green herons, who fly as though their wings were attached to their bodies with rusty hinges, are among the fingerlings' worst enemies. If they persist in making raids, they will have to be dealt with.

✺ ✺ ✺

Rebel No. 2 reports another first out here and we have verified it. A pair of rose-breasted grosbeaks has moved in. The male is brilliant.

✺ ✺ ✺

Summery weather has exploded blossoms and leaves all over the place. There is such a profusion of plants that they defy listing.

Seeking a husband

What passes for love in the animal world and ensures survival of species is so strong that Gussie, the woodchuck, has deserted the finest bed and board she will ever again enjoy to go gallivanting off in search of a husband. It was quite a blow to the Rebels, who just cannot understand how a good friend could desert them, particularly after the way they tried to make Gussie feel at home.

✺ ✺ ✺

The ways of nature seem cruel to youngsters. One of the mallards has lost her clutch of eggs to a crow. The Rebels are indignant about it. Yet, when I suggest that the crows be dealt with, they do not want that either.

Brimming days

These are brimming days. The orchard is snowing apple, cherry, plum and pear blossoms. Nests of hundreds of birds are overflowing with youngsters ready to take wing. Lilac bushes almost break with their burdens of flowers. The jewelweed is a green carpet that within weeks will be a waist-high jungle. The pines have put out their candles. On moonlight nights such as we have been having, the tender new growth glows almost as brightly as the flame at the end of a real candle. So midnight becomes ethereal with mist lying like water between the knolls and over the ponds and the creek. Frogs are trying to keep the beat, but they falter. Nighthawks range the sky, and the wind through their wings is a quick rasping.

Why must they die?

The Rebels run a regular circuit from flower to flower, nest to nest and pond to pond. They are resigned to the fact that for every young thing that survives, another three or five or eight (depending on the species) must die. For instance: One mourning dove, of the hundreds around, brought one of its two youngsters to flight age. A pair of cardinals brought but one of their four kids out of the nest. One mallard hen is starting its third clutch of eggs. Crows got the first and a mower got the second. When the Rebels ask why so many die, I have no explanation except that it is all part of a big plan to keep the trees from being broken down by unlimited flocks of mourning doves, to keep the ponds from being completely shadowed by hundreds of ducks, to keep the world in balance.

Muskrats attack

Muskrats continue their depredations. The latest assault has been on the hybrid poplar trees along the Fish Pond dike. A year ago this spring, we were able to obtain twenty-five cuttings of this tree. Fifteen survived the rabbits and the winter. From these, we obtained about a hundred cuttings for planting. The tree is supposed to attain a height of about thirty-five feet in five years. Five of the fifteen trees, though more than an inch in diameter and more than six feet tall, were cut down and eaten by the rats. The cutting job was as slick as any done by a beaver.

Most beautiful: Crimson cardinal sitting among the white flowers of a billowing hawthorn. Four species of brilliant warblers decorating the blue spruce like Christmas tree ornaments. Tree swallow shimmering green against the sunset's reflection in the water. Starling reflecting morning light as though decorated with sequins. Dog's hot, red tongue lapping crystal clear, icy spring water.

SUMMER

Oriole year

This is oriole year out here. Normally, three or four pairs of orioles haunt the leafy crowns of the elderly elms. This year, from fifteen to twenty pairs have woven basket nests. More cardinals, mourning doves and robins are about than in other years. Starlings are imitating the half-song of the orioles. Catbirds, sweet-singing cousins of the mockingbirds, are nesting close to the house instead of in the wild grape clumps along the ponds. Dogwoods, fiery red wands in winter, are now green clumps decorated with large, white buttons of blossoms. All the ponds have a spectacular fireworks display in the evenings. Lightning bugs wink on and off like the far lights of a neon-bright city street.

A first, for me: Brown thrasher, a sometimes shy bird of prickly hedgerows, following a single chick, too soon off the nest, to feed it insects. The rangy youngster, still without the long tail that distinguishes the russet thrasher, looks more like the long-legged offspring of such a shore bird as the killdeer, and races away with amazing speed when I try for a closer look.

Danger in the form of a fish lurks in Clear Pool. Breasting the recent rush of floodwater over a spillway, a northern pike made its way from the mill pond into Clear Pool and is now a two-foot-long shadow of death waiting for any fish small enough to get down its gullet.

Alien land

Pointe du Bois, Manitoba
The Rebel Gang
On Little Lakes

Dear Rebel Gang:

This is beautiful country and game is plentiful. There are deer, and we chased a bear out of a watery meadow. There are eagles, many ducks and, of course, fish galore. But still it is an alien land. Here, even in summer, survival consumes all energy.

Trees growing from almost solid rock wait a century to get as tall as a house. Songbirds need the long hours of daylight just to find enough seeds and insects to keep a family in pinfeathers. Mallards who so dearly love worms must settle for snails. There is no soil for a plant or a child to put roots into. It is a land hard as the rock that covers it, rugged as the rivers that foam around the boulders, cold as the northern lights that spill purple and white icicles down the sides of the sky.

So know this now: You are living in a favored land. During the years, if you travel, you may visit many lush lands. You may live in the tropics, perhaps even on the beautiful shores of this, the Winnipeg River. But wherever, you will find no piece of earth quite as favored as your own. So put your roots down now — deep. Then if you must leave, there will always be some part of the rich country you are part of clinging to your memories.

Your dad,
Mel

Ruthless trees

The struggle for survival is a part of every plant's life, and it is never so dramatically portrayed as by the trees. The big trees, reaching greedily toward the life-giving sun, suffocate the little trees. One species kills another. Just off the sunroom, a big basswood whips branches against the spire of a blue spruce on one side and crowds a maple on the other. Without our help, the spruce will never get any bigger than it is and the maple will lean because only those branches on the sunny side will develop.

Some trees, like some people, just cannot be kept down. Though surrounded and completely shaded by both spruce and weeping willows, the elm alongside Blue Pool keeps reaching and will surely top out unless we intervene and cut it. Among the spruce groves, box elders start from seedlings and send slender trunks spearing up out of the gloom. In a few years, their green leaves are bright above the darker green boughs of the conifers.

The short-lived trees seem to be the most tenacious. They surmount seemingly impossible obstacles. Perhaps it is because they are destined for such a short stay under the sun that they drive skyward with fervor for a brief bit of glory.

⁂

Fish Pond has dark clouds of tiny bullheads all along the shores. Small bass are jumping for flies. Crayfish sputter away from the shore by the hundreds. Turtles have taken over the logs and every low, flat bank. So winter did not kill everything in that pond.

Protecting the young

Parents of wild kids, finned and feathered, react differently to human interference. The blue-winged teal feigns a broken wing and dares to come almost within arm's length before fluttering off through the cattails. Humans out here have pursued her to see how far she would take them before lifting and flying back to corral her brood and herd them to safety. Those were long, weary treks for the humans.

Green sunfish guarding a nest of eggs actually attack and strike at the Rebels' fingers when they put them in the water. Screaming blackbirds dive to within hair-pulling distance of intruders. Little screech owls swoop out of the night, bills clacking. Mallards turn into angry, feathered bombshells and hiss while flopping against the intruder's legs. Mice flee, but the kids hang on to mother's milk faucets and are dragged to safety. Robins holler but rarely attack unless the intruder is a chipmunk or another bird.

ツ ツ ツ

New Pool, reserved since being dug for experimental crossbreeding of fish, is full of five-inch largemouth bass. While tiny, the fish escaped from Clear Pool down a small ditch and now, though New Pool is landlocked, it is swimming with bass.

Rickey is trapped

Rickey the raccoon, a free agent since he outgrew the status of a pet late last summer, came back the other day, only to blunder into a steel trap set to catch opossums that have been raiding the duck nests. It was heart-rending for the Rebels to see their old friend with the trap dangling from his paw.

At first, there seemed no alternative except to destroy the coon. Rickey is twice as large as when he left our free board and room, and a fifteen- or twenty-pound raccoon is nothing to tangle with. But you do not shoot your friends. So, we hooked a forked stick to the trap chain and hauled Rickey onto the lawn. Then I went for a large piece of canvas to put over the animal so I might try to spring the trap.

While I was in the garage, Rickey crawled into a large tar bucket, so upon my return, I quickly tipped the bucket and pinned him beneath it and put a knee on the trap spring. It opened. Rickey pulled his paw free. He limped away and started up the side of a tree. Then he looked back at the Rebels, and I'm sure he recognized them. For an instant, I thought he would come back. Then he lowered himself from the trunk of the tree and, with one more backward look, limped away through the heavy undergrowth.

⚹ ⚹ ⚹

In all the years we have observed blue herons fishing, we have never seen one capture a fish of more than a quarter-pound. But the other day on Blue Pool, Rebel No. 1 startled a heron right after it had speared a two-pound trout and hauled it onto the bank. The beak of the long-legged bird had been used like a stiletto and run completely through the trout just back of the gill covers.

To market

The cattail harvest is on. Rebel No. 1 hopes to cut five thousand or more pencil-slender cattails before they mature. After they dry, she markets them. Ambitious and energetic youngsters can find many summer money-making projects, even along country roads. A little imagination and a lot of hard work can turn creeping, crawling things into fish bait. Weeds furnish raw material for floral pieces. Watercress and mint help salads and juleps. Butterflies brighten glass table tops.

Rebel No. 2 put up a big howl when I threatened harm to the green and blue herons raiding the ponds. So now she must "ride" a regular circuit several times every day to see to it that the big birds do not steal too many fish.

Rebel No. 3 is our goose girl. Since the Canada geese love to graze, it is her job to see they get plenty of fresh, green grass. Formerly, she picked grass and put it in their pen. Now, she turns the birds free for an hour a day and herds them. The geese and the girl like it better that way.

Rebel No. 4? She just coos, chews her toes and smiles when the birds sing.

Lurking crayfish

Thousands of crayfish haunt every cranny of Fish Pond. They stare from beneath rocks, logs, undercut banks and tiny mud caverns like miniature monsters waiting to pounce and lock their pincers on unsuspecting trespassers. The winter freeze-out of fish provided them with an abundance of food, but now that the feast is over they are even latching onto fishermen's wet flies.

⚹ ⚹ ⚹

Two bird invasions this summer have us puzzled. Hummingbirds, sometimes as many as six or eight at a time, have been observed hanging in flight among the spruce trees. Cedar waxwings, always abundant in spring and fall, have also stayed around all summer.

Elms in peril

Dutch elm disease has descended upon Little Lakes. Six trees have already come down and two more are scheduled for cutting. It will surely be a tragedy if more elms succumb. It seems hopeless, however, for one individual or one village to make extensive and costly efforts to stave off the invasion of disease-carrying beetles, when whole forests nearby are turning brown as the disease sweeps through.

Welcome moisture

The earth is soft, spongy. It springs a little underfoot and there are nightcrawler and crayfish diggings on the lawn. Wheels of the tractor dig in. People and robins of Little Lakes are happy. They will not forget how hard the earth was last year and the year before. How a hoe made a ringing sound as though striking metal instead of ground. How the grass became dust. How the leaves withered and cedars turned brown. How the springs diminished. How the very air was irritating to breathe.

❦ ❦ ❦

The courage of the mallard hen in protecting her seven youngsters from the fish of Blue Pool is inspiring. Some of the trout have learned to scoop up young birds that fall to the water and they have, upon occasion, eaten ducklings. Though the mother duck keeps her kids in a tight bundle whenever they cross open water, occasionally one strays and a fish makes a pass at it. The mother immediately attacks the fish by putting her head underwater and trying to bite it. She at least diverts the fish's attention until the youngster can get with the gang so they can continue as a bundle to safer shores.

❦ ❦ ❦

Persistence certainly pays. Witness the thistle.

❦ ❦ ❦

Flies hatching in Blue Pool have a rough time of it. Not many get to the surface. The fish get them on the way up. For those that make it to the top, there are swallows and martins waiting to scoop them off the water. Should they become airborne, the pool is guarded by cedar waxwings that dart out and pick them out of the air. When darkness comes and the waxwings are resting, a squadron of bats takes over their job.

Monster in Fish Pond

It was inevitable that a monster should put in its appearance in Fish Pond. The only surprising thing is that it didn't happen sooner. The monster took a bait of dead fish we had put into the pond to catch crayfish. After much heaving and tugging by Rebel No. 2, the creature came to the surface, relinquished the fish and sank from sight. It was immediately reported as having a gaping mouth like a muskie or northern pike, great waving front fins like a sea turtle, an odor rank as that given off by long-dead fish, blazing eyes, and so on.

So this Old Man had to investigate. The monster obliged by taking a chunk of bluegill fastened to a big hook. I lifted it slowly. The water churned. What looked like flippers armed with claws broke water. A gaping, angry mouth came into the air and there was a hiss. Then, before relinquishing the bait of dead fish, the creature popped to the top like a cork. It was, of course, a huge snapping turtle who now has been commissioned president of the sanitary division, which is made up of crayfish, birds, bullheads and others. They keep the pond clean.

Popular pool

Of all the pools at Little Lakes, Blue Pool is most popular in summer. It is a haven when it's hot. Cooled by springs that percolate up through the pea gravel bottom, its depths are always icy. So the Rebels dive through the upper strata of warmed water to swim a distance below and then bob back refreshed. Some of the springs are in only a few feet of water, and visiting non-swimmers seek them out to stand over them so the icy water can creep up around their legs.

During August, the Rebels practically live in swimming suits. Then, no matter what chore or game, they can always leave it for a quick dip. It is almost possible to gauge the temperature by their number of visits. If the thermometer stands in the seventies, they are likely to swim three or four times. If it eases up into the eighties, they cool themselves six or eight times. When it hits ninety or goes higher, they never stray far and may take as many as ten, or is it twenty, swims a day.

Dumb animals?

Think fish are dumb? Perhaps, but it didn't take the bass and bluegills of New Pool long to learn that by following the rotary lawn mower around the shores of their pond, they could get in on a feast of grasshoppers and crickets, which the whirling blade spewed onto the water. Now, when Rebel No. 1 comes to cut the grass, she has a convoy of finny submarines following her.

Think geese are dumb? Maybe snows and blues are a little scatter-brained, but our pair of Canadas will graze to within a few feet of the kennels and never even raise a neck feather when the dogs growl and bark at them. Let someone make a move to open a kennel door, however, and the geese head for the safety of their own pen.

꒭ ꒭ ꒭

The fall flowers, mostly yellow and orange, are changing the landscape. Most delicate and most beautiful is the orchidlike blossom of the jewelweed. Orange on yellow, the tiny blossoms cluster like bright flames on billowing clouds of bright, bright green leaves.

Freedom and restraint

Swoop and Swirl, young seagulls now airborne, were brought out from behind wire last night and given their freedom. Like prisoners stepping from behind the grim walls of a penitentiary, the gulls were at first overawed at the immensity of the world around them. Then they were afraid. But fear vanished and their joy was something to behold as they dipped their heads into the pond and rolled the water over their backs.

For a half-hour they sported in the water. Then they clambered to the bank and spread their large, scimitar-shaped wings to the setting sun to dry. After that, they were ready to eat and, as each green sunfish was hooked and lifted from adjoining Blue Pool, they came fluttering. Then this morning, from the house on the hill, we could see them doing aerial acrobatics and flying for what seemed like sheer joy. Perhaps seagulls, like human prisoners, can't know what freedom means until after it has been denied them.

Yet prison can get to be such a habit that the courage to face freedom is stifled. Even Duke and Duchess, though they clamor each spring and fall to join their fellows in the high-flying flocks of Canada geese, are content after grazing in the clover patches to return to the security of their pens. All of us, of course, are prisoners of sorts, chained to a job, a family, and habits, both good and bad, of a lifetime. When we try to break these bonds, we become uneasy, and sometimes our consciences, bludgeoned by feelings of guilt, hurry us back to our prisons.

Freedom is relative. The dog, after wandering, comes back to lie by the pen door waiting to be imprisoned. The coyote may forage afield, but never far from the same route it follows all its life. Not only lakes imprison fish, but special areas of those lakes suitable to their survival. Discipline imprisons children, but without it, they are frustrated, irritable and lost. Freedom belongs to the hawk each day, but night makes it a prisoner. So freedom, in all its many meanings, is really meaningless without restraint.

AUTUMN

Flight plans

Mallards, silent all summer, are sounding reveille and taps with raucous quacking now that fall is approaching. They will be filing flight plans soon for their trip south. Drab drakes are starting to take on color. The molt is over and adults are trying their refurbished wings along with youngsters who just learned to fly. They are not as wary of humans now as they were during the flightless time. Now they know they can take to the air in the event of danger. While flightless, they scurried to hide among the rushes.

❧ ❧ ❧

Squirrels are so fat they waddle. It is a great acorn and hickory nut year at Little Lakes, and the bushy-tails are not waiting for the nuts to ripen. The ground is littered with shells and husks. Chipmunks, which live in scores of tunnels under and around the house, are making long trips to the oak trees these days. They stuff as many as four and five acorns into their mouths each trip and look like they've come down with the mumps.

Softening mist

Mist is on the meadows. It rises halfway up the knoll and hides the lower branches of trees. It shrouds the moon and filters sunlight. At the first morning breeze, it moves like smoke across the water. It puts a wet hand to the flowers, dims the yard light, fogs the windows. It softens and the early sun cannot glare, so turns an angry red. The mist puts a halo around the house and fills in the low spots along the road. It is the cooling night touching the scorched earth. It is the beginning of the end for summer.

King Rainey

If Rainey, the ten-year-old German shorthaired pointer, could read, he might know how he rates with the Rebels. On his kennel, second from the end, they have put a sign: King of the Kennels. This in spite of the fact that he is a somewhat obstinate and even ornery critter so intent on hunting that he has little energy left over for the kids. It surprises me to see the youngsters give this old dog recognition. The animal belongs to this Old Man and they have their own dogs. These younger animals are much more affectionate. Age must engender respect and a certain kind of affection in the young. Perhaps it is not age alone, but the long, hard life old Rainey has lived. Perhaps they sense that this old warrior, scarred veteran of hundreds of hunts, has come all the way with great dignity, always giving in to a master, but never giving up, even when death had him hanging on to life by a hair.

ᴗᵉ ᴗᵉ ᴗᵉ

Rocket, Dawn, Ringtail, Flash, Grayeagle, Tumbleweed, Dusk, Fireflash, Jet, Moon, Dove, Comanche, Cloud, Midnight, Storm, Hurricane, Falling Star, Mercury. Names of new-model cars? Race horses? Naw! Names of the Rebels' pet pigeons.

The old sadness

Cooling waters look crystal clear. Green bass are coming out of the holes to lie in a few inches of water along the shore, especially when the sun is hottest and highest. The leopard frogs are huge from feeding all summer. The tiny screech owls mourn more often. Mourning doves are flocking and, before sunup, they sit like shivering balls of fluff on sand the same color as their feathers. Blackbirds string in at night. Herons fly when the moon is bright. Ducks are restless. And when I walk at midnight along the dikes, through the dark tunnel trails in the spruce, across the high knoll white with moonlight, the old sadness is there among the first dead leaves, the dying grass.

Move to town?

Occasional visitors are appalled at the variety and endless hours of work that a place like Little Lakes entails. They groan almost aloud when they see the hundreds of tons of rock that have been lifted, pound by pound, to make retaining walls. They literally begin to sweat when they see cord after cord of sawed wood drying for the fireplace. They measure the lawn and count the hours that must be spent mowing it. They count the dollars that have gone into making holes in the ground that have filled with water and speculate on how many weeks in Europe those dollars might provide.

They see the stacks of bags of animal and bird food and think how many parties might have been financed with dollars spent for corn, duck grower, fish pellets and dog meal. They see the mud tracked from the marsh to the kitchen, the pumps that must be disconnected in winter, wiring and lights that must be repaired and replaced. So they go home happy because their life is uncomplicated and ours is not. They feel sorry for us instead of envying our lot. And we are happy for them and, for a time, sorry for ourselves.

We, it seems, had not looked on these things as work. Mostly they seemed like fun and, when some particular task wore on long enough to become laborious, we philosophically labeled it a labor of love. But after listening to these occasional friends, we sometimes sit on the porch and survey the place and start contemplating the foot-pounds of work needed to keep things moving.

I see the Rebels at their tasks and wonder if they might not better spend their time at some art center, museum or roller-skating rink. I look at the Queen of the Rebels and wonder if she isn't tired and might not be better off in a city apartment. So, at supper, I sidle into the subject. I mention how rough it is to carry water to the dogs in winter. I mention what a job it is to keep the grass from growing knee-deep. As I warm to the task, I do a little growling and grumbling about money. Then, about dessert time, I throw out the bait:

"How about moving into town?"

I wait then, rather breathlessly, for the reaction. It comes in a babble of voices.

"Move to town? But, daddy!"

And while the sometimes rebellious gang does its babbling best to sell me on the joys of country living, I smile inside because the glint of the setting sun on Fish Pond, where the sumac is turning red, has done their job of selling for them, long ago, even before they were born.

Overflowing

Never in the five years we have been at Little Lakes have the springs poured forth such a quantity of clear, cold water as this fall. All ponds are full to overflowing. Watercress is emerald green and spreading. I clipped a half bushel for the table, and the Rebel Queen said it never was so free of dirt and insects. The cold, of course, has sent the insects down into the warm water or below the earth, and clipping above the water line brings up clean, crisp cress.

For sale

Rebel No. 1 has three thousand miniature cattails dried and brushed and ready for market.

Rebel No. 3 is selling kids of the neighborhood chestnuts and acorns joined and carved and painted to look like little men.

Rebel No. 2 has finally decided that the pigeon gang is getting too large and so has sold two squabs to a friend.

Rebel No. 4 is selling nothing but smiles.

Friend of decoys

A lonely-looking grebe on Fish Pond has taken to fraternizing with the four decoys riding near the shore. The grebe, a feathery submarine of unusual dexterity, moves with only its head out of water when humans approach. By watching with binoculars, however, I can see the bird make overtures to the wooden decoys.

Fall-spawning rainbow trout are moving rocks weighing as much as five and six pounds as they gouge nests out of the Watercress Creek bottom. The males are brilliant. Their bottom jaws protrude. They are not nearly so wary as during other seasons and, if frightened from the gravel beds, they hurry back within seconds.

The fingerling trout, which measured less than two inches when they were boxed in by screens on Watercress Creek in spring, are now beautifully colored fish, some measuring six inches.

⚜ ⚜ ⚜

The dreary weather, which has discouraged oldsters around Little Lakes, doesn't seem to dampen the ardor of the Rebels. They bubble with as much enthusiasm as the springs, in spite of gray skies and never-ending rain. Everything from horse chestnuts to Halloween pumpkins to water drooling from a clogged downspout interests them.

Beauty is universal

Beauty may be elusive, fragmentary and fleeting, but it is universal. It pulsates briefly in the falling maple leaf, the shredded clouds, evening sun, a child's smile. It glows in a campfire, down a flashlighted forest path, in the bare branches of a moon-white birch, and in the floor lamp's halo around grandmother's hair.

But, what has all this to do with Little Lakes? Well, there is beauty at Little Lakes, of course, but there is beauty, too, on Milwaukee's Wisconsin Avenue when the rising sun lights up the tops of the tall buildings; in the smoke clouds of the trains and factories; in the gutter water rushing through the streetlight's circle to the Milwaukee River.

It is not necessary to live at Little Lakes or at any country place to see beauty. The most beautiful sight I remember was viewed through

Rickey the Raccoon has returned, but not as a friend.

a grimy second-story window along another city's skid row. Below in the dirty alley, a little girl of perhaps six was using a dirty little handkerchief to wash discarded yellow, red and blue candy wrappers. When the wrappers were bright, she arranged them in circles, triangles and squares along the brick roadway.

While I watched, the morning sun suddenly lifted over the buildings and lighted the alley. The candy wrappers caught the sun and glistened. The girl turned to look at the sun and smiled. And for a fleeting instant, that grimy alley was as beautifully radiant as any western mountain canyon, as beautiful as anything at Little Lakes.

Bucko is back

Bucko, the yellow Labrador, just returned from a hunting trip, "talked" for nearly an hour shortly after a recent midnight to tell all the other dogs where he had been, what he had been doing and how, now that he was back, they had better mind their manners or he would teach them a thing or two. That is how it sounded, anyway. He "talked" in many tones, from sharp barks to guttural growls. These had to mean something. And what else would a dog like Bucko talk about after having been selected as the only one in the kennel to make the hunting trip?

chapter four

YEAR OF THE DEATH WATCH

WINTER

Sad Saturday

Last Saturday was butchering day, the time when the Rebels had to decide which mallards were going to be spared and which were going into the deep freeze. Then Rebel No. 2, who is in charge of waterfowl, stood by to see that ducks selected to live did not get the ax by mistake. There had been some talk about keeping young birds for breeding stock, but when the time came to cut out those to be butchered, the four old birds were spared once again. Even Rosy van Etta, that noisy and undependable female who is always deserting her clutch of eggs or her brood, was spared. Walking with her now are Daisy, Goldie and Ringneck.

❊ ❊ ❊

Squirrels, already so fat they can hardly waddle, are coming into the bird-feeding station to add more ounces. More chickadees are around this year than we can remember. Crows sit and eye the corn but will not come in. Bluejays always fly a cautious reconnaissance before being tempted to eat. Nuthatches are stowing away every edible thing beneath the bark of the big basswood near the feeder.

❊ ❊ ❊

Now that marshes and some lakes are getting nightly coatings of ice, mergansers, goldeneyes and buffleheads drop into the open ponds at Little Lakes more often.

Never humane

Death is inevitably violent for almost all wild creatures, even at Little Lakes. Feeding during the winter keeps some birds and animals alive, of course, but it attracts many more creatures than the surrounding habitat can support. When the population of these vulnerable creatures reaches peak proportions, the predators move in.

Because there are more songbirds, there are more owls and hawks. Because there are more squirrels, rabbits and other living food, there are more weasels and mink and other killers. So even here, where killing is frowned on, especially by the Rebels, the trap and gun must harvest some rabbits, squirrels and some of those predators which the law says may be killed.

Trapping and shooting are never humane. Even when a live trap is used, the animal often becomes so frightened it panics and dies of shock. There is no easy nor any humane way to trap or kill anything. But there are, of course, some ways to ensure sudden instead of prolonged death. The water set where the muskrat or mink drowns almost immediately is one of these. The well-placed head shot with a high-powered pellet gun is another.

Though the live trap has been extolled as the best way to prevent suffering, to my way of thinking it is the most cruel. Sudden captivity is often much harder for a wild creature than death. Death is even more a part of living for the rabbit, squirrel and bird than it is for humans. Only a small percentage of most wild things even mature. Hardly any die of old age. Most, if not harvested by man, die of starvation, exposure or at the talons or fangs of some other creature.

※ ※ ※

With such a wealth of water turning the earth into a giant sponge, we are looking forward to one of the best tree-growing seasons when the spring sun finally sucks the last of the frost out of the ground. The trees, from the tiny seedlings to the giant oaks and elms, have gone to sleep with more water around their feet than in many, many a year.

Winter behavior

Winter has come to Little Lakes, and with it the strange changes that seem to come over most living creatures when the sun goes south and the cold creeps over the earth. Dogs have gone on an increased ration of cod-liver oil to give them body heat. We add suet to the bird-feeding station to keep birds warm at night. All spare greens from the kitchen have to go to the ducks and geese now that the grass is gone.

The tempo of living has slowed. The Rebel Queen and her brood of four are more content to sit with a book and munch popcorn. Even the dogs conserve heat by not exercising unless they are hunting. All fish except the trout lie close to the bottom, and the only sign of life is a slow waggling of fins. Squirrels stay denned up until midday. Raccoons come down only rarely to make a raid on the unpicked corn in a neighbor's field. Opossums wander nightly, but they clump along as though stiff with arthritis. During the days, muskrats are rarely active. Even the birds wait in the thick spruce until the sun warms the air before visiting the feeding station.

These days and the months to come are the lazy times. Though humans are far removed from the prehistoric days when we holed up like animals against the cold, there seems an inclination among some of us to turn away from the winter world and lead rather sedentary, house-warm lives.

⁂ ⁂ ⁂

Every feathered and furred thing that visits the bird-feeding station passes up every other offering to get at the sunflower seeds. Even the sparrows turn up their beaks at the cracked corn, suet, mixed seeds and scratch feed, if there are sunflower seeds in the feeder. Of course, sunflower seeds are the most expensive food. So even wild creatures can develop expensive tastes if someone else is footing the bill.

Window to water

The ice on Blue and New Pools and Fish Pond melted and then, on a cold and silent night, froze again. So now it is transparent as a windowpane along the shores and shiny as a mirror over the depths. Sometimes a fish moves up from the warmer water of the deep holes and shows itself briefly like a goldfish in a bowl. One huge bullfrog, having failed to cover itself with mud, lies as though frozen in a depression the exact size and contour of its body. The ice will not remain unscarred. Soon it will be gashed by the swift skate runners of the Rebels.

⁂ ⁂ ⁂

The Canada geese, put out to graze, headed for Fish Pond. The ice held until they got to the middle, but then broke beneath their weight. It was getting dark and there was a good chance they would be frozen in by morning. So I got on the west dike and began pelting stones as close to the geese as possible without hitting them. It started the geese moving. Inch by inch then, with the geese floundering in and out of the water, off and on the ice, I frightened them toward the east shore. Once on solid ground, Duke, the gander, set up a terrific honking and led the way to the pen. It was dark by then, but the geese evidently had no trouble finding the door because, by the time I got to the top of the hill, they were inside.

Christmas wishes

Every year, the Rebel Queen wishes we did not have to cut spruce trees to bring into the house for Christmas. I try, of course, to find a perfectly formed tree. When I bring it in, she exclaims, "Oh, how beautiful! It's a shame to cut it. I wish it were still growing." The spruce groves include well over a thousand trees, but I would not be a bit surprised if one of these years I have to go out and buy a tree from a roadside tree lot.

Christmas, as usual, was wonderful. Of course, none of us got all the things we wanted. Rebel No. 1 wants, above all, to see her singing career move along more swiftly and thinks some stage and television appearances might help. Rebel No. 2 would give just about everything she owns for a horse. Rebel No. 3 is on a horse "kick," too, but she can be persuaded to settle for less.

Rebel No. 4 wants each and every day, above everything, to be lifted to the window so she can see the birds on the feeding station. The Rebel Queen wants only more of what we have been getting — good health, comparative peace and more Christmas days like those we have all enjoyed together. We'll settle for that.

How much is a boy worth?

No man is an island, entire of itself.
~ John Donne

You believe it even when that "man" is a twelve-year-old boy who hasn't had his chance to build a better house, run a faster race, be a better father. You believe it because like the leaves in spring, the snow in winter, the birds in the trees, he was a part of the life around you, even though you took him for granted until now that he is missing.

You believe it because he gave more than ducks and pigeons to your own children. He gave them companionship, which is as much a part of a child's society as home or church. You believe it because you see the tears that well from the hearts of the children who will miss him.

You believe it because sometimes you think you see him coming up the road, standing on the hill, bending by the creek.

You believe it because there are too few twelve-year-old boys, and without them there's hardly any need for dogs, pigeons, fish, stones, skates and ducks. You believe it because your village is not quite as fine a place as it was the day before a car cut him down. And if your village has been diminished, so has your state and so has your nation.

So even though many twelve-year-old boys die every day, each death, like that of Paul Vosburg of our village, especially since it need not have happened, is a tragic waste. Because how much is a little boy worth? A billion dollars? A river of tears?

Rock pile

The Rebels know it is not necessary to go to jail to work on the rock pile. At the far south end of the place, there is a mound of forty-eight tons of stone that must be moved this winter, rock by rock, down to the shore of Fish Pond. But the job has just started. One by one, the rocks, some only as big as a fist and some weighing as much as five hundred pounds, are being rolled, lifted, tossed, levered and inched onto the tiny tractor cart for the trip. Where the bank needs riprapping, we roll the rocks onto the ice and skid them into position against the shore.

It is hard work, and the Rebels can find all manner of excuses to avoid an afternoon on the rock pile. But now and again they run out of excuses, and then the rock pile diminishes. It is a tedious way to earn spending money, but sometimes they find bones among the rocks and then they begin speculating, and pretty soon they are seeing elk and coyotes, sometimes even dinosaurs.

Fossils or unusually beautiful stones sometimes slow them down, and then, unless this slave driver is right there to keep them moving, they may sit too long in contemplation. Maybe they are getting something out of this slave labor. I do not know. Certainly they must understand that beautiful things come with considerable creative effort, even if the creation is only a multicolored stone wall for the wavelets to wear themselves to froth upon.

After two days of hard work, the mound of stone still looks as huge as it did before the first rock was moved. To the Rebels, the task seems insurmountable and interminable They refuse to believe it will ever be finished. Given reasonably good weather, however, it will be completed by spring. Even a woodpecker, pecking away forever at the world, might in time whittle it down to size. At least that is the lesson I hope they will learn. But it is more likely they will look at their calluses, remember their aching muscles and decide that the best way to deal with a rock pile is to walk around it and keep going.

Reflecting life

Snow has settled a great weight on the ice of Fish Pond and New Pool. The recent storms have pulled a white sheet over the frozen waters, and from the knoll the ponds look dead. Spring ponds such as these are mirrors reflecting life. They take their color from the sky and from the earth. They reflect summer sun and storms, birds flying over and people walking by. They capture the mood of each day. Wind makes them capricious or treacherous. Mist makes them mysterious. When the world glowers, they glower. When the world smiles, they sparkle.

Only in winter do they fail to throw back the mood of the world. Then even Blue Pool, which does not freeze, looks black instead of blue. It takes on an inky cast, a somber, almost sad mien. This is partly due to the contrasting snow lying white and brilliant along its banks. But it is also because plants are not growing and there is less oxygen in the water. Clear Pool is open along the edge where the springs bubble, but it loses some of its luster in the dead of winter. Only Watercress Creek still seems to have some life to it, especially where it ripples across white stones. The current helps the water of the creek take oxygen from the air and, though it is not half so sparkling as in summer, it still looks silvery from the bridge.

People, I suppose, are a little like these ponds, this creek, in that they reflect not only the mood of the day and the season but of life around them. If a neighbor, the kids, the boss, the milkman smiles, then so do they. And if they smile, then so do the boss, the milkman, the neighbor and the kids.

Winter's challenge

The smartest critters at Little Lakes are the chipmunks, turtles, frogs, gophers, woodchucks and all those sleepers who spend their winters covered with mud or in the grass-lined bedroom of an underground burrow. They have no fuel bills to worry them, nor any food problems at a time when such stupid ones as rabbits and squirrels are having a rough time keeping full stomachs without coming to feeding stations for relief.

Perhaps you, as I do, find winter an exhilarating time. But I wonder how long we would enjoy it if we were forced to meet the elements head-on, without grocery stores as food caches, cars to haul us around and warm houses to retreat to when the wind howls and the temperature plummets.

Wild things that refuse to hibernate or go south surely suffer. Pheasants and rabbits may look in good health as they scurry away, but before the grass turns green again, many have lost half their weight and are near death from malnutrition. Critters living near communities have the advantage of many feeding stations. Sometimes, however, the charitable ones fail to carry the feeding program to a successful conclusion. Once the weather moderates and the snow starts to melt, they discontinue feeding.

This is a most critical time for wildlife. Their resistance is already at low ebb. They have come to depend on handouts and are reluctant to forage. Natural food has been consumed, and even though they have freedom of movement, birds and animals must travel far to find enough to satisfy their hunger. So winter to them is not the exhilarating time it is for you and me. It is their enemy, more deadly even than the four-footed predators always on their trail.

SPRING

Cardinals whistling

Snow is so deep in the spruce groves that the trails cannot be negotiated except on all fours. Ponds are smothered. Shed doors are jammed shut with drifts and won't be opened until the sun does the job. Still, you can just about bet your bottom dollar the ice will all go before March does. Even now, there is open water beneath the drifts along the edge of Fish Pond. Clear Pool opens by noon of each day where the springs bubble. Blue Pool never did freeze.

And the cardinals are whistling! And the wild mallards on Watercress Creek have paired off except for one extra duck, and the three drakes are having quite a discussion about who will have an extra frau. And migrant mourning doves have swelled the flock that winters here.

Crows, which moved both north and south to get out of the snow belt, are back. They spend most of every day pestering a hawk, which in turn is making life uneasy for the birds at the feeding station.

Rabbits are out every day. They, too, are mating, and the snow will not be gone long before they will have naked babies in their nests, fur-lined hollows in the ground. Fish are feeding more frantically. Longer hours of sunlight sharpen their appetites. So, even though there's snow on the north slopes of all the roofs, even though it is still piled as high as the windowsills, the breakthrough is not far off. It could even start tomorrow with a warm wind, or the day after with a gentle rain. You've got to believe it, because the cardinals are whistling!

Plenty of work

Jobs to do: Trim the weeping willows on the islands in Fish Pond. Haul what is left of the rock pile to bolster the banks of the same pond. Finish making the birdhouses and get them up. Paint the skiff used on Blue Pool. Clean the martin house and get the tools ready for an all-out assault on the place once the frost goes and the time comes for planting poplars, pines and all the other trees and shrubs that should go into the ground.

Chipmunk holes

Snowbanks all around the house are perforated with holes the size of a shovel handle. These have been made by eager chipmunks who probably are wondering what happened to spring. When the sun shines, the chipmunks sit with their heads halfway out. Occasionally, one or another starts across the snow crust for the bird feeder, but changes its mind before getting there and scuttles back to its warm den. Chipmunks hibernate, but this is the time of the year for getting married. They need food, since their underground caches are probably empty by now. So we poured corn down the holes, hoping it will tide them over until the sun gets to work on the snowbanks.

Losing battles

Mice and muskrats are number one and number two on the list of the ten most wanted creatures at Little Lakes. Never have they created so much havoc as during this last winter of the Big Snow. Mice have been especially destructive. Operating under cover all winter, they have entirely devoured the roots of some hybrid poplars nearly fifteen feet tall, and now that there is no snow to support the trees, most of them have fallen over. Those trees represent a considerable investment, especially in work.

Now that the mice can find forage, the muskrats are leaving the water to girdle those few remaining poplars. We took every precaution to protect the poplars. We were even tempted to spread poisoned wheat near the root systems, but did not because we were afraid many birds might die.

We had to make a similar decision in dealing with elm tree disease, since the beetle is surely the number three nuisance at Little Lakes.

Our elms are being sprayed with DDT. We were reluctant about spraying, but after thinking it through we decided that whatever birds died from the poison could shortly be replaced, but it would take a hundred years to grow those stately elms.

Nuisance number four are the chipmunks. We do not want them to disappear any more than we'd like to get rid of all the muskrats or even all the mice. But when their colonies get so large that they undermine garden walls, house foundations and sidewalks and steal everything that hasn't been nailed down, it seems something should be done.

It seems every animal or bird does some damage. The duck flock so fertilizes the ponds that they become choked with vegetation. Sparrow nests clog eaves and spouts. Crayfish stray in subterranean tunnels, then pop up and clutter the lawn with little clay steeples. Cardinals and robins, battling their own images, crack windows. Hundreds of grackles stunt spruce growth by breaking off the leaders.

In short, to believe that nature can maintain a balance is sheer nonsense. We are aware that we have created such desirable habitat that nature cannot possibly maintain equilibrium. Still, even in a wilderness, nature rarely strikes a balance. The history of almost every wilderness is one of the lack of balance. It is feast or famine. Trees take over and deer disappear. Then a fire comes along, the trees go, and deer populations skyrocket. Ruffed grouse sometimes reach fantastic populations, then drop off to nothing. There are many or there are few snowshoe hares. In burned areas where nature's match, the lightning bolt, has started fires, weed plants and trees very often dominate.

There is no balance in nature. If anything, nature is continually off balance. There are some, of course, who claim overproductive creatures should not be discouraged. They argue other creatures and disease will keep them in bounds, eventually. Meanwhile, I wonder what Little Lakes would look like. The elms would surely be dead. The dikes would be ruptured and the ponds dry and the fish dead. Maybe even the house would fall over where woodchucks or chipmunks finally created a crater big enough to topple it.

Death watch

These are the days of the death watch. Even as all the earth comes alive, the Rebel Queen and her brood are searching for death. Daily patrols go along the dikes, among the spruce, across the high knoll and down through the swale. All eyes are on the ground, looking for dead robins, flickers, woodpeckers, juncos, chickadees and cardinals.

Sunday, a week ago, was "spray the elms" day to save the trees from disease.

Little Lakes has some ten elms to the acre. This is considered a high concentration so far as insecticide contamination from each tree is concerned. What is more, a high wind spread the poison over a wide area. This will increase the danger to birdlife. Aerial-feeding birds will be spared, since the ponds were on the downwind side of the spray. So martins, which arrived Wednesday, are safe, and the swallows may not be harmed. Many of the birds, if they die, will not be found on the ground. Nuthatches, flickers, woodpeckers and creepers will crawl into hollow trees as they sicken.

The Rebels are perturbed. They have not called it murder yet, but maybe they are thinking that it is. It is hard to explain how a tree is a living thing, too. They will not buy such logic as exacts death from one innocent species to preserve another.

Each day, individual patrols go out to search the grounds for dead birds. Robins are nesting in the contaminated area. Many bird species — doves, cardinals, martins, chickadees — are feeding where the insecticide was used. Everyone at Little Lakes is hoping that by some miracle the birds will come through unharmed.

Woodies

Monday's sun glistened on the many-colored head of a drake wood duck, and the Rebels were enthralled. For five years we have been trying to entice a wood duck couple to make our home their home. We sent to Minneapolis for an expensive, all-metal house and placed it where the ducklings could drop right from the nest into the water.

Joker arrives

It was a great week in many ways. The new horse, Joker, arrived in last Sunday's snowstorm. The littlest Rebels had a hard time sleeping Sunday night, and Monday when the Rebel Queen looked out she couldn't see the mare for kids. Naturally, every neighborhood child would have liked to ride her. But they are polite children, and though they waited around hoping they could climb aboard, they did not ask. We had to disappoint the children, because Joker is not a pet. She is a spirited animal and likes to go into a full gallop as soon as there is weight in the saddle. One or another of the youngsters would surely have been injured had they been permitted to ride. Rebel No. 2, who is 12 and has had some experience, was able to hold Joker in, so the new horse got some exercise.

First to die

We found the first dead bird, a robin, on the fourteenth day after the Sunday on which the elm trees were sprayed with DDT. On the fifteenth day we picked up a mourning dove, and next day we found two more robins. During the next two days, we found no dead birds. Scores of robins and doves are nesting in the contaminated areas. Some of these robins moved in after the area was sprayed. Apparently the effect of the spray on the robins was not as lethal as expected. But it is difficult to assess damages. Though it is unlikely that many more birds will die, there is no way of knowing how many perished and were carried off by animals or hid before dying. There definitely is a decrease in the bird population since the spraying.

Ferociously free

No birds are so ferociously free as the hawks. Even if captured while young, they are not likely ever to become tame. Theirs is a wild, high-flying life. They have contempt for people and a hatred for any hands that dare to handle them. They, more than their cousin the eagle, are symbolic of the proud arrogance that conquered our frontiers. We were reminded of this when neighbor children came bearing a stunned red-shouldered hawk that had been struck by an auto. Gradually, it recovered its senses and spread its wings wide to attack. Its pale golden eyes glared defiance. Since it was unable to fly, we placed it in a wire-roofed pen. But the proud one refused food. It refused water. In three days it died rather than accept favors from man, who must always be an enemy.

Drummers drumming

Drums resound. Some sound tinny. Others rattle like snare drums. Some boom like the big bass drums any good marching band must boast. The drumming starts early, sometimes before sunrise. It continues even after sunset. The drummers are broad-shouldered flickers, birds with strong bills and with neck muscles vibrant as the mechanism of an air hammer. They pound away on the roof and hollow trees. One has as its special drum a tin pail abandoned on the shores of Fish Pond. Another has driven the martins mad, for it clings to the side of their house and hammers on the little hardwood chimney. The birds are not looking for food, nor are they trying to hammer out homes. The rat-a-tat-tat-a-tat-tat is all part of the mating ritual.

❊ ❊ ❊

Sleep after the first light is almost impossible because birds are shivering the morning with song.

※ ※ ※

The Rebel Queen, most optimistic of the Rebel gang, starts looking for leaves on the trees April 15. We always assure her that they will not come until May 1. This year, however, they did not green up the place until the middle of May, and even then the hickory, swamp ash and even some of the linden trees and oaks had no leaves at all.

SUMMER

Back on course

People put a lot into living and, sometimes, living takes a lot out of us. It is the same way with nature. Only trouble is that people often haven't the time, ability or desire to pay the price for mistakes, while nature is willing and has forever to correct the ones she makes. Take Watercress Creek as an example. Spring floods ripped it wide open, changed its course, altered its banks, ripped out its plant life, gutted it to the gravelly core. Already, sediment from upstream is putting down an earth bed for watercress. Already new banks are settling to the side of the water's flow. Already the current has discovered that the old way was best. We should be so lucky.

※ ※ ※

Birds continue to die six weeks after the elm trees were sprayed. Adult birds known dead: thirteen robins and two mourning doves. There is no doubt more have died. The red-headed woodpeckers and nuthatches have disappeared. Adult birds are not the only victims. Now the day-old and week-old young, those nestlings that have absolutely no resistance because of their tiny bodies, are dying. Along the footpaths, along pond banks, beneath the spruce, up under the oaks, everywhere, are fledgling dead discarded from the nest by their parents after food still contaminated by the poison killed them.

※ ※ ※

Sometimes twenty or even thirty painted turtles crawl out onto a long floating dock in Fish Pond to sun. Then, when someone approaches, they clatter for the water like so many tanks and the sound is enough to set the skin on one's neck to crawling.

Beneath the stars

Northwoods, Wisconsin
The Rebel Gang
On Little Lakes

Dear Rebel Gang:

There was starlight last night, and I stood outside awhile and thought about being home. Then, because the mind is such a wondrous thing, I was home. I walked the trails and moved in a small circle of silence, because crickets and frogs hearing my boots in the grass stopped rejoicing to listen. But soon as I had passed they picked up the beat and joined in the far-flung chorus.

Sometimes I sat down. Then, after an interval, there was no circle of silence because crickets chirped right by my boot toes and frogs croaked close by my side. But I had to sit perfectly still and remain silent. If I cleared my throat, moved a boot, even lifted a finger, the circle of silence was there again.

June, of course, is the month for inventory, and what is an inventory but an annual count of your blessings? So I hope that you are about your business and when I get back off the road you can tell me how many bluegills and bass spawned, where the blue jays and cardinals nested, how many ducklings are hiding in the rushes, how many tree swallows are occupying nesting boxes. And did we get any new wrens, and are all the robins dead because of the poison used to spray the elms?

And how many orioles have hung nests in the higher trees? And does the moon still lay a light through the music room window, or has the linden tree grown so tall there is no white path on the green rug this year?

Today I will fish for bass where the limestone ledges have water-worn caves. Tomorrow I think it will be muskies where lifting coontail lays a green underwater reef. Next day, trout in the turbulence of a stream roaring at the rocks that try to stem its flow. Then, if there is a quiet time, I will come at evening to see if bluegills will lift to a popper. But sometime and somewhere along the road I will know it is time to turn back. Then we'll walk in the starlight together.

Jumper

Joker, the horse, is getting to be a jumper. Not content merely to ride the mare, Rebel No. 2 started her leaping logs and now has her going over a rail some three feet off the ground. The horse, somewhat perplexed by this turn of events, sometimes comes to a jolting halt right in front of the bar and the Rebel gets the western saddle horn rammed right into her midriff.

※ ※ ※

Rebel No. 3 has lost any love she might once have had for Duke and Duchess. Every time she turns them out to graze, they try to outflank her in a wild scramble for Fish Pond. Then the sixty-pound Rebel has to turn on the steam to get out ahead of them and drive them back to the pen.

Shaping up

The fruits of many years of backbreaking labor are beginning to be harvested. Canary reed grass stands six feet tall on the dikes. Wild berries are abundant everywhere. Fish Pond's two tiny islands are verdant with weeping willows whose branches sweep the water. The shore of New Pool is secure with grass. All manner of trees and flowers are trying frantically to outgrow and smother neighboring species. Water tumbles from all the pool outlets over rocks, making much music. Little Lakes is shaping up.

Fish inventory

The bass, green sunfish and bluegill gang in New Pool face a food shortage because there are so many of them. Perhaps the blunthead minnows we have been transferring there will put meat on the table. The pond trout are ravenous. At feeding time they can feel my footsteps from as far as twenty to thirty feet away. Like kids at the sound of the dinner bell, they come speeding toward shore. Put a fly among them and they will ignore it. Throw some pellets on the water and they feed. Some fish, these spoiled, modern day, hand-fed trout.

Minnow traps in the crystal waters of Clear Pool attract all manner of hungry customers. The commercial fish pellets used as bait put such aromatic odors on the slight current as interest crayfish, sunfish, bluegills, blunthead minnows and even bullheads. Some sunfish, wider even than the small trap mouth, somehow manage to squeeze into the glass trap. Inside, magnified by the glass, they look twice as large as they actually are. Once inside, all creatures gorge themselves and then begin to search frantically for a way out. The resulting maelstrom of churning fishes never fails to fascinate the Rebels.

Counting the toll

We will never fully know the destruction wrought by DDT. Robins, either late migrants or birds moved in from other areas, are again fairly abundant. Many blue jays, young and old, died, but we do not know whether it was from the poison. Martins deserted, but maybe the starlings chased them away. There are no red-headed woodpeckers around this year. There were no wrens up until about ten days ago, but now one is chatting in the apple trees. The swallow population is way down. Normally in the evening all ponds have good flights of swallows picking off insects.

The grackles, once so abundant, are depleted. We have no complaints about that. The cedar waxwing population is up. It is difficult to tell about the cardinals; they are so secretive. Mosquitoes have been rare, and spiders have practically disappeared. Four more elms have the disease in spite of the spraying.

Breaking out

Like people, certain animals show extraordinary traits while the rest of their tribe travel in the same old rut. To the list of unusual critters, add Joker, the Rebels' mare. Her objective is an unworked garden, white with clover, in which she is occasionally permitted to graze. To get to this garden, she must leave her pasture through a gate with a six-inch, hook-type latch on the top and another about eight inches off the ground.

One day the Rebels forgot to fasten the bottom hook. Shortly thereafter, Joker was in clover. She was put back into the pasture, but did not even wait until the Rebels were gone to unlatch the gate. Using her teeth, she lifted the hook and then nudged it aside with her muzzle. The second hook on the bottom had her baffled for about two days. Finally, she found it. It was only minutes then and she was back in clover. Now a heavy section of log lies in front of the gate. Joker is puzzling over the obstruction. Perhaps soon she will find a way to roll the log back and get the gate open.

Savage side

The veneer with which civilization has glossed our sometimes savage instincts occasionally cracks at boxing matches, dogfights or western movies. Even the young and tender-hearted can be carried away by a savage scene. We saw it happen at Little Lakes when a mink came up on the hill and invaded the duck, goose and pheasant pen right during the middle of a bright day. Rebel No. 2 came hurrying into the house to tell us the mink was making a raid. The Rebel Queen had unsuccessfully tried to deter the animal with a landing net.

So I said: "Turn Bucko loose."

Bucko is gentle as a kitten except when it comes to cats, mink, raccoons and the like. He routed the mink out of a prickly ash stand, drove it beneath a lumber pile, growled it back into the open and then, with such fury as the Rebels have never witnessed, killed it. The Rebels are dead set against killing spiders, mice, snapping turtles, any living thing, but when Bucko closed with the mink, they were one with the dog, and it was surprising and even shocking to see the vicarious thrill they got from the killing.

When it was over and civilization once more took command, they were sad, of course, that such a beautiful creature had been killed. But when the mink was screaming, the dog growling and the blood spattering, they were ten thousand years removed to such savage times as even history would like to know more about.

⚜ ⚜ ⚜

The little green herons are flying in small formations now that youngsters are on the wing. Great blue herons are visiting, which would indicate that some have done with their rookery duties. Sometimes there are upward of fifty mourning doves taking gravel on the road right after sunrise. Brown thrashers live in the prickly ash hedge beneath the chokecherry trees.

Floral succession

The seasonal succession of flowers is well on its way to a flaming, fiery fall display. Starting in spring, the blooms progress from timid violets and pastel Mayflowers up the color scale to burnished, high-standing, flamboyant blossoms. Purple phlox, richly colored as royal velvet, are competing with the tigers, those burnt-orange lilies along the knoll drive near Fish Pond. Brassy-looking daisies are everywhere the mower hasn't been; in a week or two another daisy variety standing on seven-foot stalks will bloom. Then the flaming sumacs. Then, frost.

⚜ ⚜ ⚜

A rejected mourning dove infant, given for adoption to a pigeon couple who had a teenager ready for flight and two eggs already incubating, got a warm reception. But after a couple days the pigeon parents suddenly had a change of heart and tossed the youngster from the nest. The Rebels brought it to the house and, though they could keep it alive, it was not doing well. So they tried another pigeon couple, but the tiny, still-blind mourning dove died.

⚜ ⚜ ⚜

Most beautiful sight of the week: Mayfly on the kitchen door brought inside to cling to a sweet potato plant. Fragile wings like fairy lace.

Amber abdomen, curved like a scimitar. Antennae fore and aft. Bulging multicolored eyes which change with the light from the window. Graceful creature, born to dance but one day and then die.

Reprieve for Ralph

Rebel No. 2 thinks she witnessed a small miracle. Ralph, a grouchy snapping turtle, so snarled a bullhead setline that this outraged bullhead eater hauled the culprit up the hill and went for the gun. Rebel No. 2 was given the burial detail. Nearly in tears, she went for the spade but made a prayer in her heart to St. Francis, the patron saint of all animals, that Ralph be spared.

When I put the shells into the gun, it jammed so badly that execution was delayed fifteen minutes. By then, Ralph had disappeared. Rebel No. 2 did not hide the critter, but she knew where it had disappeared to. Though Rebels No. 1 and 3 were asked to search for Ralph, for some strange reason Rebel No. 2 was not asked to join the posse. She reasoned, therefore, that she was not strictly conscience-bound to reveal Ralph's hiding place, which happened to be the cleft base of a big elm. Time after time the posse passed within inches of the fugitive, but finally abandoned the search.

Several hours later, we saw Ralph waddling down the hill toward Fish Pond. It was then Rebel No. 2 admitted all. Yet I allowed Ralph to go free, because who on earth can argue with heaven and let such an august one as St. Francis down?

✻ ✻ ✻

Joker the mare has not only won the hearts of everyone out here but has taken over nearly every square foot of the place. She roams freely, and only when the mosquitoes get too fierce does she come galloping back to get relief in her stall.

AUTUMN

Lights in the sky

When is the last time you looked at a star, paused to contemplate the nighttime sky? It might do you good, especially if good fortune has been your lot and you are beginning to believe all the nice things your neighbors are saying about you. Not even the boss can put you as quickly in your rightful place as a few minutes among the stars. If the money has been rolling in, promotions have been your lot, friends have been especially complimentary and the old head is beginning to swell, there is nothing like a little stardust to shrink it. Nothing, not even the whole world with all its millions, amounts to much out where the universe begins.

I was stargazing and thinking such thoughts the other night when the Rebels joined me in front of the picture window. But the young ones saw nothing except sparkling, beautiful lights. They were enthralled. To them, the skies at night are as friendly as the fields, and the stars exciting, but only as flowers are.

Scientists are taking the glitter out of the skies and reducing the sun, moon, planets, stars and whatever else is beyond, to orbiting bodies capable or incapable of being invaded. The Rebels are aware of this, yet it does not tarnish their enthusiasm. To them, the sun is still the source of warmth and a joy to see, especially after a storm. The moon is still a lantern to light the lawn and turn the green grass white. So, too, the stars are still something to wish upon, friendly lights in the sky.

Labors of love

The dogs, horse, pigeons, ducks and even the geese are lonesome now that school has started. They see the Rebels briefly in the morning, but the rest of the day they must be content with such bird and animal company as their penned associates provide. Along about the middle of the afternoon, they become restless. Then, if the Rebels are late in getting home from school, the dogs begin to pace, the horse lifts its head more often, the pigeons congregate on the cote roof to wait, and the ducks gather at the pen gate.

When the Rebels finally come, the shouting starts. The dogs bark, and when the ducks hear the children's voices, they quack. The pigeons hover and alight on the ground, then go up again in a multicolored cloud back to the roof of the cote. A whistle brings Joker galloping to the fence. She whinnies and, for a while, the place sounds like a zoo. The Rebels, after a brief hello, duck into the house to get out of their dresses and into trousers. Then the feeding begins. Supper is often getting cold on the kitchen table and the Rebels are still scattering grain or lugging water or pitching hay.

Once when, in an emergency, I did the feeding and went from stable to poultry pen to kennels in a swift ten minutes, I wondered why it took the Rebels so long. So I spied, and I learned that hay and oats alone will not feed a horse. There must be apples, or perhaps carrots, or sometimes fistfuls of fresh, green grass. On special days, the gift goes wrapped in a ribbon.

There is no haphazard spraying of grain to the ground, no dumping of matted leaves or baled hay. Like all acts of love, it is a careful giving. The rabbits cannot survive on grain and ordinary greens. They get every vegetable and fruit peel from the kitchen, and oatmeal in a special dish, and corn mixed only to the proper proportion with oats, and fresh water even when there is plenty standing. The eggshells must go to the ducks, and the dogs get every special kind of meat treat a kitchen can turn up.

But it is not just the accumulation and distribution of treats that takes so long. It is sitting to dinner with each, and feeling complete when they eat with relish, and worrying when their appetites wane. Then, of course, each duck and pigeon must be accounted for, each of the five dogs needs at least one pat, and the mare, who is learning to kiss, must have her short training period. Then there is saying good-night to each and every one, as though he or she were special, and checking again to see that doors are closed, the bedding is adequate, and the animals are happy. It is caring so much, and that always takes time.

Kitchen mouse

My morning cup of coffee sipped in the solitude of the kitchen before the Rebels are stirring has become more interesting because of a mouse that spends its nights beneath the stove. The instant the light comes on, it makes a run for its exit hole beneath a corner cupboard, but upon seeing my slippered feet in the way, it turns and races back beneath the stove. The mouse, beady-eyed but quite harmless looking, usually has enough courage on the sixth or seventh attempt to race across my feet. But now the Rebel Queen has learned about my friend and has decreed that it must go. The Rebels side with me and the mouse, but you know who will win.

Screech owls hunting

Tiny screech owls are on their hunting roosts in oaks, elms and maples, and on moonlight nights they mourn more often than when the moon is down and the sky is dark. And perhaps they really are sad, because now the lush days are ending. Soon grasshoppers and moths, mice and tiny songbirds will have died, gone south or gone underground. Then the owls will have no time to sit and cry and snap their bills, because they must hunt hard if they would survive the winter. Twice since we have lived at Little Lakes, one of these owls has used the big maple that shades the sunken garden as a hunting roost when the big yard light is on. The owl watches the lighted garden and swoops down when a moth moves across it or an insect stirs in the artificial glow. So even owls, who hunt at night, seem to like a little light to see by.

Robber baron

No robber was ever dressed in finer plumage or practiced his art with such deadly skill as the great blue heron who has been driving his stiletto of a bill into the trout of Clear Pool. No thief was ever so secretive or so ruthless or so without conscience. The slate-blue bird is probably four feet tall and has an even wider wingspread. It sneaks into the pool after dark from some hideaway along the Fox River. Then it stands like a statue until a trout swims within striking distance. One night it killed at least a half-dozen fish and left them on the bank. The largest fish measured twenty-one inches and weighed more than four pounds. Each night the heron kills, and those fish small enough to be swallowed go wiggling down its long neck. But the larger ones of more than two pounds are left to die.

One night I left the powerful floodlights on, hoping this would discourage the striker. But when I stopped the car on the bridge while en route to the office the next morning, there the bird was. It fled the instant the car door opened.

⚜ ⚜ ⚜

Two maples are flaming. The others are still green. Leaves of the flaming maples fleck the ground like big sparks of fire.

Can you hear it?

There was no wind to rustle the yellow leaves of the big maple that spreads like an umbrella just outside our bedroom window. Cold had silenced the frogs and crickets. Only a little light from the stars sparkled on the frost where the lawn dips down to Fish Pond. The Rebel Queen, in bed next to me, had lifted to an elbow.

"There!" she whispered. "Do you hear it now?"

I heard it. It was like the sound of a child crying in its sleep. So I got up, climbed the stairs and went from bed to bed. All the Rebels were sleeping, so I went back down. The sound was clearer, nearer now.

Then, I knew. "It's the hounds," I said. "Listen. There are three dogs, but the one you really hear has a high bell of a bay."

I looked at my watch. It was 3 a.m. Yet someone was still hunting raccoons, and the hound pack was somewhere along the river, running hard but smoothly and coming nearer and nearer.

It was a lonely sound. As I looked from the dark bedroom through the window at indistinct shadows of trees, it seemed the hound pack was the only living, moving, articulate thing in a big, black, deserted world. I hoped it would run the coon close, right beneath the bedroom window. I wanted to hear the pack sweep by. I wanted to hear its sound diminish into the distance until there was only the mournful belling of the one. But the dogs turned, and then there was nothing because the wind was down and the night so still.

Dying for love

Trout very often die for love, literally. It happens during the honeymoon, and usually the fatalities occur among the bucks. The injuries that eventually kill them are suffered either while they move stones to make the nest or while they battle other male fish. Rainbows are dying at Little Lakes now. They are some of the fall spawners developed by commercial hatcheries. Rainbows normally spawn in the spring. Those that do not die often come off the spawning beds scarred for life. Some of the wounded become infected, and a white fungus covers their open sores. The female deposits eggs in the rocky nest and the male covers them with stones. Then, in about fifty days, the youngsters are born. After they have consumed the egg sac, they worm their way to freedom through the pile of rocks. So life for the trout is a tough time from beginning to end.

Remains of summer

Beneath the blue spruce trees, a brown volleyball. On the banks of Blue Pool, a swimming cap. Beneath the swings, a pair of tennis shoes. Frozen into the water in the bottom of the boat, a trout fly. On the sidewalk, a roller skate key. On the clothesline, a sunsuit halter.

Inside the cellar but close to the door, two pairs of skis. On the workbench in the garage, ice fishing tip-ups ready for repair. Back of the screens, still waiting to be put away, a pair of freshly varnished snowshoes. On the auto dash, a windshield frost scraper. Leaning by the kitchen door, a snow shovel. Waiting in bags, salt and sand.

Plague of mice

Mice have the Rebel Queen frantic. As soon as she catches one, two or more enter the kitchen to take its place. Some are not ordinary house mice, but white-footed creatures with a passion for hoarding. They filled one vase half-full of popcorn seed. They got into a five-pound bag of bird seed and began hauling that off to caches. Mornings,

*Tending the animals means more than a haphazard spraying of grain
to the ground. Like all acts of love, it is a careful giving.*

while I am having my coffee, I hear them rattling around in a top cabinet with as much noise as a couple of raccoons might make.

"When will it stop?" the frantic Queen wants to know.

I tried to catch one in a cabinet. It jumped over my hand, dropped seven feet to the floor and scurried down a hole. I know where the mice are getting into the house. It is a tiny break in the concrete. If the Rebel Queen will make me some pigs' knuckles and sauerkraut, maybe I will tell her where it is.

※ ※ ※

Six cherry trees and four apple trees that have lived long and useful lives will shortly become logs for the fireplace. The trees have grown old and gnarled. Year by year they have become less efficient in producing fruit. Even so, it seems a shame to cut down even one of them.

Pool renovations

Blue Pool and Clear Pool are under construction. For ten days, their manicured banks and settled bottoms have been ripped and gouged, widened and deepened by huge machines. Now, where there had been four to six feet of water, there is ten to twelve feet. Clear Pool will be half again as big as it was. There will be a concrete overflow with a ten-foot span to carry off floodwater. Now, with mud splattered from road to dike to creek to knoll, the prospect of either pool again being beautiful seems remote. But already Blue Pool has taken on such a deep shade of blue that from the house it appears to have been lacquered with a bucket of liquid sky. Clear Pool has such depth that, looking from the bank into the wind ripples, one has the illusion of falling, falling into a bottomless well of clear water. The mud will disappear. Grass, flowers and new trees will have it green again. By next August, the scars will be all but healed.

Fatal mistake

Daisy, one of the mallards elected to survive the annual butchering, got caught up by mistake and went under the ax. There were tears in Rebel No. 3's mashed potatoes that night. Daisy was her favorite.

chapter five

LONG LIVE THE QUEEN

WINTER

Temper tantrums

Dogs guard their right to love and be loved more jealously than do the Rebels. Since old Rainey has been moved from the kennel to the basement, Bucko, Ace, Sergeant and Captain take turns having temper tantrums. When they see this old dog out being exercised, they roar with rage. When their barking avails them nothing, they go to their beds and sulk. Rainey, meanwhile, struts as if he owns the place. When his four former kennel mates are turned loose for a run, he bristles and starts pushing them around. One of these days, of course, he is going to get his ears beaten back. Though they have a truce with members of the opposite sex, younger dogs are not above jumping on an old man dog if he gets too cocky.

⚹ ⚹ ⚹

This is tree-trimming time. From weeping willows, basswoods, apples, cherries, maples and spruce, we have sawed and chopped enough wood to build a small house. And now we have about seventy-five weeping willow saplings to plant in spring, and fifty or more hybrid poplar cuttings and a basement full of hickory, oak, apple, cherry and maple chunks for next year's fires in the fireplace.

⚹ ⚹ ⚹

A hawk has come to live. It dives through a pigeon flock and the birds explode like white fireworks. It soars over the ducks and they scurry. For a couple of blocks it followed a rabbit the beagles were driving and then made its dive, but the rabbit bounced to safety in the briars. So far as the Rebels can determine, the hawk has been living on mice.

Helpful snow

Deep snow does not mean trouble for all wild animals and birds. Mice thrive under the snowbanks. It furnishes them warm roofs and protection from predators. Living in their dusky world of tunnels, they grow fat on weed seeds and roots of plants. Mice have no need to come out into the light. Some go an entire winter without looking at the sun.

Crows, too, thrive when the snows are deep. There are more road kills of birds and animals, since they use the plowed places as a runway. What's more, a crow can spot a dead animal or bird at great distances when the world below is white. The deep snow has no effect on birds that live on insects whose homes are in trees. Only weed seed eaters have difficulty getting food. The deep snow even puts rabbits up to where they can get at untouched saplings and buds. Snow works in many ways to benefit wild creatures.

When life is hard

Most beautiful sight of the week: A cardinal scarlet against a green bough of spruce decorated with a white patch of snow.

Hardest job of the week: Thirty bales of hay dumped in the drive and dragged by toboggan a hundred and fifty yards to the stable.

Most disconcerting event: Five squirrels emptying the bird feeders before the birds can lunch.

Most discouraging: The continued grip of winter.

Life is sometimes hard at Little Lakes, especially for the Rebels. For every sunny, warm day of swimming and riding it seems they must put in two dreary, cold days of shoveling manure, carrying water, feeding animals and birds. Sometimes I think it is too much for them, and that I have made a mistake by encouraging such a rigid routine.

But fathers are always worrying. If they are not worrying about making things too difficult for their Rebels, then they are worrying because they think they are making life too easy. Meanwhile, the Rebels survive and radiate joy no matter what the circumstances. Only real hunger and cold, it seems, can pinch the spirits of youth enough to keep them from bubbling over.

I think it must be age that makes us lose our enthusiasm for winter. It wasn't too many years ago when winter seemed as pleasurable as summer. But now, by mid-January, I have had enough snow and cold and can think only of the warm, sunny days still so many weeks away.

⁂ ⁂ ⁂

Can't wait now for spring. Want to see Clear and Blue Pools when the bulldozer has leveled the ground gutted from their bottoms and spruce and cedar have been transplanted on the raw earth. Want to see the canary grass spring from seed along the shore. Want to watch for the first tender leaves on the willow sticks that will go into the ground the day the frost goes out. All of winter's work becomes meaningful in spring.

⁀ ⁀ ⁀

The deepening of Blue Pool did not come off as well as we had hoped. Instead of thirteen feet of water over which to erect a ten-foot-high diving board, we ended up with a maximum of nine feet. Now the height of the diving board will be six feet.

Struggling pheasants

These are rugged times. Snow has crusted and even the pheasants cannot scratch through. So they wander far these short winter days, and when night comes their crops still are not full. At Little Lakes they come at night to the spruce groves seeking shelter from the wind. They peck listlessly at spruce needles on the low boughs and then, as the world becomes shadowy, they squat where the branches are thickest to wait out the night. We put corn out, but often they fail to find the feeding stations, and there is no way to drive a pheasant to dinner.

Trails and bridges

People are trail makers, bridge builders. Inherent in our make-up is the urge to lay roads through the wilderness and span turbulent waters. Sometimes it is almost a disease, this desire to make the way easy, to see a trail open, to watch a bridge vault over a bay. Much as we love the wilds, there is fascination in hacking out footpaths through the dense spruce groves, in throwing a bridge across the ponds or the creek.

The first trails at Little Lakes were bumpy, stony, brushy, weedy pathways through the dense spruce woods around Fish Pond. That was not enough. We smoothed the trails out. Finally, we even moved some. What is it that makes us want to smooth the edges and wax the way from place to place? I do not know, but whatever it is, it played a vital part in lifting cities from the prairies.

Bridges are even more fascinating to build than trails. Even a small footbridge across a tiny creek has a special significance to the man who makes it. Though he cross it a thousand times, the man often pauses to see how his bridge is holding up. He finds pleasure in walking on it.

Right now, we are building two bridges over portions of Clear Pool. One will span Watercress Creek where it empties into the pool, and the other will cross where the new overflow spills water down to the mill pond. They are utility structures. To visitors I suppose they look ugly, surely the work of an amateur. But there is as much satisfaction in building a bridge, I suppose, as in writing stirring music.

Stalking goldeneyes

A wild whistling always announces extreme drops of temperature at Little Lakes. The goldeneyes, driven inland by cold, seek out the warming waters of the springs and Clear Pool. When they see a human approaching, they take off, air whistling through their primary wing feathers. It is easy to crawl up on the goldeneyes. The birds dive for food, and the time to move forward is while they are underwater. Recently, I got right to the banks of the pool while five goldeneyes were searching for larvae and mollusks below. When they bobbed to the surface, there I was, and each duck, on sighting me, kept right on lifting into the air.

Joker is a riding horse, and she does not take kindly to pulling a load. But, with a little coaxing, she decided to make the best of a makeshift harness and hauled the Rebels around on a toboggan. She even dragged small trees, which had been cut, to the burning pile.

I bought a new cruiser's ax and have been finding sets of muscles which seem never to have been used. It is a nicely balanced ax, and gradually I am learning to act merely as the fulcrum while the weight of the head provides the momentum for a clean cut.

Never is the dogwood as red as in February. Against the green spruce, the pencil-sized branches look fiery in a slanting sun. Canary grass is golden. Cattails are a soft, velvet tan. Bare patches of raw earth where wavelets wash ashore are black onyx. Underwater rocks, cleaned of algae by the cold, sparkle beneath ripples. Birch is white, weeping willow branches a high, bright yellow, and mist each morning leaves frosty lace on alders. Even February is beautiful.

Most breathtaking? This winter it has been the sunsets. With crimson regularity the sky catches fire each evening where the Fox River valley is held to the west by a high hill. Sometimes it is a smoldering, darker red, low and holding to the hill. But often its flames leap across the sky and put bright reflections on ranks of marching clouds. Then the word goes around the house, from room to room, child to child: "Have you seen it? Just look!"

True or false?

Earliest spring? Who can tell when there are still nearly four months to wait for summer? But the first red-winged blackbird has arrived. Mourning doves are mating, and each new day vibrates with their cooing. The starlings sing a softer song from the high branches where the sun comes earliest each day. Mallards are bowing significantly to each other. Moss is green, like grass, where the wind does not strike it. Clear and Blue Pools are completely free of ice. Fish Pond's ice has an old, veined look and a gray pallor. Each warming day brings a quickening of activity among birds, animals and even fishes.

A few northerns have come to the current of Watercress Creek. The colors of spring-spawning trout are fiery, and the males have developed undershot jaws. Even cottontails are abroad during daylight, and there are skunk tracks along the muddy horse pasture path. Let's hope it is not a false dawning, and that winter does not come back quickly before the doves have eggs to incubate and whole colonies of newly arrived blackbirds sit huddled for days while the wind heaps snow over nesting areas they have staked out. Spring is a time of promise and hope, but it is also a treacherous season. The sun glows warmly, enticing birds north and all creation to flower. Then, in one hour, the heat is turned off, and the skies darken when the wind comes beating down on the earth to cover it with snow, sleet and death.

SPRING

Becoming a lady

Lipstick, a yen to wear heels and sudden modesty are sure signs that a little girl is turning into a little lady. Sometimes the change is slow. Other times it comes with lightning speed. Rebel No. 1 made the transition gracefully and gradually. Rebel No. 2, who loves horses better than people, wavered. One day her face would be spotless, her hair curled and combed. The next day there would be mud on her cheeks and a rat's nest in her hair. Then, quite suddenly, she made the jump. We noticed it one day before breakfast. She was in old clothes instead of school dress.

"Why?" we asked.

"You know I have to feed the mare and clean the barn," she answered. "But is that any reason I have to go to school stinking like a horse?"

That other world

Dear Rebel Queen:

Sneaking off for an unscheduled vacation in the hospital may be fine for you, but this ranch really is in an uproar. The Rebels are going to school without their coats, and sometimes even their socks do not match. Instead of chicken, steak and stew, I have been reduced to hamburgers, hot dogs and beans, out of a can. The begonias have not been planted because nobody knows quite how. There are no razor blades, and I have been using hand soap to try to soften my whiskers.

The lawn is a mess and the garage has blown full of last year's leaves. We are out of aspirin tablets and vitamins for the baby, food for the dogs and bedding for the horse. The bills are all stacked on your desk and I can't figure how much money we have left in the bank, so I am afraid to pay them.

But seriously, Ma, even if now you do not think the grass will ever turn green or the violets ever turn purple, believe me, they will. And, come summer, the flash of an oriole in an elm or the rasp of a cricket at night will seem all the more wonderful because you have had a peek into that other world humans are always wondering about.

Love,
Mel

Water everywhere

Wet feet are the order of the day. On mild days, ruts in the road carry as much water as little mountain streams. Puddles stand everywhere in the pasture. The Rebels have ceased hauling water because the horses drink from the puddles. Clear Pool has no ice at all, and Blue Pool is more than half open. Fish Pond has water atop the ice and looks as though it may open with the first warm rain. Only New Pool gives no indication of wanting to break its ice chains.

Leaves clogged the outlet of Blue Pool. Water went up over the bank, and a new creek formed where the overflow found its way to the mill pond. This delighted the Rebels. They had another little stream they could jump the horse over. Water has seeped into the garage and into the dog kennels. Fortunately, the dogs have platforms to jump on to get out of the water. But still they go to bed each night with wet feet.

Song-filled mornings

There is no sleeping mornings unless the windows are closed. The deep, persistent silence of winter has ended. Dawn is greeted by hundreds of birds. Blackbirds trill and mourning doves coo. Grackles puff up, let their wings droop and hoarsely woo their mates. Robins scream alarm when another robin invades their territory. Around the ponds, there is the sound of running water. From the stable comes the plaintive whinny of an imprisoned horse who would like to be out in the muddy pasture.

Squirrels sound like stones rolling off the roof. Chipmunks rustle last autumn's leaves. The penned Canada geese sharply protest being confined. Starlings imitate all manner of birds, and sparrows chatter as they trail nesting material into the martin house.

Winter may enjoy an encore, but the sounds of spring will overwhelm any return of howling winds carrying cold and snow. The die has been cast. The pools are free of ice and sparkle in the sun. The willows glisten with new vigor. Mallards have eggs in nests around Clear Pool. Cardinals whistle. Flies hatch in stagnant backwaters. Trout are ravenous and slurp pellets off the water in a frenzy of feeding.

Watercress is shiny green as a polished emerald. Grass grows where a warm spring pushes out of the sand on the shores of Blue Pool. Brush willow has soft catkin tufts. Skunk cabbage shows purple and will soon burst into bloom. Horses and dogs are shedding. The ground is springy underfoot. Bluegills are coming out of the cool deep to the warmer shallows. Crows come silently to the tall elms looking for nesting sites.

Kites fly and gravel spurts to the spinning of bicycle wheels. The Rebels are almost ecstatic. At long last, the endless chain of snowstorms has been broken. The sleeping earth is coming alive, and if spring is here, can summer and vacation time be far behind?

Magic moon

The moon works magic. When it is bright and shiny, the birds awaken, point their beaks toward the sky and warble. It happened that way Tuesday night. Little Lakes was dressed in shimmering robes of silver. The weeping willows were gilded, and even the gnarled oaks looked soft. Through the bedroom window, the lawn was a long pool of shimmering grass. From the hill, the ponds looked milky in the moon. The sky was almost as bright as day.

Then, at 3 a.m., a robin warbled. A mourning dove took the cue and began cooing. Within minutes, a chorus of bird voices came through the bedroom window. There was no sleeping then, so the Rebel Queen and I went to the kitchen and drank a cup of coffee. In the kitchen, the chorus sounded distant, unreal. But when we went back into the bedroom the birds filled the place with singing. It was at once eerie and wonderful, but there was no sleeping until we closed the windows. Then the muted singing furnished a comfortable background of sound on which to fall asleep.

Aggressive swallows

Tree swallows, most graceful speedsters, have taken over the birdhouses that stand on poles rammed into the mud of Fish Pond and Clear Pool. They fight off any trespassers. The brilliant male swoops down, often within inches of the trespasser's head, while the plain little female sits on the house and chirps approval.

Redstart visits

Another bird, a redstart, thrilled the Rebels this last week. It was first sighted by Rebel No. 2. The redstart's beauty of form and plumage, and its graceful motions, place it at the head of the wood warblers. The bird fairly dances through the trees.

Shick-shack

Rebel No. 3 has been spring housecleaning. Along with her neighbor friends, Barbara and Annie, she has been cleaning the one-room house which stands on the shores of Clear Pool, almost completely hidden by spruce trees. The children have scrubbed the floor and washed the windows and will paint the porch. They call the place their shick-shack, and they sleep there summer nights. That is, they go there to sleep, but often the party lasts until 2 or 3 a.m., and that is keeping late hours when you are only ten.

Timid Rebel

It is hard to understand why children raised under identical circumstances react differently to situations. The three-year-old Rebel is a timid one. She likes the quarter-sized painted turtles so long as they stay in their bowl. Frogs are fine along the shore or in someone else's hands, but not in hers. Yet she thinks a slimy fish is soft and fine to touch. Spiders and hornets enthrall her — at safe distances. Any dog or any horse is a friend, and sometimes I think it is a miracle she still has all her fingers, because when she feeds these animals their teeth touch her hand.

Dangerous places

There are many dangers at Little Lakes. Some of the pools drop off abruptly to twelve feet of water. The mare does not always mind her manners. The dogs, lovable and gentle as they are, may never be completely trusted. There are rotary mowers and tractors. The boat, though stable, can be tipped. There are poisonous berries, and sometimes the poison ivy comes back. Even the fins and teeth of the fish can inflict wounds and cause infection.

So we must always be on guard. The Rebels must be taught to know the harmless from the harmful. They must learn how to handle a horse and a dog, how to fend off an attack from a gander without injuring the bird. There is no denying that we worry. But the Rebels are more resourceful than we give them credit for. From tiny on, they ask before eating a berry. Water is their friendly enemy. A mower is a fiendish instrument that must be handled like dynamite with a lighted fuse.

They delight in roasting marshmallows but respect the fire for what it can do to them. Every day they must be on their guard, and they know it. But, if anything, instead of making their life miserable, the dangers around seem to give them a certain kind of pleasure. Still, we worry.

New house

A new white ranch home recently went high into the sky with speed that made an old fashioned barn raising, to which all the neighbors used to come, look like a slow-motion movie. Occupants for the new home arrived April 14, but the paint had not yet dried, nor was the roof completely in place. An all-out endeavor was necessary. So, while a snowstorm raged outside, the builder enlisted members of his family to help finish the structure. It was delivered Sunday, and on Monday we carried it to the shores of Fish Pond. We took the old house down, fastened the new one securely to the tall pole and raised it on high. There it is now, silhouetted against the sky, a home with twelve rooms for the martins to live in.

A better way?

The robins are busy building nests, but few will live long enough to hatch the eggs they will soon be laying. If this year's march of death approximates that of last year, most of the robins will die within the next four weeks.

Right now, there are dozens of robins building in the cherry and apple trees, among the pines, high in the elms and maples, everywhere. As they work, so does the poison with which the elm trees were sprayed. The robins assimilate the poison as they eat contaminated worms or drink from contaminated puddles. Eventually, they lose the power of flight, sit and shiver, and then die.

The Rebels know what is going on. They saw it all happen last year. For nearly a month they had a daily burial detail, and the job of scouting the acres, picking up dead birds and covering them with earth. There was as much sadness in the beginning as in the end. It is the same story with the grackles now that this dictator has decreed the death penalty because hundreds upon hundreds of birds are raising havoc with the trees.

I thought that in time the Rebels would reconcile themselves to the fact that some wild things must die so others might live. But it has not happened. They will not face up to death. Perhaps it is because they are children, and only maturity enables people to face facts. But I am not so sure this is the case. I think they do face the facts, and that is why they cannot reconcile themselves to this slaughter. Their questions indicate they feel adults responsible for killing grackles and robins are not using alternatives that might save both the trees and the birds.

"There must be another way," they claim.

Of course, there must be another way, and there surely is. The trouble is the adults are involved in so many things they consider more important that there is neither time nor money to develop selective poisons that will not harm the robins. They are so busy with the "big things" that nobody has time to find a sure-fire way of scaring the grackles out of the spruce instead of shooting them down. Maybe the children are more mature than the adults.

Expectant geese

After two unproductive years, Duchess, the Canada goose, has a huge nest of grass, leaves and down with five big eggs in it. The Rebels are ecstatic. Duke is beside himself and chases every living thing brazen enough to enter his pen. He even pummels the mallards who share his quarters. We have seen no reign of terror quite so tyrannical. Instead of setting up housekeeping in one of the barrels or boxes placed in the pen for that purpose, the geese built a home right in the open, within a few feet of the six-by-four "swimming pool," which had been community property. Now the pool is forbidden ground to the ducks, and feathers fly if any dare to encroach on the goose domain. Even the pigeons do not escape the wrath of the royal pair, and Rebel No. 3 is not permitted in to scatter food. Rebel No. 2, using a tin pan as a shield against their assaults, stands them off while she scatters grain.

⚶ ⚶ ⚶

Rebel No. 2 has found a snipe nest, which she visits regularly, hoping to witness the hatching. Last spring, she saw killdeers pop from their eggs, dry in minutes and become fluffy little birds that ran about wildly while the mother put on a broken-wing act to turn attention her way.

⚶ ⚶ ⚶

Once in a lifetime! Two scarlet tanagers in the low branches of a small maple. A cock cardinal above them and, still higher, in an overhang of basswood branches, a Baltimore oriole. Too much! Too much!

SUMMER

First elms fall

Four diseased elms went crashing this week. One was a giant, and the rings on the stump put its age at near one hundred. Even with spring spraying, the community of elms seems doomed. But at least the dying is delayed. If the elms all went at once, Little Lakes would look like a battlefield where artillery has ravaged the forest.

⚶ ⚶ ⚶

We have planted more ferns beneath the blue spruce and pine trees. Delicate plants, they break easily. The first plants brought down from Door County four years ago are now doing well. They stand in the shade of a gnarled oak and an umbrella-shaped elm.

Goslings arrive

Duke and Duchess are being congratulated upon the arrival of two goslings. If the Rebel Queen had given birth to triplets, the Rebels could not have been more excited. Now the geese will not permit the mallards to nest. They are intent on making life miserable for Rosy van Etta, Goldie and all the ducks. So it appears the geese and their two goslings may have to go into solitary confinement so the ducks can get on with their job of raising kids.

⚜ ⚜ ⚜

The cardinals who came to the bird feeders during the winter with as much caution as might be accorded a booby trap seem to have lost all their wariness. Now, even though nesting, they sit and whistle in the big basswood tree right alongside the house, while the Rebels are raising a ruckus directly underneath.

Just one Rainey

There is a fresh grave with a bouquet of purple phlox on it at Little Lakes. Rainey died Tuesday. Death did not come easily, nor did the Old Dog accept it graciously. He complained bitterly even with his last breath because his legs would not lift him. Most amazing is that he lived as long as he did. Death stalked him from the day he first came to us as a pup. He should have died the morning he was swept beneath the ice of the Milwaukee River, or the afternoon he dived through the window of a moving car because a hunter had shot a ruffed grouse along the roadside.

It looked like his time had come the day he crossed a railroad trestle over a river with a train bearing down on him. Only terrible determination got him back the day he stepped into a steel trap. Rainey survived being suffocated while wearing a culvert like a corset, probably because he was more dynamite than dog. He recovered when a kennel mate broke a tooth off in his skull, probably because he was hardheaded in more ways than one.

A virus that is ninety-nine percent fatal had him prostrate once, but with the Rebel Queen's help, he clung to life and recovered while being nursed on a blanket next to the kitchen stove.

Perhaps he was not the smartest dog who ever lived, but when a duck named Aristotle kept biting him during practice retrieves, he wisely went into the marsh and buried the mallard — alive.

But if he was as fine a hunting companion as any man could ever want, he was also a kennel boss, and kennel bosses have troubles. During one fight on the banks of the Brule River, he accidentally grabbed me and sank his teeth right down to the leg bone. Another time, he brought me bouncing out of a sickbed with a 104-degree temperature sans everything except pajama bottoms to stop a fight on a motel lawn right downtown in Winnipeg.

If Rainey ever spared himself, I do not remember the time. He would hunt until he dropped, and a field of sandburrs couldn't stop him any more than a briar or thistle patch. Once he tried crashing through a barbed-wire tangle to retrieve a downed pheasant. We had to stop in Princeton, and a people doctor just back from a duck hunt sewed the gashes in Rainey's belly and a front leg. Before the day was over, however, Old Dog had torn out the stitches and was hunting as though nothing had happened. His last big hunt was on sharptails in Manitoba, and he capped a terrific performance with such a fool trick as picking up a skunk.

I like to think, now that Rainey is gone, that he liked me. But I never was quite sure. He stuck with me like a fly to flypaper, but sometimes I think it was only because I was the key to every hunting paradise he ever knew. But maybe it wasn't that at all. Maybe he did like me. He wouldn't hunt with anyone else.

There are still four dogs in the Little Lakes kennels. There undoubtedly will be others down through the years, but there will never be another Rainey.

So, the Rebel Queen and all the little Rebels are in mourning, and all the droplets on his grave aren't dew. I'm in mourning, too, because I know this fall, sometime and somewhere, I'll be stepping off the road of an early morning into a glade shining white with frost to await the sunrise. There will be a hunter's moon slipping out of the sky, there will be pearly clouds on the horizon. But, Rainey won't be there.

Faithful muskrats

Muskrats aren't much. They are not even smart enough to select a pothole with enough water to serve them throughout the year. That is why motorists see dead muskrats along the road. They are run down while changing homes. As for muskrats predicting winter weather, that is malarkey. If they knew what was ahead, they would not always be freezing out of their homes. So it is true, muskrats aren't much, except when it comes to being faithful to their families. In this they excel, and a mother muskrat will make perilous journeys in daylight to bring food to her young.

Right now a mother muskrat has a litter of young beneath a high bank on Fish Pond. The pond is practically without food. So the mother must swim across the pond, laying herself open to attack from the air, then climb the east bank where dogs and cats prowl. Here, she cuts down plants, grasps them between her teeth and swims back. It is an odd sight. Sometimes the muskrat is completely camouflaged by the salad she has cut, and it looks as though part of the lawn were swimming away. When she reaches the far west shore, she has to dive to the underwater entrance of her burrow. Sometimes the load of greens so buoys her up that she has a difficult time submerging.

It will not be much longer before the young muskrats will be able to forage for themselves. Then the mother will resume night feeding. But as long as the kids can't leave the burrow, she will brave anything to bring food.

ン゛ ン゛ ン゛

The sun was just rising when I looked out the window through a haze of golden rain. A little breeze had come, the minute golden petals of the linden tree blooms were falling and the slanting sun rays made them sparkle like drops of water.

Uncut grass

Rebel No. 3 does a lot of the grass cutting at Little Lakes, and lately we noticed unmowed swaths. One time, an entire triangular area went nearly to seed before she put the mower through it. It turned out there were small frogs in the grass, and she could not bring herself to move the mower across any areas in which they might be hiding. The large triangular area? She had seen one tiny toad, and when she could not find it to move it to safety, she just let the grass grow.

Sadness never lasts

The wonder of being young is that the spirit renews itself like the earth after a rain, and sadness passes even in seconds. If the Rebels are sorrowful before breakfast, they are brimming with joy before the milk glass is drained. If they are enemies at bedtime, they are friends by the time they have said their prayers. If they are disappointed when sleep comes, they are hopeful at dawn.

It seems no tragedy can stifle their ardor for living. Their emotions are like the sunshine among the leaves, the wind skimming rain across the water. Yet even the young must come to such solemn moments as scar their attitudes. It may be the death of a chipmunk, or the sudden flash of lightning across a bedroom ceiling, or a branch scraping on the roof at night. The most careful discernment is often not enough to see that a subtle change — a deepening of feeling, an awareness of suffering — has become an undercurrent in the young one's life. This is because the laughter, tears and anger pass so rapidly that the image of a youngster is as a pond reflection shattered by a stone.

Horse or hippo?

Meet a horse who thinks she is a hippopotamus. When heat holds the land in shimmering waves, Joker likes nothing better than to go for a swim in Fish Pond. Once in, she is reluctant to return to shore, but rolls in the water purring like an overgrown cat. Upon entering the water, she dunks her head until only her ears are visible. One dunking is enough, however, and after a swim she stands or lies in the shallow water like a human too happy to come back out into the heat. Then the Rebels have a job getting her back out, but who can blame the horse? There are no flies underwater, and all the little irritations — where an insect drew blood or a wire barb nicked her — are quickly soothed.

A mockingbird of the north has Joker in a tizzy. It seems the catbird has learned to imitate the piercing whistle the Rebels use to summon the horse. Now, throughout the day, Joker hears the whistle and comes to the gate looking for the Rebels.

Signs of fall

Tree swallow kids flying in family flocks as they skim insects off the water. Blackbirds flocking. Black-eyed Susans blooming. Raspberries drying on the vine. Grapes swelling to where they are ready to purple. One- to three-inch bass of this year's hatch pecking away at the fisherman's bass bug. Young screech owls away and on their own, but mourning, perhaps, for their parents to feed them. Dew beading grass and fog holding the hollows. Cool nights of a week ago and a fire in the fireplace.

Breathtaking: Morning glories entwined in a small spruce so the blooms look like Christmas tree lights. Dayflowers, blue and fragile, in the parched, brown lawn. A hundred red-, white- and black-spotted goldfish shining at the sunny surface of New Pool. Daisies running rampant through any cover spared by the lawn mower. Watercress Creek, silver where the sun knifes through overhanging trees. Brown cattails so velvety among their slender swords of greenery. Cedars, high now, and billowing up a bank like green clouds. Fresh freckles on a child's face and gold where the sun has bleached her hair.

The best times

The best times at Little Lakes are sunset, night under the moon, and sunrise. It seems there are always a few clouds for the sun to set afire before going down. Under the moon, harsh outlines become hazy and the trees, buildings and even people take on a gauzy, soft look in the half-light. Then, when the sun rises, all the freshness of early morning lifts from the springs to be felt.

Goslings grow up

The young geese begotten by Duke and Duchess are full of wing now and, except for size, look like adults. Their white markings are sharp. Their legs are sturdy, and almost every day the old ones run into the wind with wings spread as if to teach the youngsters to fly. That is the sad part about having wildlings back of wire. They must be wing-clipped lest they fly away. But the Rebels try to make up for the loss of freedom with much food and excellent care.

Nighthawks and whip-poor-wills

Four nighthawks, those big-city birds that nest on the flat roofs of buildings, are using the air lanes above Little Lakes. We rarely see them, nor do we hear the wind thunder through their wings when they dive.

I wish we had whip-poor-wills at Little Lakes. Every time I hear them, I am reminded of a lush, green meadow on Marquette County's lower Mecan River. Here, the big brown trout would rise to a mayfly almost any June or July, and the whip-poor-wills would whiplash the night with their cries.

Back to school

It is a sad week. How would you like to get back into shoes after having had the dewy, cool grass tickle your bare feet every morning? How would you like to walk and sit so properly as a dress requires after racing around in shorts all summer? How would you like to have to look a teacher in the eye instead of seeing your own reflection in the big, brown eyes of a loving dog or horse? How would you like to smell the varnish on a school desk instead of flowers on a breeze? Or listen to a lecture on English literature instead of learning your poetry firsthand from the throat of a songbird? So, it is a sad week for the Rebels, and they have been going around with long faces since it suddenly dawned on them that school was just a few more dreams away.

Change comes quickly

So quickly, the change is noticeable. The elms are ragged. The pasture is brown. Colors of asters and sumac and the high yellow of the sticktight replace the flamboyancy of tiger lilies. The water weeds are going down. The ponds sparkle with more clarity after each chilling night. Chipmunks and muskrats are even busier than during the summer. Robins are flocking and young blue jays are raucous as they find their voices. Even the stars sparkle with increased intensity. Summer is sick. One frost now and it will die.

AUTUMN

Night time

The moon intrigues Rebel No. 4. She thinks there are several moons, because at 6 p.m. she may see it in the eastern sky and then, before going to bed, directly overhead. The moon intrigues all the Rebels. It softens the world. It is comforting to have it shining when the sun goes off duty. It puts shadows on the bedroom floor and a patch of light on the wall. It is both mysterious and friendly. It lights the road and the paths to the ponds.

Sometimes it is only a sliver of silver in a daytime sky. Often it is a ball of red on the horizon, whitening as it lifts to look down. It is a comfort, because when the moon is out there are no storms and the tree branches do not beat on the roof and the sides of the house. It is no strange, cold planet but a warm reflection that means all is right with the world it shines upon.

Night is a fascinating time for those who can tear themselves away from television long enough to be thrilled by it. Right now, there is hardly a moonlight night on which birds of one species or another are not migrating. The herons and the ducks are most in evidence. When a lone heron or a small colony arrives over a pond or lake in the nighttime, it immediately calls out and is then directed to a roosting area, either in trees or in a marsh, by those already in camp.

After moonlight, the mist that nightly holds the low places in its scarf of white is the most beautiful. Sometimes it looks like white water with trees growing from it. Other times it seems the earth is smoking, especially when an errant breeze sends the mist curling up around bridge abutments and low tree branches. Soon now, a frost will crystallize the mist and there will be a white morning. Then the flowers will droop and the grass will lie down.

Frosty nights will change things. The sooner they come now, the better. The air will be crisp. Stars will shine more brightly. The moon will be luminous. Owls will talk and ducks will hurry. Sounds will be sharper when carried by dry air.

Rebel No. 4 loves Concord grapes, so when we raided the vines for jelly and jam, we left some clusters behind. But we left only the high clusters, so now the peanut of a girl has to jump to satisfy her appetite for grapes.

Chores undone

Work that won't get done: Hundreds of spruce trimmed to the height of a man's head, a hundred small spruce transplanted, six to ten elms killed by elm tree disease cut down, the final hundred yards of Fish Pond rocked in, stepped-down pools installed in the sunken garden, swinging bridge built over Clear Pool, New Pool poisoned out and planted to trout, thousands of bushels of leaves burned, and so on and on and on.

Clouds of cress

Watercress was never so verdant as now. It rises in green clouds in Watercress Creek below Clear Pool. Few if any wildlings eat the cress, not even the muskrats. So there it stands, cold and crisp, waiting for us. Mint is disappearing along Watercress Creek. Perhaps it is because of the inroads being made by canary grass. Poplar trees and canary grass are the two most ambitious plants, except perhaps quack grass and Canada thistles.

Silver-gray ghosts

Ghosts haunt Little Lakes. Silvery gray creatures, they wait until dark before coming up out of the earth or the giant hollow of an aged tree. The ghosts are opossums. Ghostlike they roam now, and they may still roam if there is an earth a million years hence.

Tempering springs

Temperatures on and around Clear Pool remain higher than anywhere else at Little Lakes. The springs, gushing from the earth at forty-eight degrees, "steam" when the temperature drops. Rabbits know about the warmth, and they fashion their forms within inches of the water. Birds, too, are more plentiful near the pool, and ducks stay on the water around the clock to keep their webs warm. The "steam" from the pool and Watercress Creek rises to the willow and spruce trees and freezes to a sparkling white glaze. In summer, the pool acts as an air conditioner. It is always a few degrees cooler along the shores than elsewhere.

Ace joins Rainey

There was another fresh grave when I returned this week from a Canadian trip. Now, old Ace lies next to Rainey along the fence line where the currant and gooseberry bushes will soon be laden with fruit.

Ace and Rainey were traveling companions for more than ten years. Together, they saw the sun come up on pheasant marshes. They saw the frost melt in the glades where the ruffed grouse came to dust in the sun. They knew most of the duck marshes in Wisconsin, and a few far away. They saw bluebills come busting off Lake Superior and into the mouth of the Brule, mallards settling on Sinissippi, teal whizzing over the brown flats of Muskego, and wood ducks tooling back into the marshes along the Mississippi.

They hunted every manner of game, and though each was a specialist, either one could pinch hit when the other was sick or injured. Ace never had the stomach Rainey had for hunting. He was good, but he preferred to live like people, and when the ice formed he let his partner do the retrieving.

Though his father, Black Panther, was one of the nation's greatest, Ace's fame was in being a friend to man. I cannot remember that he ever bared a tooth or uttered a growl, though he was pummeled in turn by each of the four Rebels when they were still too young to know that a finger in an eye can hurt, a yanked ear will ache.

Cancer caught up with Ace. He must have had it quite some time before it was discovered, and he must have suffered. But he never complained. Two of the Rebels were able to get to the hospital to say good-bye to him. They brought him home then, and wrapped him in a warm blanket before lowering him into his grave.

There was many a wet eye around Little Lakes, and one little girl cried herself to sleep. But mourning is a luxury when there are the living to be cared for. So the Rebels must leave off the weeping to feed, water and clean up after the other dogs. They must look to the chickens and Canada geese and groom and exercise the horses. But they will not be forgetting Ace, even if each lives to be eighty. Any maybe from his life they will take something to help them through the years.

Because he was one gentle creature who never complained about those things for which there was no remedy.

❀ ❀ ❀

Duke, Duchess and their two young Canada geese pay no attention to the many flocks of relatives going overhead. Last spring, before the couple had any kids, they honked constantly every time a north-flying flock came into view.

Tequila

Tequila, a recently arrived palomino gelding, is adjusting to Little Lakes. Joker, the quarter-horse mare, still bites and belts the good-natured palomino, but not nearly as much as when the two were first pastured together.

Tequila was rightly named. He has a kick, and the Rebels have to be alert or they are likely to wind up with hoof marks. The dogs are not safe in the pasture when Tequila is roaming it. He comes prancing in, rears and comes down with front legs stiff, trying to cut down the dogs. He chases strangers, and one day the Rebel Queen made the mistake of trying to herd him into the stable. Tequila promptly switched his rear to her and began kicking. She fled to the house.

Sometimes, though, I think the horse is only showing his high, good spirits and really would not hurt a fly. He is careful not to step on any living thing, and so far his flying hooves never get anywhere near the Rebels. The only one the aggressive horse listens to is Rebel No. 2. She can handle him as though he were a kitten. Once the horse begins to get regular workouts, he will have no stomach for chasing people and animals out of the pasture.

Waiting days

The cardinals still whistle at Little Lakes, but we seldom hear them now. The moon still lights up the night, but for all practical purposes the shades might as well be drawn. Squirrels still chase each other in the hickory trees and rabbits gambol on the lawn, but no one notices. The sun still shines, but not in our hearts, because the Rebel Queen is joined in mortal combat with a dread disease.

All we wait for is the sound of her voice in the middle of the day, in the middle of the night. All we pray for is a word of hope. Still, life goes on, and when Rebel No. 3 becomes bored while herding the horses so they may graze the banks of Clear Pool, she makes friends with the fish. Using food pellets to tempt them, she gathers twenty to thirty trout with-

The Rebel Queen lives on in the flowers and trees she planted, in the children she bore, in the friends she made, in the hearts of all who knew her.

Using food pellets to tempt them, she gathers twenty to thirty trout within a few feet of her position on the bank. They recognize her now and are unafraid. Several permit her to reach into the water and pet them.

The unfortunates among the trout are her favorites, and they have names. There is one with a deformed spine, another blind in one eye, one with a deformed head, five or six cripples who get fed first, who are among the favored few.

There will be no hickory nuts or walnuts this year. Weeks before they are ready, the squirrels are eating them. But there will be grapes. They are plump now, ready for purpling.

Water surely is life. Standing high and dry, the purple and white phlox shriveled in the sun. But then we directed a steady stream of water from Fish Pond among their dying blooms. Within days, they came back to life. Now they stand proud and pretty, a long slash of brilliance alongside the sun-browned lawn.

More ghosts are joining the once proud and lofty colony of elms. Bitten by the bug, they die a little at a time until the sun can glare through their bare branches. The bark warps then and peels away. Then they stand white and ghostlike, mere skeletons of their once verdant and crowning glory.

So that's how it is out here at Little Lakes these waiting days.

Long live the Queen

The Rebel Queen is dead. Long live the Queen. May she live in the flowers and trees she planted. May she live in the children she bore, in the friends she made, in the hearts of all who knew her. Little Lakes cannot be the same, but there never will be a day that something around the place will not serve as a reminder of the times she walked across these acres. Because she was no queen in ermine seated on a throne, but a mother and a helper with dirt under her fingernails and sweat on her brow.

Her mark is everywhere out here. It is in the white stones that hold in the banks of Fish Pond, on the buildings and fences she helped to paint, along the hedges she planted. The years may change Little Lakes, but a hundred years from now some child may lie back on the grass under a towering cedar, and there will be shade then because the Rebel Queen hoed the weeds from around that seedling struggling toward the sun. So, even though the Rebel Queen is dead, we can truthfully say, "Long live the Queen."

BOOK TWO

Introduction

"A widower's weeds, watered with a little love, become flowers again."
With those words, Mel Ellis brought back "Notes From Little Lakes" after a two-year hiatus that followed the death of his wife, Bernice. When the column reappeared in The Milwaukee Journal on January 24, 1965, a new Rebel Queen, Gwen, had come to Little Lakes.

"For those who knew her," Ellis wrote, "Rebel Queen I was physically a considerable woman. Rebel Queen II is pint-size. Underneath, where it counts, both have hearts as huge as heaven must be."

With Gwen at his side, Ellis continued the slow transformation of his property into a mature and thriving wildlife community. Gwen, especially adept with wildflowers, rescued many from the paths of encroaching highways and transplanted them into the Little Lakes soil.

In time, the family phased out formal flower gardens in favor of wildflower plantings. Amid all the natural beauty, Ellis mused, planting tame flowers seemed "a little like gilding the lily."

As for the Rebels, the two oldest, Sharon and Suzanne, had moved on to raise families of their own, leaving three sisters to tend the horses, dogs and all manner of wild and tame friends at Little Lakes.

As Little Lakes came of age, Ellis found his voice as a writer. Within months of the column's return, readers began to see his lyrical side. He turned from mere reporting on life at Little Lakes toward evoking the beauty he saw around him and refining the warm, sensitive touch that won him recognition as "a poet of the land."

As Book Two begins, Rebel No. 1 (Debbie) is fourteen years old, Rebel No. 2 (Gwen's daughter Dianne) is eleven, and Rebel No. 3 (Mary) is six. The writings in this section, spanning 1965 through 1973, describe memorable times at Little Lakes and offer the finest examples of Ellis' prose. The entries are arranged to portray Little Lakes against the backdrop of the four seasons.

~ T.J.R.

❧ ❧ ❧

chapter one

WINTER

Early winter

Early winter: spawning trout caught tightly around the gill covers by a trap set in Watercress Creek for muskrats. Ducks, crowded by ice from the mill pond to Clear Pool, then, as the temperature drops, on up into the flowing water. Plethora of squirrels, eleven under one maple, streaming like hungry refugees to crowd beneath the bird feeders. Brown swirls of sparrows, in from the stable, to wait in the trees until the bigger birds make room before descending in a cyclone of feathers for their share of food.

Starlings hanging like sequined ornaments on the suet swinging from a limb in a mesh bag. Mourning doves, fluffed against the cold, looking for gravel in tire tracks. Nuthatches caching sunflower seeds beneath the shaggy bark of a hickory. Rabbit hunched into a muff of fur where brown grass threads up between the spreading green skirts of a spruce. Opossum, eternally hungry, looking to warm, for a moment, its bare feet where a trail has been blown clear of snow.

Goldfish, swarming up beneath a thin skin of ice on New Pool for their last look at the sun until next spring. A painted turtle, poking its head up in the horses' watering hole in Fish Pond, only to dive back down to the relative warmth of the muddy bottom. Mournful grackle, alone on a limb, the rest of the colony having flown to warmer climes. White-footed mouse, a bird scratch of tracks from one hole in the snow to another. Crows, high and black against the paper sky, waiting in an oak for appetites to send them patrolling the highways for road kills.

Pale worm, briefly pink on the black ground, where a white rock spreads heat it has gathered in from the sun. One white-faced hornet left, frozen to the side of the paper house that once was home for hundreds. Hunting owl, wing prints where a mouse was. Dead ant, frozen into the clear glass of a hanging icicle. Cardinals, flashing like flakes of fire.

Solitary hawk, the whole sky to himself. Torpid fly, still living where house heat warms his crack where window meets sill. Ladybug on a bathroom curtain, carried in from the cold on a coat collar. Spiders, looking out through the lattice of their window webs. Big black ant, scurrying to keep ahead of the fireplace flames eating the wood chunk in which it lived.

Brilliant glitter of a butterfly, waiting in a chrysalis on a cattail. Maple seed beneath the snow, waiting to become a tree. Raccoon, found a frog and ate its head and entrails. Mink, left the claws and shining armor of a crayfish on the ice.

Hollow-tree bees, all whirring to keep warm. Deer mouse, at home in an old bird nest it has roofed over. Black beetle, shell shining like a piece of coal. Late fly hatch, preserved in pond ice. Muskrat houses like raisins in white frosting.

White weasel, ghost trailed by the black tip of its tail. Flashing, fighting blue jays with angry crests. Frozen shrew, worm in its mouth, as if eating even in death. Shell-shocked pheasant, safe at last.

Early winter, time for dying, except for the defiant.

Careful steps

To walk on ice so clear the world of water goes down, down, past gently moving coontail, past a swimming fish to where white stones mark the pond's bottom, is like walking on thin air, and the Rebels move as though each step might be the one to break the window over this liquid world that has never been so clearly close, even in summer while they were swimming in it.

Sometimes the ice is like that, as smooth and transparent as nothing at all. There is no comparable experience, so the Rebels never quite get their breath back until boot soles or skate blades have scuffed the ice and at last it seems to have some substance.

But I must always test the ice first. It is a rule the Rebels favor because, being country bred, they are not anxious to throw themselves into just any adventure without first considering the risk. So they hang around the kitchen door waiting for me to finish breakfast.

This morning I am not so quick to dress because the first evening grosbeaks have come, and I am watching a female of modest attire accompanied by two males in yellow jackets. But the family of red-headed woodpeckers, which has decided to stay north, gives them only seconds at the feeder. I watch and wonder if the grosbeaks will stay, or if the competition is too much and they will seek out more solitary forests where birds do not gang around because some family sees fit to feed them.

Then I go to the basement for boots. Eventually I come to the shores of the ponds. Blue Pool is open all along the shore where the springs are, and Clear Pool has no ice at all, but Fish Pond is frozen. I try a patch of ice, and cracks go in every direction like zigzags of white lightning. So I search for thicker ice. In a protected place the footing seems firmer, and I try. Though it creaks, it does not crack, and I know it will hold.

Yet this sure knowledge does not still the tremors of wariness as we look down, down, through the thin, clear ice into this other world of water, a universe of its own with strange life forms clinging to air bubbles or straining oxygen through red gills, and where now lie buried frogs and turtles awaiting the sun of spring.

Keel! Keel!

Death was there and we never knew it. So all morning we wondered, where are the birds? On any other day, as dawn pushes darkness to the west, they come at first light from the trees that crest in every direction. But this morning there was not even one of the ubiquitous sparrows, not a chickadee or a nuthatch, nor even the blue jay, whom the devil himself might find difficult to frighten.

Storm? Well, there were a few clouds on the hill that holds the river, but mornings they are almost always there. Cat? Not that anyone could see, but cats are careful, so we beat the brush and the yews, to no avail. Weasel? Mink? None would chance the light of day here within the shadow of the house.

Perhaps just for once every bird at Little Lakes had a full crop and all were resting now where thick conifers break any wind. That had to be it. What else? Noon came, but the birds did not, and then we knew something had happened, because on any other day, without exception, there would be starlings sunning high in the top branches of the tall basswoods. Now, nothing.

So I went looking among the spruce that crowd into groves, all the way through to the bank of Fish Pond. Up the hill. Down into the marsh. Along the creek. Back into the pasture. Nothing. Not anywhere. Except once, three chickadees and a nuthatch where the conifer branches were thickest. So I went back to the house, and Gwen and Rebel No. 1 went to Milwaukee, and Rebel No. 3 went to a friend's house, and so I was alone to watch from a place on the couch where I could see, through a picture window, one of the bird feeders.

Then a flash of feathers. Arrow on scimitar wings. Swift between birch branches. Talons balled for a strike. Talons quickly opened to close again in an iron vise. Death beautiful as a spreading wing. Smallest of the falcons. Most colorful too. Sparrow hawk with a burst of jet speed down and then up again as a chickadee dived into the yews.

One? Likely two. Poised on high branches. Waiting. Ready always to strike. Needing songbird or mouse now that grasshoppers were gone. Swifter than a wind cloud. Silent as fingers of fog. Lightning thrust. Little killer calling now.

"Keel! Keel! Keel!"

Birds believing.

Catch the wind?

Save me a bag filled with sunshine for the days when the winter is cold. Put away a morning of bird songs for when the birds have flown. Net me a basket of moonbeams to spread when the night is dark. Gather a garden of flowers to spill when the earth is stark.

It started when one of the Rebels asked if she could catch a bottle of wind and keep it. Without thinking, I said: "No." But, of course she could catch a bottle of wind or the sigh of a pine, the splash of water, the pink of dawn, just about anything she put her mind to. And there's no magic to it, only the need to really feel, see and hear. Really seeing is simple. It takes only such humility as can get the eyes to look past one's own nose.

The wind was gusting up to fifty miles per hour the day the Rebel wanted to know about bottling some. It was finding cracks in the house we'd never suspected. It howled, shrieked, moaned and whimpered. It twisted trees, and a Colorado blue spruce of thirty years lay over. It sprayed water into branches of overhanging trees to hang out icicles. It raked the weeping willows clean of dead branches. It swept up the broad lawn to get the last leaves into windrows against the fence. It tousled the horses' manes and turned their tails along their flanks. It tipped the ducks until they turned so that the wind could flow with their feathers.

Into the night it blew and tossed a linden's limbs until there was walking on the roof and thumping in the attic. It whipped the yews to a frenzy of fingers up and down the bedroom walls. The dugout basswood log, flower box in summer and bird feeder in winter, crashed and spilled some frozen flowers. The wind shredded clouds and then swept the sky so shiny clean the stars looked polished. Then all of another day it cut deadwood until late in the afternoon when it rested and hungry animals and birds hurried out for a snack before bedtime.

Sad song

Northwoods, Wis.
The Rebels
On Little Lakes

Dear Rebels:

Last night, I heard a coyote howling, and it was a sad song, perhaps because the little wolf remembers that when winter comes, the days of feasting are over, and that many times before the snow melts he will curl up footsore and hungry. Of all Northwoods creatures, the coyote, originally a little desert dog, will probably suffer most in this cold and alien land it has chosen to call home.

Deer suffer, too, but they at least have the company of their own kind as they yard together in valleys for protection against icy blasts. The coyote must keep moving or starve. To find one mouse, it may have to lope ten miles. To search out a single whisky jack roosting low enough to be plucked, it may have to hunt a week of nights. For the reward of a single snowshoe hare, it may have to wait along a hare's runway for a month. To trap one grouse in its night camp beneath the snow, it may have to hunt out an entire forest.

It caches no food as do the beaver and the red squirrel. It cannot hibernate like the bear or the woodchuck. It may not even run in packs, as does the timber wolf, so that combined strength might enable the killing of a deer. It is not the coyote's fault that it does not store food, hibernate or hunt in packs. The little wolf has no choice. It was ordained by nature to be a loner, running only with its shadow across the frozen wastes.

In its desert country, the lone hunter that loped tirelessly and silently across the flat lands found more rats, mice, snakes and jack rabbits than a pack moving noisily through the sage. So the habit stayed with him. Occasionally, he may run with a companion, but during most of the winter he goes it alone. The miracle of it all is that he survives. I have never found a coyote dead of natural causes, nor have I heard of anyone who has. But I have heard of hungry coyotes who have eaten gloves or belts and even chewed on auto tires. I have heard of coyotes eating not only a handful of grapes dried on the vine, but part of the vine, too. Any patch of fur with enough hide to give half a calorie is gobbled by the gristly little ghost. Snowshoe webbing makes material for feasting.

Leave a sandwich wrapper and the coyote will eat it for the wax. Though its narrow jaw is not powerful enough to crack old bones for a smidgen of marrow, the coyote will gnaw endlessly until the bone is worn through and he can tongue out a few ounces of energy.

To understand how this is, you must know that the Northwoods is in no way like Little Lakes. Though winters are sometimes severe at Little Lakes, the animals always have enough hunting to stay in good flesh. By comparison, the denizens of the Northwoods are spread over such vast areas that the land seems barren. To see the Northwoods in the grip of winter is to see a white, freezing, frustrating land. Many animals and birds, including squirrels, beaver, muskrats and even mink, freeze out or starve. Deer sometimes die by the hundreds. But not the coyote.

Leave some axle grease in the sugarbush and the coyote will eat it. Pare your horses' hooves along the forest fringe and the coyote will feast. Spread chicken bones with the manure and he'll smell them out. Merciful death that ends the deer's suffering has no time for the coyote. In his heart, the need to survive is so strong that before the spring thaw he sometimes is a rack of bones held together by rubber bands. Still, he remains a runner with the wind, wanting the comfort of death but never finding it. Maybe that is why tonight, as I listen, the coyote's song sounds so sad.

Your Dad with love,
Mel

Christmas Eve

In keeping with the season, nature has decked out Little Lakes with her own ornaments, and if she has not been as garish as some might like, she makes up for it with a subtlety that wears well. Only the most insensitive can endure for long the brilliant lights and brassy loudspeakers in the tinsel-draped, gaudy world of downtown. After awhile, it is a relief to get away from the hurdy-gurdy of the streets to the softer lights and the quiet of home.

There are reds at Little Lakes, but they are used sparingly. Only the dogwood branches interlacing the low boughs of the green spruce and the chains of nightshade berries looping from branch to branch are vivid. Even the greens of the cedars and all the other conifers are subdued, almost coppery. Silver is used sparingly, too. Only where the creek glistens in the sun or light glances from the shiny ice is there a knife-blade shine. There are some icicles on the rocks, but they are translucent and seem to absorb rather than reflect light.

There are browns of every shade, from tawny canary grass to deep velvet brown cattails, which stand like fat tallow candles with little spikes sticking through like wicks. Where Watercress Creek widens into an open pool, there is blue, none of your washed out blues, but a color with substance, changing shade only slightly in the wind. There are vines, golden in death, and multicolored stones washed by water. Dried grapes, still purple, grow out from vines thick around as a man's wrist.

There are whites: Frost rime on a bridge, and sometimes snow in scarves on spruce boughs, and covering like cotton the branches of the big trees. There is milkweed silk, exploded from a dry pod, an ethereal shimmer of white caught up in the brambles. Sometimes over all there is the rose-colored reflection snatched from a sky at sunset. Then, as night lifts from every little place, shadows change all texture until the moon gets high enough to gild the scene with a soft, white light. Then truly, it seems like a holy night.

Animals in heaven

This is the Rebel Queen's story about how the animals got into heaven:

One day a child died and came to the throne of God, who asked, "And how do you like it, now that you are here?"

The child, shy in the presence of God, could make no truthful answer. God saw she was frightened, so He said, "But, come now. Of all men, surely you can talk to Jesus."

The child looked into the eyes of God and then it was easy, and so she said, "My dog. I left him, and the priests say there is no place for animals in Your kingdom because they have no souls."

God frowned. "But did the priests forget to tell you that in Me all things are possible?"

The little girl remembered that the priests had truly told her that. "They said it," she said.

"Well, then," God said, smiling, "do you want your dog with you?"

And the child nodded and was happy, and that is how the animals got into heaven.

Killer cold

The air is so clear that windows of houses on a distant hill shine in the sun. Only when it is very cold and the air is bitingly sharp can I see them. Sounds, too, are strikingly loud when the mercury sinks below the red zero mark. The crack of an ax against a tree trunk hits the stable and echoes back, and I never noticed it in summer. If a squirrel walks across the sidewalk, I can hear his tiny nails clicking on the cement. Voices from all the way uptown are near and clear. A pin in the dead grass catches my eye, and I can see the colors of a scarf on a skater way over on the mill pond. There's little moisture in the air, of course, and sights and sounds are intensified. The biting cold brings everything into sharp focus, but it is no friend of mine. I hate it.

Cold creeps craftily. It blisters, breaks, bulges or cracks everything it can't kill. It comes almost without warning in the night, stealthy as death itself. Then, in the morning, the cherry red comb of the Muscovy drake is frozen black, the dogs' ears hang like frosted leaves, the horses' nostrils are white-rimmed with ice, birds are fallen and hard as stones. Wild ones or domesticated, all suffer. The cold saps even the house dog's vitality and he gets stringy. And cottontails lucky enough to survive come to spring little more than skeletons held together by thongs that once were full-fleshed muscles.

On especially cold nights, ice on the ponds creaks, groans and booms as hairline cracks streak from shore to shore. Snow underfoot squeaks, wheels of the wheelbarrow screech, bridge boards crack as though breaking. Even rocks are torn asunder when moisture in their tissues expands as the cold freezes it.

I can abide heat or wind or snow or even deluge, but I hate the way cold creeps beneath windowsills to wilt African violets, the way it digs through mittens to freeze the Rebels' fingers. I hate it because it kills and cripples beautiful trees and flowers and cardinals and people. I hate it because it has no character. Storms at least shriek or moan. Thunder rolls and lightning flashes. No one can mistake the warnings. But cold is invisible. It comes like a ghost. There is no sign except the frosty tracks it leaves, and by then it is too late.

Even the Rebels hate the cold. They go out into it to skate or ride or sled, but they hate it. Cold is a ghostly, cruel force that brings pain to their fingers and ears and might injure or kill a bird or animal friend. They learn to tolerate and even thrill to lightning and thunder. Each year, they become less frightened of high wind and are more inclined to take delight in watching the trees bend before it.

But savage cold that drops temperatures to well below zero always frightens them. Perhaps that is because I have so persistently warned them to be wary of frostbite. Having been cold's victim more than once, I continually preach about the dangers of freezing.

I have a healthy fear of fire, too, but I do not hate it as I do cold. Fire gives all kinds of warning. It has color and smoke and smell. But cold is like the shaft of an X-ray. It penetrates and the victims never know they have been victimized until it is too late.

Cold fells thousands every year. Cold breaks dams and causes floods. It overtaxes heating systems and starts fires. It is the indirect cause of asphyxiation in a hundred instances. It brings icy roads and accidents. It tempts people onto thin ice. Name a winter accident and perhaps cold was its underlying cause.

But most of all I hate cold because it comes like a stab in the back. Rain or wind or snow make frontal attacks. These elements even have a certain dignity. But cold is only sly and only treacherous with freezing fingers to wrap death around the unsuspecting.

The rabbit in winter

Perhaps we should not be so quick to write off every animal's seeming acumen as instinct. If Little Lakes' cottontails live through a winter's night, if they elude the many predators and find enough to sustain life for one more day, perhaps it is because there is at work a mind of sorts, something a little beyond a species' inherited reflex for action.

Granting that most rabbit actions are the mere flexing of such sinews as have been fashioned by countless generations of cottontails fleeing down whatever trails were necessary for survival, it would still appear they are gifted with a wild sort of fortitude that sometimes calls for personal and individual invention necessary to fit circumstance.

I track one rabbit from its day camp in a woodchuck hole, and I see how it remembers to stay among the brambles because it knows no owl can penetrate them. Then when it must leave, it does so with long leaps to a shelf of spruce shadow, and follows in the protection of this evergreen skirt to the sunken garden, where it remembers how, during more prosperous times, here were all manner of tender, growing things.

But now there is nothing and the rabbit is cold. I know this, because one night I saw through the picture window how the snow came streaking like white knives, and I know how the wind must have upended the rabbit's fur, driving in its needles of ice.

Now the rabbit would, if it could, return to the woodchuck hole and the comforts of that cavernous place beneath the frostline where it is always warm. But it must eat! So it jumps the wall and goes up under the bird feeders. Digging down, it finds some sunflower seed husks and eats a few. But this is small nourishment, so it goes to where last winter it found white mulberry saplings. When it discovers wire around these, it goes to the wild rose hedge, but is disappointed to find the succulent hips are buried beneath a drift.

Back swiftly then, but never going so close to the doghouse as to cause an uproar, it finds the sidewalk, and here it tongues at the sprinkle of salt — a dark, moist place where we melted the ice. Down the eight steps to a lower level and out to the squirrel feeder. But the snow has covered the corn, so rabbit raises itself. Ears moving constantly to trap any sounds of danger, it looks to where the brush willows are an indistinct bank in the blinding snow.

Perhaps the owl will not risk this wind, so the cottontail races down a trail the Rebels have plowed with the tractor, but turns off suddenly to come to rest in a clustering of cedars. Here, trees resist the wind. It is quiet among the crowding trunks. Snow sifts through softly. There is some box elder, but it has been gnawed so many times the bark has toughened into a bitter scab. So there is nothing except to cross the snow-covered ice of Fish Pond.

The rabbit comes to the fringe of cedar to survey the frozen white raceway. There is nothing to be seen except the snow and the willows, so the rabbit races across. Among the willows, it lifts a little and neatly cuts a twig at the exact place where next spring's catkin lies beneath the scaly bark. The green morsel is not much larger than the head of a pin, but the rabbit quickly cuts other twigs, each time getting a smidgin of green. When it must move on for fresh foraging, there is a crazy pattern of twigs cast about like jackstraws, already disappearing beneath the falling snow.

The rabbit eats for several hours. Then a fox, which earlier had been frightened up from the Fox River marshes by snowmobiles, comes over from the neighboring property. Though the rabbit has never before seen a fox, there is an instant warning. The rabbit waits until Reynard's intentions are clear, and then the race is on. Even if the cottontail is incapable of reasoning, of working out a problem, it knows the fox cannot follow down the narrow confines of the woodchuck hole. So the rabbit sleeps again beneath the frostline, and the fox walks off along the dike, across the road, past the greenhouse and to the marsh to see if there are any mice.

It was no such a night as brings the rabbit to its bed with a bulging belly, but there was enough, and who knows but on the next night perhaps there will be corn at the squirrel feeder, or the wind will blow the wire from around the mulberry trees, or the Rebels will have spilled sunflower seeds while filling the feeders. Or maybe the rabbit will take a journey down the road and hop off into a lilac bush to see if there might yet be some buds, if the snow has come high enough so it can reach them.

So at least the rabbit remembers, and surely it is capable of making a choice. So it is at least the handmaiden if not the master of its fate.

January thaw

Today, spring was a thin trickle. It coursed in thousands of tiny veins beneath the covering of ice and snow to add freshness to our four ponds. And if the cold must come again and freeze the mud, now so softened as to take its first faint print, it will never stay as long. Because if the buds do not swell for another month or even two, there will be other days like this, and each time the already pregnant earth will swell to accept the running waters so it may give birth. And that is the January thaw, a beginning.

The impatient time is, of course, in March. Then, deer and cottontail, coyote and fox, and even humans are ready for the rebirth, if for different reasons. Perhaps only the crows can wait, because the snow is going, the casualties of winter are uncovered and there are plenty of carcasses to feed upon.

But if winter lingers into April, man has reason to be upset, for there is a weariness of spirit. If the animals need sustenance so their bodies may survive, man needs warm winds and sunshine if only to satisfy what some call his soul. Still a man of many summers can even tolerate a cold month of May, because he never doubts that warm days are ahead. It is only the very young who are never quite sure, unless all the signs are right, that summer will come.

Icy rescue

It happened again. Night came. Supper was on the table. But the Rebels had not reported in. We went to the picture window that looks out on the stable through a clump of conifers and birch, but there was no light there. We went to the window that looks out on the kennels. No light there. We decided to put on coats and go look, but then we heard the basement door. So we went down, and there they stood, almost sheathed in ice, wet through, hair straggling, bodies steaming.

"What in the world! It's eight below out! What were you doing in the water?"

Embarrassed, yet a little proud. Still panting and shivering. Frightened at what we would say, but hoping we would approve instead of being angry. The story came out in short bursts of speech, a sentence at a time, about how they had rescued four ducks, which the creeping ice was trapping in an open hole beneath the Clear Pool spillway.

The ducks had been living at a widening of Watercress Creek, but the unrelenting cold had finally narrowed their world. Now the ice was about to get them. So the Rebels jumped into the water. After a wild chase that sent water, snow and ice flying, they finally caught the ducks and, in the dark, carried them all the way to the headwaters of the creek, because it does not freeze there and they would be safe.

"Are you mad?" they asked.

And all we could say, without actually condoning such foolhardy behavior, was, "Get those clothes off! Take a hot shower! Supper is waiting!"

But I think they knew I was secretly pleased, because I could see it on their faces at suppertime. I was pleased, because I thought that if they could be so concerned about four ducks, maybe someday they would be just as concerned about people who need help.

Solace in the stable

I like sometimes to go to the stable alone and sit on fragrant bales of hay to listen to the horses stomp and the mice scurry. I am not sure what it is, but just running oats between my fingers and then digging a hand down among the kernels of corn renews my faith in the earth, and I feel it cannot fail us. Even the smell of leather — saddles, bridles and halters, all soaped so they are supple — tells in some immutable way that all restraints are not lost, that rules are still made to be obeyed, that in the final reckoning man's impetuosity will be curbed.

But of course things change. There are no red-headed woodpeckers this winter because their favorite tree went down. We miss seeing them at the bird feeders. Even the kingfishers, who usually wait until there is not enough water to dive for fish in Watercress Creek, have gone. It is a strange beginning of winter. But, inevitably, the sun will again come high enough so day will outlast the night, and then winter will be but a memory. Where snow once suffocated the earth, all manner of flowers will present many rainbows of color. If you cannot wait, there is always a trip south, but do not expect to see all the colors Wisconsin has to offer. There will be brilliant reds and blues and variations of all the gaudy colors, but the pale, creeping blooms that carpet a richer Wisconsin will be missing.

So perhaps that is why I find solace in the stable, because here are the fruits of the earth, flowers of all kinds mixed with the alfalfa and timothy. There is the harvest of last year, and I know as a bright-eyed mouse looks out from a dusky corner that, when the stable is empty, there will be another harvest, the harvest of a new year now in the making.

So I sit awhile and chew on a stem of hay and give the horses each a handful of corn, even if they are fat from overeating, and then I go back into the house and listen to all the doomsday reports on television, or read more dire predictions in the newspaper, and I feel that maybe it is time for some reporters to go back to the stable and sit on the bales of hay and let oats run through their fingers and look into the wide-eyed innocence of a horse's eyes. Maybe they will get a new slant on the universe of events and know that in one kernel of oats there are as many miracles as anywhere else in the world.

Hawk in hand

I knew when I walked into the kitchen that either the Rebel Queen had had a spiritual experience or we had won a hundred thousand dollars in some sweepstakes. What really happened to her was more exciting. For more than half an hour she had held a wild red-shouldered hawk in her hands after it came to a cracking halt against the house because it failed to pull out of a dive through a flock of songbirds at the south side feeder.

She was alone in the house when the resounding thump brought her bouncing and dripping from her bath to look out the picture window. There, wings askew on a mound of snow, lay the hawk. Above, its mate soared and screamed, but the big bird on the ground neither opened its eyes nor lifted its head.

A granny nightgown was closest at hand, so, donning it, a jacket and floppy red boots, the Rebel Queen went out to see what succor she might offer. The hawk was inert, curved beak slightly parted, sharp talons balled and tense. Gingerly, she gathered the wings tight to the body, picked the hawk up and held it. The hawk's mate circled a few times, keening, then flew off. The Rebel Queen walked around the house through the deep snow with no plan, nor any idea how to proceed.

It was below zero, but Rebel No. 3 was due home from school in fifteen minutes. Perhaps, if she waited, between them they might confine the still-breathing bird so it could not injure itself on regaining consciousness. But Rebel No. 3 was late, and the granny nightgown, besides being conspicuous, was poor protection against the cold. So the Rebel Queen started toward the garage, thinking there might be enough room for the big bird to maneuver there without hurting itself.

Then, while she was walking, the magnificent hawk lifted its head, opened its yellow eyes, closed its beak and relaxed is talons. She held it for a while longer, and then gradually relaxed the tension of her hands. As she did, the hawk shuddered, shook its feathers into place and then, when she lifted it skyward, opened its wings and flew to perch in the nearest blue spruce. It was still perched there when Rebel No. 3 came home. Then it went back to its element, the air, and with steady wingbeats flew in the direction its mate had taken.

Shivering, the Rebel Queen went inside, but the thrill of having held such feathered power in her hands would not leave, and when I came home a few minutes later her eyes were still glowing.

Out of the shadows

In death, even of a tree, there is consolation, if you look for it. This is difficult to believe, especially as we look out the sunroom windows at the huge elm logs sprawled across the lawn like wooden carcasses. The most gigantic of all trees at Little Lakes, the elms succumbed to Dutch elm disease, a microscopic ailment borne by a tiny beetle. One by one, they died, until more than a hundred and fifty stood bone-bare against the sky, and then came crashing to earth as the snarling saw ripped through them. Last to perish, though still standing, is the giant alongside the walk that divides into a Y to service the front and back doors of our home.

But now that the elms are down and there are no high-flung branches, underneath there will be a quickening of growth. One special cluster of slow-growing blue spruce, previously smothered in shade, will put forth longer leaders, round out and flourish. Colonies of young oak, ash, maple and poplar, until now destined for minor roles, will spring more quickly to creditable size because the elms no longer shade them.

In the areas that are now open, wildflowers have sprung up in profusion. Mushrooms carpet the elms' burying grounds. We pick morels there to smother broiled steak.

The horses have more pasture. And while once the great umbrella-shaped trees shaded us from the hot summer sun, their wood now warms us in winter. We are accumulating enough wood to keep the fireplace bright for many years. Larger logs will become bridges and boat docks. Small, straight pole branches will become split-rail fences.

We all loved the elms because they were so stately and so reminiscent of days when only settlers and some Indians knew them. But few birds could use the tall trees. It seems only the orioles needed the dizzy heights of the monarch elms, the orioles and an occasional flicker hard-headed enough to hammer a home in the bone-hard boughs. Now, with the lifting of the undergrowth, there will be more nesting sites for robins, mourning doves and cardinals, and more berries, too, in their bush pantries.

Perhaps best of all, elm saplings are lifting where the old roots died. They have grown from seeds the last giants gave the wind to spend. And their growth rate in the old stump beds is phenomenal. It will be some generations before Little Lakes again has towering elms, but the time will come. Meanwhile, there is no dearth of shade. Hickories and maples, lindens and willows, spruce and pine and cedar, ironwood and black cherry and chokecherry, hawthorns and oaks, hundreds still stand.

And the youngsters, already forgetting how it was when every other tree was topped by tall elms, feel no sadness. Though they momentarily mourned the passing of each elm, they quickly gave their affection to those living, and now they climb other trees and nap in their shade.

Character builder

The recent week of zero weather certainly strengthened the core of character in the Rebels. Ten below or thirty above, the two youngest Rebels spend most of their waking hours outdoors. Like little animals, they have become so acclimated that when the thermometer gets above freezing, they start shedding. Let it get to fifty degrees and they are begging to go barefoot. Last spring, Rebel No. 2 was so insistent that we let her do so, even though there was snow on the ground. She ran until her feet were red. Being outdoors seems to make the Rebels healthier physically, and it certainly makes them tougher mentally.

Still, to take a collection of ducks from behind wire to Watercress Creek so that they may swim requires a special kind of mental fortitude when it is five below zero. And during the past week, each morning before dawn, the Rebels had to open the water hole where the horses drink from Fish Pond. They had to reopen it when day was graying. Sometimes the ax and shovel were so sheathed with ice that they had to be banged together before any work could be done.

Then there were the water containers for ducks, dogs and rabbits. Each night and morning, the Rebels brought sets of pans to the basement to thaw out while alternates with fresh water were already freezing again in the pens. There was manure to be moved and the bird feeders to fill and some live traps way down across the white bridge to be checked. And sometimes in the dark the snow squeaked so loudly underfoot, it was Rebel No. 2 who said, "I thought somebody was following me."

And when all the animals and birds had been cared for, there was drifting snow to be shoveled from the walks and plowed from Fish Pond to prevent freezeout. Often it was zero, sometimes below, and often the wind out of the northwest was so cutting even the cottontails made only exploratory trips before returning to shelter.

But the Rebels had to be out in it, so, at supper, I tried to placate them with somewhat exaggerated tales of how my family once crowded around a potbellied stove with isinglass windows before we raced upstairs to an icy room where irons, heated on the kitchen range and wrapped in flannel, had been put beneath the blankets. I told about chillblains, frozen fingers and monumental drifts we had to carve through to get from the house, and how, after awhile, we walked in the road because, at least, the bobsleds left a trail we could follow.

I talked of water pipes freezing, and how we brought snow in to melt so we might drink, and how school was never closed because, being a Spartan breed, we would not have dared use the weather as an excuse to stay away.

Then, it occurred to me that my generation was no more dauntless than any other, that the hard core of character might be as well fashioned in a house with automatic heat as one that burned wood chunks, and that a boy did not have to walk a mile over snowbanks to prove he was a man, because when he got to school there was a whole new concept of thinking to take the place of such primitive character builders as snow shovels and axes, picks and crowbars.

And if it was a most difficult thing to admit to myself, I knew it would be doubly hard to tear down my image in the eyes of the Rebels. So I came through the back door of their minds by suggesting that perhaps if some of the animals were eliminated, they would have less work; if we moved farther south, there would be fewer cold days to face up to.

Then I got my surprise because, even if the Rebels did not credit their chores as aids in character building, they were satisfied that life would be dull without a challenge. Because how could the fire ever feel so warm again if, first, they did not almost freeze their fingers? And how would supper ever taste so special if, first, they did not wrestle an ax and shovel over a frozen water hole? And how could the sun shine so brightly if they never came down the long path in darkness? And how would lying down on a bed and pulling soft, warm covers to their chins be such a delight if their muscles were not tired?

So I was vindicated, or at least some comforted, except that I resolved not to regale them further with tales of my youthful hardships. Well, not often, anyway.

Sabbatical

Days are getting longer. Soon the sun will invite us outside earlier and entice us to stay later. So, how the indoor days? Put to good advantage? Or squandered on complaining and wishing for warmer weather? Was your wintering a bore or a blessing? Time to turn the covers of a book and discover some other's world and how he lived in it? Or frittering away minutes that cannot be retrieved? Perhaps it is my age, but by the time summer has run its brazen race and the autumn parade of color has marched the route, I am ready and glad for the long nights. I can come to my typewriter, book or restful reflection, and outside there is little to tempt me.

When darkness comes long before dinner, I can come to the luxury of slippers and the easy chair with no qualms about the growing grass or any voices through the window. In winter, peace settles over the world. Then there is time and the inclination to look back on where we have been and forward to where we are going. In spring there is such a quickening of spirit that the mind becomes quite breathless. Summer relegates it to a minor role while the body swims, motors, gardens, barbecues, runs some mad race right down again to the freezing days. Winter. Sublime sabbatical.

But I do not spend all my time inside. On a sunny day, I like to go down to where Clear Pool is held in a cup of conifers and there be amazed how flies can hatch in freezing weather. And I like to go to the pasture to see the horses sleep in the bright reflection of the white stable, eyes dreamy, bodies too lazy to lift to a touch. Then, I spend a few minutes on the hill where the wind can cut me so I can come to the bright fire in the basement and stand rubbing my hands over the flames. It is a fine feeling to come from winter to the fire's warmth, back to peaceful pursuits.

Never ugly

Dead elms ugly? Not against a stormy sky with their bony fingers white in the lightning. Not when sunset warms the bare branches with a pink glow. Not when decorated with waxwings or doves and flickers or red-headed woodpeckers.

Dead elms ugly? Not when multicolored fungus builds exotic shelves on trunk and branch. Not when grape or nightshade or morning glory climb beyond the first fork and take blossoms into the sky.

Dead elms ugly? Perhaps sad to see. Perhaps lonely as only the dead can appear lonely among the living. Perhaps even grotesque. And always a reminder of the mortality of all things, even such giants as can spread shade over an entire house. But never ugly.

Fragile signs

Yesterday a cardinal's piercing whistle announced that already a peppery cloud of flies was probably lifting from among the rocks along Watercress Creek. I couldn't believe it was already that time, so I looked at a thermometer in the shade. The temperature had not risen above freezing, but I went to the creek anyway. Sure enough, in a windless, sun-warmed corner, insects were hatching.

I put my hand to the stones and they were warm. So I went to the dog kennel where there is an extra thermometer, took it back to the creek and, laying it among the stones, watched the red thread that measures life lift to forty, then forty-five, and finally stop at fifty-six degrees. Then I had to believe, and if there will be no sudden burgeoning of green softened by the pastels of spring for perhaps another two months, there will be signs on all sides. And I saw another on the way back to the house. Where a young maple stands in the shade of two tall basswoods, a squirrel was tonguing frantically for each tiny trickle of sweetness.

I have watched that maple for fifteen years, and I cannot remember a leaf unfurling earlier than the second week in May. So why is the tree sending up sap when tomorrow wood-cracking cold may freeze the very fiber in which its lifeblood is coursing? Perhaps it is because all life is so impatient that it takes only a hint of spring to produce a pulse strong enough to swell a chrysalis, bring a chipmunk up through a hole in a snowbank, send a skunk walking across frozen fields, tempt a spider from a crack in a board, force a piercing whistle from a red bird's throat.

Perhaps it also explains why my children forget their boots, scarves and hats. Why the Rebel Queen sweeps a sidewalk that minutes later may be covered with snow. Why I go to where the current is a black gash through the ice of Clear Pool and hopefully, with numb fingers, cast a fly when the fish know perfectly well the time has not arrived to expect insects on the menu.

Our ancestors once migrated, and I wonder if there is not in all of us such an intuitive urge to follow the sun that, trapped as most of us are, we all but go to pieces upon a hint of spring. Our ancestors measured their lives by the winters each managed to survive. So there is probably an inborn desire to have the dark, cold days behind so we can mark one more year on our own calendar of life. Why else, if we do not have an intuitive fear of winter, do we so welcome even the most fleeting and fragile sign of spring?

The great impatience

There will be considerable agony and ecstasy during the next six weeks. It will be the time between promise and fulfillment. It will be the misery of muck and the miracle of green. There will be dandelion gold next to the wall where the warm reflections raise ground temperatures. There will grow a fringe of pencil reeds, each thin as a match, where warm springs bubble from the earth. There will be gullies of gumbo where the horses go to water.

Already we have had a preview. The killdeers called and there were geese passing. There were ruts in the road and sticky mud on the white garage floor. I walked to see how it was. There was snow coming down thin as mist with no promise that it would come to anything more. Clear Pool was the color of a plum under the low sky. There were white-throated sparrow tracks in the mud. A fish rose and swirled. I peeled back the brown edges of a green spear of plant too quick to believe a promise. A cardinal whistled once and then thought better of it and was quiet.

Would that it stayed crisp until the time for creation, lest the unfolding tendrils be cut so sharply they will not come again when the sun is warm to stay. But it won't. And some crocuses or tulips or violets will lift to the false promise and be killed back to their roots for this season. Perhaps that is why the bulbs must be set so deep. If the ground softens, they cannot come all the way to sunlight before another freeze keeps them from breaking the crust. There have been years, and we remember them, when the trees were coming to full leaf, and the cold came quick, sharp and fast to turn the green to black, and it was a spring of thin foliage and a summer of less shade.

What is with this impatience? This need to flower? This urge to come from the dark places into the light? Why can't all things wait their time and just be careful and comfortable in the protecting earth? Why must they hurry to put forth a leaf and be nipped by a cold and little-caring world?

And what of the birds? Why can't they wait? What drives them? Geese by hundreds all over the sky, looking for open water where there is none. A flicker at the bird feeder when March is only one day old. Scores of grackles in the spruce. Robins on an icy lawn, shivering in a freezing rain. All up from more productive fields and forests and warm, blue bays.

It is not time yet, so why do they come? No need for nests now. No place to build them, because snow comes intermittently to bog and bough. But they come. Blackbird cocks in red epaulets are in the marsh, and there they cheer any sun, but mostly sit disconsolate among falling snowflakes. Is it a compulsion to come home? And is home the place where they were born and where they in turn will give birth? Is it because, of all things, the hatching of youngsters is the most important? Is that why they come here singing, but their southern sojourn is mostly a time of mute waiting to go back north again?

Something drives them inexorably, else why would they come when blizzards cast snow in drifts to the boughs they perch upon? They

Though the rabbit has never before seen a fox,
there is an instant warning.

come long before the buds and bugs that feed them. They die, sometimes in flocks, because they could not wait one week, two weeks
more.

I see them. Ducks circling and circling. I hear them. Killdeer's plaintive query. I touch them. Feathered body frozen in the snow. I feed
them. Whole colonies sometimes. What brought them here weeks, a
month ahead of schedule? Must they come, because it is here, and only
here, that there is some purpose, some reason for living? Is everything,
all of it, in the nest they build, the eggs they lay and the clutch they
feed to send south? Are they nothing if, in living, they do not guaran-
tee perpetuity to the robins, grackles and geese of tomorrow? I wonder.

Rebels leaving

Rebels are leaving, and their tracks remind me that some day soon the snow outside my window will record only the activities of squirrel and rabbit, cardinal and cat, because there will be no more children at Little Lakes. But to think of Little Lakes without children is to think of summertime trees without leaves. Every gate here was built so a child might reach and open it, every path fashioned for little feet.

Already I sometimes come after a fresh fall of snow and, sitting on a woodpile among the trees that encircle Clear Pool, listen to find if on the wind that sings through the spruce needles I can hear my children, all young again. And sometimes I can, and mostly there is laughter. But sometimes, likely on a wind change, I hear a sharp cry of pain, and then the soft sound of such sadness as almost brings tears to my eyes.

So I walk out of the spruce and stand by New Pool, thinking of other winters when the sled track was curved so the riders might end their descent on the slick pond ice. But even though this year there is no slide, I see flying scarves, though I am not practiced yet enough to hold the visions of rosy cheeks.

I walk the path beside the vines and, beneath the arching limbs where willows have wept their leaves, I am startled to hear the sharp ring of a skate blade, though no one is skating. I turn my head a little and look up toward the house, but there is no snowman standing there even if a moment ago I saw the quick black flash of its charcoal eyes.

So what is this? A child throwing snowballs that melt before they reach the ground. A heart traced in the snow. Face fingered on a frozen pane. Odor of wet wool. Quick, cold kiss. Lost red mitten. Icicle held between white teeth. Frost, like white lace, on a scarf. Feet flying. Arms swinging. Eyes bright. All brief. Flashing. Gone.

chapter two

SPRING

Just one spring day

How will Little Lakes look in a few days? Will the sun shine? Will the spruce still be wearing white mantles of wet snow? Will all the ponds except Clear Pool still be ice-covered? Will chipmunks still shiver on the sidewalk in front of the sunroom door before making tracks back to their warm, subterranean homes? Will there still be only one red-winged blackbird waiting in the marsh, or will the entire churning vanguard of males have arrived to await their women? Now, one warm day makes all the difference. The Rebels may go to bed one night along with the rest of the cold-weather residents and awaken to a dawn swarming with big and little birds back from the south.

More lovely

I think that I shall never see
A tree as lovely as a child.

Rebel No. 2: How'd you like to be a tree?
Rebel No. 3: Oh, I don't know. Why?
No. 2: Gee, just think how tall you'd be!
No. 3: Yeah, and all the things you'd get to see!
No. 2: Nighttime, too. You'd be out here all night when everyone else is sleeping, and maybe things like raccoons and possums would crawl up into your arms.
No. 3: I never thought of it that way.
No. 2: And maybe you could remember all the Indians who used to live here.
No. 3: Gee!
No. 2: Maybe they even used some of your branches for spear and arrow shafts.
No. 3: Maybe they even made handles for their fish spears from your limbs and then picked up your deadwood to smoke the fish.

No. 2: Man! You could look down on every living thing. There isn't anything bigger than a tree.

No. 3: I'd like it. But, how about winter? Wouldn't it get cold?

No. 2: Maybe. But look how warm that spruce looks with all its needles. But actually, trees don't get cold.

No. 3: What do you mean?

No. 2: They just pull in their blood, right down to their roots where it's warm.

No. 3: But a tree can't move.

No. 2: Who wants to move? Everything comes to a tree. The rabbits come and the ducks fly over and the birds build their nests right in your arms. And just imagine how many miles you could see, especially if you lived on a hill.

No. 3: I never thought about it, but you sure could see just about everything, probably to the end of the world!

No. 2: Not to the end of the world, you dope. But even if you walked all day you couldn't get to see all that a tree sees just standing still.

No. 3: But wouldn't you be scared in a storm?

No. 2: Heck, no. A tree can take a storm better than people. Trees bend. People get hurt because they won't bend with the wind. A tree wouldn't live long if it didn't bend.

No. 3: I'll bet the wind feels good blowing through your branches.

No. 2: Probably a hundred times better than when it blows through your hair when you're hot.

No. 3: Why do people cut trees?

No. 2: Some dumb people even go around picking flowers.

No. 3: But you pick flowers.

No. 2: Sure, dizzy. We plant some to pick. And then there are some that will grow better if you pick them. But you gotta know, and you don't go around cutting down trees.

No. 3: Maybe you don't. But a lot of people do.

No. 2: That just proves how dumb people are.

I know that I shall never see
A tree as lovely as a child.

Broken promises

Spring, more than any other, is the season of broken promises. Warm, soft and inviting one day, she has but to switch her skirts and the mourning dove eggs freeze, the Canada goose is without water, the rabbit litter dies. There is no doubt that the amount of light plays a more important part in creation than the temperature. So, before this month is out, the doves will already have laid eggs, and it is only by being prolific that the species avoids extinction. If they depended on one clutch a year for survival, they would have perished long ago.

But the promise of spring is so necessary in the lives of every winter-weary thing that no one ever lampoons her for her fickleness. We forgive her everything, because in her smiles are reflected all the bright days of summer and the warm nights when insect music keeps the universal beat. We shrug off her whims, her unpleasantness, her discomforts, her cruelties.

Some people are still victims of the seasons. Then, when the salmon run or the geese come back, they can fill shrunken bellies. Then, when the rice grows, they rejoice. Then, when the trees blossom, festivals are in order. It is spring again! There is green in the brown canopy of winter. There is glistening water cutting through the gray, rotting blanket of ice. Buds swell and show pink beneath thin, brown scales. Bloodroot is unblemished white. Crocuses open and close with each passing cloud. Daffodils put forth swords of green. Tulips spike the earth. Sap wets eager trees. There are songs in the air and in our hearts. So what if tomorrow is cold? Today it is spring again!

Our Pool

How much will one gallon of sweat produce? How long after the pain can a man remember? I think about it with a pillow bracing my back, and I know that after a few days I will not reckon on the sweat or the pain it took to produce still another baby.

Our baby — mine and the Rebel Queen's — is a lannon stone pool in the heart of a triangular tangle of day lilies, iris, elderberry, raspberry, gooseberry and canary grass. It is shaded by a spreading linden tree and edged by a stately row of spruce. It is a tiny thing, as pools go, and anyone not contributing to the work might lift an eyebrow when we estimate it took six tons of fieldstone, several tons of lannon stone, a half-ton of mortar and six (or was it sixty?) gallons of sweat. Complicating construction, we tapped a spring that would not be contained, and we often worked hip-deep in an icy gruel of mud and water. We had set aside two days to produce this baby. We were in labor ten days.

The tiny, new pool will be called Our Pool. That is because it was the first major endeavor of two families, which a little more than a year ago were joined as one. Compared to Fish Pond, Clear Pool, Blue Pool and New Pool, Our Pool is only a glint in the sun. Its inlet is banked high on each side with fieldstone. I had a visitor just after I treated one side of the wall with muriatic acid. Standing back, I watched as the acid did in minutes what erosion might require years to accomplish. Hidden colors surfaced. Deepening light and shadow sharpened the weathered carvings of centuries. As the streaks and strands of red, onyx and green began to show, I turned to the visitor intending to say: "Now, how about that?" One look, and I knew he saw nothing but a pile of dirty rocks. But I tried.

"You like it?"

"Yeah, it's fine. But what's it for?"

"Well, it is a sort of live box. A little fish pond. A kind of..." I stopped suddenly, realizing it was for nothing. That is, unless you believe there is a place in this savage world for such practically useless things as poems, paintings, flowers, fleecy clouds, and that contortion called a smile. Because that is all Our Pool really is: A small smile on the face of Little Lakes.

Constant struggle

Within a wildlife area as confined as Little Lakes, we must decide almost daily whether to permit nature to have her way or go ahead ourselves to shape the face of these acres according to our abilities. If we have put trout in a pond, we may permit the kingfishers and herons a reasonable share. But if they become greedy, the birds are routed. If we have planted spruce, but grackles annually retard their growth by perching on and breaking off tender new leaders, corrective procedures must be followed.

Last week, we ordered some white water lily tubers. Once before, we had planted them. We got a bountiful and beautiful crop, which muskrats promptly devoured. The same has happened with duck potato, water iris, spatterdock and wild rice. So, we had to weigh the thrill of seeing a swimming muskrat cut a rippling vee across the calm of the evening waters against the delight of an annual resurrection of water plants. There is no formula to follow. Mostly, it is deciding which plants or animals must receive preferential treatment.

Brush willow, spreading like excema, may prevent erosion, but in solid stands it suffocates everything else. Wild cucumbers may trail fragile white necklaces of flowers in summer and leave lacy seed cones for winter, but in climbing, they kill the conifers. Grapevines provide fruit for us, and for birds, but they strangle with boa constrictor tenacity anything they can get their tentacles around. The list is long, the struggle forever.

The curtain rises

Actors and actresses who annually cavort across the stage of the Little Lakes Summer Theater have mostly arrived and are now in rehearsal, so that by the time school lets out the curtain will go up on what should be one of the finest shows ever staged here.

Already the flickers are practicing on their bongo drums. Squirrels are rehearsing incredible aerial acts. Kingfishers are practicing their death-defying dives. Cottontail clowns expect they will have a dress rehearsal no later than Saturday. This year, the dragonflies are expected to spruce up their act with a little backward flying. Hummingbirds have not been heard from, but the jewelweed crop looks good, so it is likely they will renew. Options have been picked up by most of the robins, though there has been some infighting about the billing.

Orioles, who complained last year about the lack of high-rise staging since the tall elms went down, have sent word on ahead that at least two pairs will be on hand. In addition to the regular acts, there will be walk-on parts for the fox and raccoon, and the woodchuck promises to play most matinees. Water acts will be staged on all four ponds. Trout can be expected to exhibit their skills by arching out of the water to take insects in full flight. The water-walkers will go skating across the liquid surface as though it were solid concrete. Thousands of water-bugs will race their teams.

Evenings there will be the death dance of the mayflies. Mosquitoes will perform such magic as turns wrigglers into winged insects, and the butterflies, as usual, will try to upstage them by turning from caterpillars into winged creatures of indescribable beauty. There will be industrial exhibits as wasps build paper and adobe houses, ants throw up incredibly complex communities, and bees manufacture waxen combs and then fill them with honey made from nothing more than the juice of flowers.

Crayfish will exhibit their skills at castle building. Moles will show how to drive a tunnel without excavating. Spiders will parachute and free-fall, then save themselves with almost invisible strands of silk. Herons, cranes and bitterns have been invited to participate in a frog- and fish-spearing contest, and the terns have been asked to repeat their aerial ballet. Evenings will be given over to the symphony, and the frogs are already warming their throats in the sun so that they will be in voice to keep the beat while, overhead, nighthawks and bats sweep the skies in fantastic nighttime displays.

The crickets will add their excitement, and it is hoped a screech owl couple can be engaged to lend an eerie note. Efforts will be made to sign on a wood duck couple so there will be a tumbling act when the youngsters are ready to leave their tree house. Mallards are returning their contracts and will provide troupes of downy ducklings.

Already in rehearsal are gophers and warblers, chipmunks and song sparrows — altogether such myriad performers as should make this the extravaganza of the decade. What is more, the show promises to be well staged. A thousand, ten thousand flowers have been promised. Maybe a million or two million leaves will provide a green canopy and backdrop. Lilacs, cherries, apples, honeysuckles, roses and scores of trees and bushes will ornament the theater entrance and the stage.

There will be drama, the life and death struggle in the sometimes stark and tragic tradition. But there will be lighter moments of comedy, and of course there will be situation shows for those who disdain the more heady stuff. As usual it is a benefit performance for people caught up by the atomic excitement, a free show for humans to whom the concrete encroachment is becoming a terrifying reality. So plan on it. Besides the show at Little Lakes, there will be plays on tour all across the country.

Refuge in the hay

Weep not if you lived your youth before radio, television or the automobile habit. You had the haymow. Of all the passing institutions that mark a people's struggle toward the allegedly better life, none is so missed as the cavernous barn stuffed full of sweet-smelling hay. In the mow, we had hilarious times. The mounded hay provided soft landings for daring leaps, slick slides and acrobatics we would never have dared on less forgiving material.

But we remember, too, the days we climbed the ladder and crawled far back to hide a tear. Here was refuge and, aching inside, we lay consumed with some sorrow until the scratching of mice, the steady comforting sound below of cows and their cuds, soothed the real or imagined hurt. Slowly, the sorrow diffused and, lying back, we could see the dust dance on slender shafts where cracks in the barn let through blades of sun. Then a youngster was one with the world, cradled in its harvested bounty of timothy, clover and alfalfa, intertwined with wildflowers holding still their sweet perfume. Comforted, we climbed back down and came blinking out into the sun, where in minutes we forgot what it was we had crawled into the hay to cry about.

The Rebels have hay to play in, though it is in abrasive bales. But, never having jumped a daring twenty feet, they do not miss the thrill. Never having made a hiding place so cleverly the search might come within inches without discovery, they are content without it. Without knowing, they are just as happy to manipulate the bales into long tunnels, high skyscrapers, impressive forts, dark dungeons and many-roomed homes. And the jostled bales smell sweet, even though modern farming tolerates no wildflowers in the hay crop. Still, we who remember cannot help feeling just a little sad that this hay is not intertwined with faded though fragrant flowers.

Battle from above

One time, from a high place, beyond seeing range of the blood, I saw a battle unfold. At that altitude, it was fascinating and even beautiful as Mustangs swirled in graceful combat with Messerschmitts, as Thunderbolts charged at treetop level to strafe snaking lines of trucks. I saw Flying Fortresses lumbering along as Focke Wulfs pecked away at their formations. There were Liberators, looking like flying boats on cloud water. And the bombs grew great white smoke flowers on the earth. And I forgot they were dealing in death.

Today, many years since that unbelievable afternoon, I sit on a hill out here and my mind goes back, because a great battle is raging all around me. Blue jays and starlings dive to strafe the squirrels as they dare to try to cross the open lawn. Tree swallows competing for nest boxes swirl and dip and dive in aerial combat over Fish Pond. Red-winged blackbirds peck away at bomber formations of crows and herons. Martins swoop down on English sparrow squadrons and drive them to the ground. Robins attack robins in screaming dives. A svelte little hawk plummets through a grackle horde and scatters birds in all directions. A cardinal is swift on the tail of another cardinal.

But the bird battles rarely end tragically. Defeated tree swallows leave the Fish Pond area for less desirable homes on Blue Pool. A ruffled robin settles for a nesting site beyond the orchard. Sparrows leave the martin house to build beneath the eaves of the stable. Crows retire to the dense forest and herons to their rookeries. Then, except for occasional differences of opinion, usually settled with only threats, the birds live in comparative peace until the next great battle of spring.

Just another day

My day: Walk in the morning freshness while the grass is wet. Sit on the white bridge with the sun on my face, listening to the flickers keep the beat for a hundred more melodious birds. Breakfast. Post office. Session on the typewriter cut short when I remember that the lawn-sprinkling system must be connected. Wrench in hand and to the big green tank hidden among the spruce. Examine a woodchuck hole. Lean to look at a growing columbine. Check the dove nests in the spruce.

Lay the wrench next to the tank and down the trail to Fish Pond. Sit in the sun among the cedars, fragrant now. Watch bluegills rise. See bass swim by. Watch eleven turtles on a log crane their necks toward the sun. Dream. Lunch. Siesta. But no sleep. Outside a window, a robin goes to and from a nest in a blue spruce. Outside another window, a squirrel hangs by its toes to get maple buds.

Down to Clear Pool. Skunk cabbage in full furl and ferns showing. Trout holding in the current of Watercress Creek, shifting only to intercept hatching flies. Tree swallows iridescent. Green herons complaining. Back to Our Pool, where crocuses still bloom and day lilies are a foot high and water sparkles like a jeweler's showcase. To Blue Pool and into a lawn chair and drift to sleep. The bell on the hill sounds supper. The hum of traffic — workers returning from the city.

After supper, into a boat with the Rebel Queen, and we flick a fly to the bluegills. But then the fly rod lies idle over the stern and we watch the bird procession and the sinking sun and the night lifting from the valley to shroud our white house on the hill. To the kitchen. A look at the front page. There, people are busy. They will take care of the world. A late lunch. To bed and, warm in the darkness, I remember the wrench, still among the spruce where I went to connect the lawn-sprinkling system. Maybe it will rain.

No beauty in death

Death is the banquet table to which the living must come for sustenance. So the rabbit dies to feed the fox, and a tree goes down to form a seed bed for other trees, and the fish fertilizes the flowers, and in every living thing, including you and me, and all around the world and without exception, death is the necessity on which life thrives.

But, it is never beautiful. And whether death comes while behind the wheel of an auto, amidst the flames of an explosion, in the wreckage of a tornado, or while asleep on our own sheets, it is a devastation, a destruction. And when I see it so clearly, I have no stomach for telling the children about how their rabbit, dog or bird is fulfilling a destiny by bringing to the banquet table more food for new life. Because they are not concerned with some other life, but only this one, which has gone while they held it in their hands.

Dying may be a necessity, but it is never noble, except perhaps in purpose. So I will not go again with words of comfort to where the girl sits in the sunken garden with the dead rabbit in her arms, but let her shed the tears and hold the rabbit until she has wrung her heart dry and will part with it in her own good time and on her own terms.

It is necessary, I know, that the hawk must kill to eat to live, but it would be a deceit to say there is anything beautiful about it. In the hawk's swift sweep? Yes. In the piercing scream and the yellow glint of its eye? Yes. In the deft strike? Yes. But in the death there is only a beginning of corruption, and in this I must hold nature responsible, because surely her ingenuity is such that she might have found some better way.

So when the bird in my babe's hands opens its bill and gasps for life but blood comes to its throat to strangle it, I will not tell that child how wonderful death is because it guarantees life, lest that youngster know me for a liar, since this is not a wonderful but a terrible thing to have a warm creature grow still and cold and stiff while she is holding it.

Risky business

Yesterday it was wild asparagus and morels and bluebells and trilliums and white and yellow and purple violets, all manner of flowers and some plants that none of the several flower books identify. First we went to look at them in Salentine's woods, where there are rivulets of white above the dead brown leaves and purple patches along the edge of the maple wood lot. Then we went to the Erasmus woods, where the Rebel Queen filled a cardboard box with plants. Back home, she and the smallest Rebel put them carefully into the ground.

Transplanting wildflowers is risky business at best. To be uprooted from their native places and brought to alien soil is a shocking experience that requires considerable chemical adjustment. Take the shooting stars. They did not like nor could they tolerate the soil to which they were transplanted. But instead of giving up and withering, they moved to more kindly quarters. Now they are beginning to flourish in many places of their own choosing. Dutchman's breeches, though still showing and flowering, obviously are not going to make it. They only hang on. Each year, their foliage becomes more sparse and the blooms fewer.

The wake-robin seems to have found its niche beneath the towering willows and is spreading healthy plants in an ever-widening circle. The adder's-tongue hit it lucky, too, and now there are twenty or maybe fifty spotted leaves sprouting for every one planted. For the bloodroot, it is good and bad. The plant with the pure white flower has done well next to rotting logs where winter's accumulation of fodder has kept the grass down, but where grass competes, the bloodroot died.

Jack-in-the-pulpit still grows, but the plants are not high and hardy and will probably disappear. Trilliums will stay, but it is obvious they will not spread beyond specific wooded areas. White violets, apparently less hardy than their purple cousins, are having trouble extending their range beyond the branches of spreading spruce trees. In time, it seems, the growing spruce will shade them and they will die from lack of sunshine. So it goes. Each plant, to prosper, must have habitat it can at least tolerate. We see it every spring. It means looking for a habitat at Little Lakes that most resembles that from which the flowers came. But the Rebel Queen has a talent for rubbing the soil between her fingers and looking at the slant of the sun and ciphering the way the land will hold or lose its water.

In praise of dandelions

From the white house on the hill all the way to the ponds, the short-cropped green grass is golden with dandelions. I have seen few sights so beautiful, and I wonder again why people spend millions of dollars to destroy this flower. I suppose it is because the dandelion is as common as stones. If there were only a few and these in danger of extinction, the dandelion would be held in great esteem and every measure taken to preserve its golden sunburst.

It is a flower with all the attributes of greatness. Impervious to cold, it blooms while other flowers wilt, and if there is no place except a crack in a sidewalk, it will edge out and lay a coin of gold on the gray path. Its tender roots are a salad for a gourmet. Until you have eaten dandelion salad, you cannot know how crisp and flavorful a green can be.

Its hollow stem can be woven into necklaces or bracelets or made into curls for wearing. Laughing children put the flower close to a soft chin to gauge a friend's appetite for butter. Then, when the flowers' time of brightness has passed, the lawn becomes a giant, fluffy, white cloud. A child can spend an hour or a whole day to see if, in a single breath, she can blow all the seeds from a flower stem so they float like tiny parachutes on the breeze to sow themselves for another bright carpet of gold in another spring.

But as people today want the land poured to concrete so it will be uniform from horizon to horizon, so also they want their lawns to stretch in a monotony of green like a carpet laid outdoors. If there is one dandelion to interrupt the greenness, they crop its golden head and dig its roots and throw it on the trash pile. It is the measure of conformity at any price. Sometimes I think we would pluck the clouds from the sky if we could, so there would be nothing but solid blue, and all our horizons would be comfortably the same and safe.

Tough old hag

Indifference to suffering is an animal trait that startles some people so that they turn from the real world of nature to a Walt Disney concept of the wild society, because they simply cannot stomach reality. The sight of cock robin eating a worm alive and without killing it is acceptable because the victim, after all, was only a worm. But when a lion drags down a gazelle and starts chomping on its still-writhing innards while the little antelope looks back with pleading and helpless eyes, it is too much. But it happens every day. The owl, on catching the rabbit, does not bother to kill it, but only hangs on and proceeds to eat. Even the domestic cat is not always anxious to kill, but only to catch, and often it deliberately keeps its victims alive so they may provide diversion before dinner. It is rarely the predator's specific intention to kill, but only to immobilize, and where that is not possible the hyena, coyote, wolf or bobcat will try to get a mouthful from its still running victim.

Brutal? Gruesome? Yes, but it is nature's way, and only people with fuzzy ideas are likely to invest their bird and animal friends with good will toward all. But, why bring it up? Partly because the television shows are misleading youngsters into believing the animal world is one of loving tongues, wagging tails and cuddly fur.

I will go along with fairy tales for preschoolers. They serve a purpose. But it is almost insane to make youngsters believe that lions and tigers and chimpanzees are their friends if only they will be kind to them. Children should know that even their dogs and cats and horses are not far removed from the years of savagery, and that even their friends can be treacherous. And, all that aside, youngsters should know that nature is not a kindly old lady but a tough old hag with poison ivy in her hair.

To love a tree

To love a tree so much that you must cry when it splinters into a heap of kindling is to remember about all the chipmunks who lived among its roots, the orioles who yearly hung their high nests in its branches, and the squirrel who sunned each morning on a southern limb. To love a tree so much that you must cry when it falls is to remember how it was wrapped in snow each winter, how it put forth pale buds of promise each spring, and how it spread a leafy canopy against every hot sun of summer. To love a tree so much is to remember how you raced around and around it, and touched its rough bark to your soft lips as you tried to reach around.

To love a tree is to remember how it loomed black and familiar on dark nights to tell you the kitchen door and safety were only a few steps away. It was the big tree right by the sidewalk, the tree anyone doing dishes might look out upon to watch the cardinals fly from the bird feeder to its branches to perch and crack sunflower seeds. It was the enormous tree you braced your small back against a hundred times while eating a cookie and drinking a glass of milk. It was the tree that reached its branches out to the bedroom window. It was the tree that kept the sidewalk dry when it rained. It was the tree. The big tree. Well, it is down now and you must dry your tears and find another tree. Only when you are old will there be a time to cry again for the big tree you tried to reach your arms around.

Like the wild ones

Many of us have longed for what apparently is the carefree existence of one or another of our friends in the wild society. We may, perchance, wish to sun on a limb all day like a squirrel, take our living right off the front lawn like a rabbit, court and coo the hours away like a mourning dove, or bask in the warm shallows in the shade of a lily pad like a bass.

Surely, I relish the incredible journeys my mind can make into worlds of thought where no dog or cat, owl or hawk, or any other creature can venture. But still I am envious because my dog can smell out such fragrances as I will never know and, on a hot July night, can literally hear the corn grow. I am envious because the hawk on high can count the spots on a frog where I can see no frog at all, and the owl can sail through the forest at night without touching a branch while I bump into the trees. I envy the kingfisher's hovering flight and the hummingbird its feathery jewels, and wish there was some extension of myself I could turn to the sun as a tree does its leaves.

In thinking these thoughts, I neglect, on seeing the spider only waiting, to calculate how long it took to weave its web. On glimpsing a woodchuck in clover, I give no thought to the arduous hours it spent digging a den in some gravel hill.

Still, I would borrow the equanimity that permits the grasshopper to bask in the hot sun all day with never a thought of winter, or even tomorrow. And I would guard such contentment, if I had it, as comes when a full belly makes the lion lazy. But I am what I am, and if I pay too high a price to ponder on the imponderable, I would like, if only for a little while, to come like the cat and crouch unseen in the shrubbery, knowing about the nightcrawler that has just poked its head out of the ground, feeling the warmth of the bird above so I would know just where to pounce, and even hear, perhaps, the singing of the spheres.

Hot and rainy April

Hot for an April day. Sun glistening from every pond. Goldfish shining red and massed like a field of water flowers in the warmer shallows. Bass in schools. Big bass and little bass, patrolling the shores and coming cautiously to investigate a twig, a splashing pebble that sends up a bubble from the bottom. Bluegills darting. Nervous because the bass are near. Nervous because the kingfisher's shadow is on the water. Trout hunting. Silver fish with crimson stripes angling up for an insect. Bullhead backed into a crayfish hole, whiskers dangling. Thinks I can't see him. Thinks he is safe. Foolish bullhead. Sucker for a worm. Anxious birds trailing grass and string and paper and feathers of other birds into the trees, into nesting boxes. Quarreling, fighting, loving. Grackles, iridescent in the sun. Cardinal, a blowing, burning leaf. Flicker, raucous carpenter. Warbler, flick of an eye in a bush. Hot for a day in April.

Rainy April day. Iridescent green tree swallows flying low. Robin under bough shaking beaded rain from its feathers. Willow catkins from gray to silver. Ducks hilarious. Jewels on grass blades. Ponds speckled, like old, gray barn boards shot through with insect tunnels. Dogs sleep. Horses turn their broad behinds to the rain and stand with hanging heads. Pines washed green. Cedars shining. Nightcrawlers looking for love stranded on wet sidewalks. Buds sheathed in crystal. Cat stepping gingerly, shaking a wet leg. Frogs up on the lawn. Redwings sitting silent as black mourners. Crocus closed. Current quickens. Squirrels in their hollows. Stones washed. Reflections in a puddle. Smoke flattens and spreads. Sky close. Ground soft and a whole spring full of plants taking advantage. Rainy April day.

Age of discovery

Maybe ten is the age of awareness. At any rate, this is the year of great discoveries for Rebel No. 3. It has all been there every other year during all her life, but this is the year she is really seeing it and coming wide-eyed and so excited she must whisper because each discovery, bird's egg or flower, fish or cocoon, is so amazing it must be reported in awed, hushed tones.

Deposits and withdrawals

A welcome of warblers, a whitewash of anenomes, a crawl of gophers, ten skips of chipmunks, a shade of May apples, a burst of tulips, a purple rain of violets, a fragrance of lilacs, a flaking of Mayflowers, a sunburst of marigolds, a swoop of swallows, a flame of cardinals.

A vigor of young rabbits, a chatter of squirrels, a burst of buds, a lode of morels, a song of wrens, a glitter of dandelions, a ripple of waters, a silver of sunshine, a mane of clouds, a shelf of turtles, a fellowship of robins, a high swing of orioles, a hammer of flickers, a complaint of catbirds, a trill of song sparrows.

These were some of the entries in our passbook after a visit to the bank to weigh the costs of work against assets and to see if our investments have paid off. We go to the bank every spring because that is the time entries are made in the pages of our savings account. Sometimes winter has wiped out a portion of our investment, but usually there has been an increase, and that is the way it was this morning when the Rebel Queen and I walked together to inquire of the banker.

Of course, reports have been filtering in all along because the Rebels cannot wait for our day of accounting, but must run a daily reconnaissance to gauge the growth of all things newly arrived. So we started by counting new trillium plants and balancing the new total against the old. Then we measured the increase in wake-robins, but had to make estimates only on anemones and Mayflowers and every species of multicolored violets because there was such an abundance.

We counted bloodroot and jack-in-the-pulpit and discovered a contribution — both species in places where we had never planted and they had not grown before. Sweet charity. Then, though it was only early May, we found shooting stars already blooming. Usually we do not expect much from them before Memorial Day, at least not in any abundance. And we counted ten blooms in a single trillium clump, so there was an interest rate of fifty percent.

These days, every day is payday. Interest on our investments has made us wealthier than we had dared hope, and the work blisters, the pulled muscles, the aching backs, the cuts and scratches, the evenings of exhaustion, all are forgotten as, like misers, we count our riches. There were times we thought we would never make it. Mostly we faltered when days of disaster shook our resolve. Floods, drought, high winds, or devastating snows might wipe out the work of weeks. Then we would fall into bed convinced that it was all a mistake and that, come morning, we would sell out, take any quick profit that had accrued, and settle for a less arduous life on some easier street.

But sleep healed, and every dawn held forth new promise. Then, spirits further warmed by hot coffee, we would tackle tasks at hand to inch forward. It is not all over, of course. It never really is. There is always work, but who cares if at the end of the day there is time to add up the profits, count the gains and be amazed how twenty years of effort has made us as rich as, if not richer than, any man on earth?

So we did not get to Africa as we had promised ourselves. So we lost weekends and scuttled vacations. Now they would be but memories and, as wonderful as memories can be, how can they compare to such riches as we now can count every hour of every day, riches that continue to grow with the announcement of each new dividend?

Like last fall. First day to fill the bird feeders, and out of the forest of spruce we planted, watered, trimmed and cajoled into becoming giants, came payment in a swirl of pine and evening grosbeaks. Up from the cedars, rooted to cover a barren, rocky pond shore, came a dividend of nuthatches and chickadees, and off the hill of honeysuckle and junipers came cardinals, and from nobody knows where came a rufous-sided towhee, until the yard just beyond the kitchen window was a whirlwind of bright colors.

Like today. A payment of eight bluegills from a pond carved out of a marsh morass, fish to bend the tiny fly rod, fish to please the palate at suppertime. Like last spring. A dividend check of thirteen fluffy, bronze ducklings hatched in a grassy nest where once only white stones grew hot in the early summer sun.

Like the Fourth of July. A whopping dividend when three deer decided that we, in cooperation with the good earth, had finally created habitat worthy of living in. Like last Christmas. A present of eight goldeneyes, frozen out of who knows where, in the springhole to feast on freshwater shrimp, which had come to live among the lacy roots of the water plants we had rooted here. Like last Memorial Day. Another surprising payment when a gray fox took her kits out of the hillside hole to hunt mice along a meadow trail, which had once been a gravel road.

Like every day when the sun silvers the water, and every night when the little screech owls whimper, and like next fall and the fall after when the oaks, hickories and walnuts will pay such a dividend as can be shared with the squirrels. Such are the bonuses, the dividends for cooperating with the good earth. These are the interest payments, compounded almost daily. All this — flowers in spring, red leaves in fall, high hawk in summer, sparkling ice in winter — makes yesterday, tomorrow, every day a payday.

Withdrawals? Enough wild asparagus for one meal, and one dwarf iris bloom for a special bud vase.

Wind at the door

This day, the wind breaks trees it cannot bend. It churns to dust the new-plowed field and carries it to some other farm. It lifts a building, bangs a door, flirts a skirt, frolics with hats, catches my breath. This day, the tree swallow slides so far from the force of it that it cuts short its pond patrol. Insects are caught up and carried away before the swallow can catch them.

And, where yesterday there were half-a-hundred, today there are no grackles or robins on the lawn because the wind would blow them away. And if a flicker dares come out from his hollow tree, he hurries around to the lee side and hangs tight. Branches toss, and sometimes it is enough to lift a mourning dove off her fragile platform of sticks, and then her white eggs go rolling.

No sparrow tries, on this day, to carry string or feathers or any other thing to the purple martin apartment, lest the wind catch it in midair and, levering on the load, carry bird and nesting material away. Now, if a heron comes, it does not sit out along the marsh edge where the fishing is good, but dumps right in among the reeds and rushes, only too glad to be out of the sky.

Then, if a crow tries for a place on the other side of the woods, it must crab sideways across the sky, and in the end settle for any refuge, but preferably where the trees are thick enough to stay the thrust of the wind. Only ducks sometimes defy the wind and let it whisk their flocks at speeds of more than a hundred miles an hour. But then they stay for the night in some strange slough because to go back the way they came would be too much.

So no hawk sails. No oriole weaves. Nor does any bird sing about how it is the springtime for such celebration. And the squirrels do not try for the tender leaves, because it would be suicide to go out far on any branch, nor do the bees try the flowers, lest they be dashed to death, and the butterflies have crawled into crannies.

Nor does the woodchuck come out onto the lawn because, under cover of the wind's wild howling, any meat-eater might get within striking distance. And even the dogs and horses are upset, because once long ago they were wild and then the wind whipped away such scent lines as might have warned them of approaching danger. Even fish swim out from the shallows where restless waves churn up mud, and the frogs sink deeper into the marsh and pull down their blinkers so the tossing rushes cannot damage their eyes.

Then, where yesterday every stone and every log was wearing bright-colored turtles, today there is not a single one, and even crayfish stay buried in the mud.

It is the wind. Wearing away mountains. Leveling forests, sanding smooth the face of cliffs. Creating tides. But also, lest we forget, mating one tree to the other, and scattering seeds from pods even the frost could not crack. That is the wind. Invisible, yet leaving tracks where it touches. Voiceless, yet playing on every grass blade, tree, rock and house, a hundred tunes. Intangible, yet pressing, a force to scatter sand or cities. Odorless, yet scented with the sea, desert, forest and fields.

At my door, thrusting to come in.

Glimpses of spring

Quick glimpses around Little Lakes: goldfinches like a host of bright dandelions on the green lawn. Bright warbler jewels among the new leaves. Swales purple with wall-to-wall violet carpeting. Jack-in-the-pulpit preachers rigid on green and purple lecterns. White waves of anemones washing down a hillside. Spring beauties laid in fresh, pink sheets on an old brown leaf mattress. Green asparagus spear. Floating white mist of Canada lilies. Arching Solomon's-seal. Silent bells of yellow bellwort. May apples unfolding tents. Flick of adder's-tongue. Skunk cabbage spreading umbrellas. White carpet of strawberry flowers with ripe, red promise. Trillium chalice.

Of plants and children

As witness to the budding, growth and flowering of five girls, it occurs to me that the cultivation of spirits does indeed pay off, even though, unlike the asparagus, it does not happen after a single warm spring rain. Lest there be any doubts, my role in this gardening project has been minimal, and the weeding and watering have been left largely to two women — one wife who died and the one who now keeps the earth loose around their deepening roots. If I have had any part, it has been at best that of a catalyst, administering such occasional injections of inspiration as I felt might stir them out of the comforting shadows into having a go at it in the hot sunshine of reality.

Now this is an ordinary procedure, a common experience of all parents who plant kids. Still, even those who have faithfully adhered to the most rigid procedures become apprehensive on seeing, for the first time, sudden signs of uncontrolled, rampant growth at about the age of thirteen. It seems there comes a time, even in the life of a child, when, like the asparagus, it must go off in all directions, producing a branching wilderness of frightening possibilities. Then the soft spring shower may be almost too tender a compliment, and the growing plant-child goes far afield to be watered by more caustic, worldly rains. It is sometimes heartbreaking. Here the heart of my heart, the soul of my soul, loses patience with such slow, steady growth as characterizes the good healthy plant. Then, suddenly, bird songs and a field of flowers are not enough, the sky of wind-blown clouds worth never a second glance.

So, being a conscientious gardener, you backtrack to see where, during the growing and formative years, you went wrong. Then you ask yourself over and over, "Did I inhibit by pruning too much? Did I over-fertilize, and is that why my child-plant now puts out such tendrils as become entangled, like an uncontrollable vine, with all manner of alien growths?"

We planters all go through it. Our gardens grow all manner of child-plants, no two the same, except in this sudden impulse to sprout in all directions even beyond such confines as we have so carefully fenced. I have agonized, like all the rest, when turtles and mice, horses and dandelions, smooth stones and pretty butterflies, are put away for the bright lights, the motor's roar, the tires' squeal, the rock band's blare. Four times now I have asked myself, "Why?" And right now, with the last plant in my garden of kids getting ready to go off on her own tangent, I am once again fearful she may not find her way back.

Of course, by now I should know better. I should know, having watched first one and then another go moodily up the stairs to spend endless hours alone with what thoughts I can only guess, that someday she will come down those stairs. If you are a planter of kids, you will know. And if it is no easier the second, third, fourth or even the fifth time, at least you will be able to chart the progress of such junglelike growth as takes the child-plant through the new and strange places.

But then, happily, one day you may come of an evening and your child may be with you. Then perhaps you will hear her say, "Lord! Look at that!"

And you ask, "What?"

Then, if she says, "Why the sunset, of course!" you will know that she has come back, returned to the garden you worked so hard to make a fit place in which to grow.

Down now, winter

Spring. Late, wet and cold.

Swallows, no insects to eat, down to the ground. Luminescent blue-green wings fashioned for flashing low on arching flight spread in helpless, hopeless gesture. Starving.

Winter will not go, though millions pray for his demise. Torpid fly. Buds waiting to burst. Bloodroot waiting to open its white star. Bass needing to bed. Morel puckered by frost, inert. Cold turtle up from the mud, craning its neck from floating shell, and still no sun.

Down now, winter, down into the grave of winters past. Bury your old, arthritic bones. You have had your fling of snows and biting winds. Away with your rain and mist and fog. Do you want the young and naked doves to die? Is death all that you are really good at? All things suffered you in silence. They paid their dues. So take your victims. There are so many. Be satisfied with the carcass of the fox and the trillium root from which you froze the juice of life. The still living now must lift.

Your time will come again, and all too soon. So take your cold hands off the shivering grass. If you delight in white, save some of your frost for next November. Your months are gone. What kind of season are you to stay for April and squeeze even through the door of May?

Treacherous to withdraw, tempt millions north, and then sneak back again. No friend of mine when you wear out your welcome. Did I turn your head with sharp, crisp praise about the shadow and shine of your sculptured drifts? Is that the reason? You want more brisk words about your brittle ways? Your glance of white? But maybe this time I will say how you deceived the trusting moth out of the cocoon so that it fell back from the bright window, wings frozen. This time I will tell about eager earthworms caught and killed crossing the cold sidewalk. You will get no praise for sending the woodchuck chattering back below. Nor will I reach for praise appropriate to tenacity, because there is no virtue in such stubborn pride as strikes the glint from dragonfly wings before they have their chance to dry.

You are a reprobate, sullen as your gray skies. An old man moaning a northwind dirge. A sick season waiting to pervert the Lady Spring. Better you had died on the robust gust of a blizzard. Then no man might know you as less than roaringly heroic. But to keep creeping back to thump the things already dead makes a ghoulish specter of your vigorous reign. So you bow my head and I walk with dispirited stride through your icy rain. How can you count that as a victory when, in your time, you might have caught my breath and crowded me back through the door?

Or don't you care? And is it that you are reluctant to give the stage to a lady because, even when you were at your biting best, you knew someday she would surely upstage you? Is that what it is? Jealousy? For that the bluster? Because even you must thaw and disappear down rivers of sunshine? Because, tough as you are, there is none so tough as can resist the gentle ways of spring?

Still a hunter

Once a hunter, always a hunter, and if I now come unarmed down fence lines, through meadows, or up and across hills that take my breath away, I still move with a careful, quiet stride and with eyes alert to all such surrounding signs as might indicate that in the grass, among the thickets, back of the trees, my quarry lurks. Having walked so many thousands of miles to creep within gunshot range of a graceful deer, lumbering moose, slinking puma, I still employ the careful stalk, even though now my quarry has no legs to flee, nor any wings to fly. It may be I am a throwback, one of those genetic freaks of nature with the instincts of a Stone Age ancestor surfacing here and now in an age that has no need for such talents as caution me to walk softly in the shadowy places.

Whatever! Once away from the house, instinctively I shorten my stride and, walking toe down first so as not to announce with a heel thud or the breaking of any branch that I have come, I sometimes get to see a mink at play, a fox dozing, a cottontail nursing, though that is not why I am abroad. My quarry these springtimes, though no less adept at blending into its surroundings than a squirrel who has decided to become a lump on a limb, will not be alarmed so that I must take up the chase, but only wait, once I have found it, to be snapped up and popped into the gamebag I carry across a shoulder.

Then, even as I once did, while watching geese work a decoy spread I have arranged, I stand immobile, though my eyes, instead of searching the skies, roam over the ground prying all such hiding places as new green grass, unfurling skunk cabbages, leafing wood lilies, spreading May apple umbrellas, all the sudden junglelike lift of spring.

But my hunt is no haphazard thing. I have come in many other springtimes. I know about such places as my quarry is likely to lurk. So, just as I would not expect to find a mallard flock in any forest, nor a coyote among the trees of some southern wood lot, I know what acres to avoid and on which to concentrate. Also, just as I would never take the last quail from a covey during any autumn because it is in my best interests to leave progenitors, so too, during other springs I have not cropped too closely, so there remains seed stock for what other April and May days may still be on my calendar. What is more, even when I am no longer able to pull on bird shooters for these spring hunts, I will have some satisfaction in knowing I have left enough for my children and theirs.

So tomorrow, with dew diamonds yet glistening, I will come down the steps and stand for a moment to relish the fresh morning air, feel the first warming rays of the sun, hear the orchestration of the great bird choir, and then be off to where the wild asparagus waits, off to where the wary morel lurks camouflaged in the litter of brown bark from some dying trees. Then, when I find first one and then the other, I will kneel to deliver the coup de grace with as much reverence as I once felt while putting my sharp hunting knife to the jugular of a downed deer.

Then, in cream or butter, garnishing steak or toast, zestful with perhaps vinegar or onion, pungent in gravy or fragile in soup, touching and running fragrance through many a mundane dish, my wild asparagus, my wary morels, will match the succulence of any venison steak or browned goose breast.

To children leaving

Know these things, dear departing Rebels. You cannot stay, not forever. It is the way of the world, so you must go. But before you go, know these things well, as in your pigtail days. Know that come deserts or mountains, far lands or near, whether one flower box or wide-flung fields and forests, know that you, too, are of the earth. It will comfort you, tree in Brooklyn, geranium on sooty window ledge, lichen on mountaintop, for unless you deny it, using whatever guise — fame or fortune, tragedy or triumph — you will find some solace.

But, should you deny it, think to come back. Know that whether you wear sackcloth or satin, your humble origin is one with the solitary blade that struggles from a crack to spread grass on concrete. Know that in these there is healing. Wrap your hearts tenderly in the dewy, green leaves of home so they will stay fresh for planting. Then, when the season is right, root yourselves and the years will grow strong dreams.

But if first you come upon barren soil and must cross arid deserts, know there are lush valleys. Then, draw the memories of what you have learned close around so this heart you hold may not shrivel with despair. Some day, then, you will come to a place and you will know it is home. And do not grieve. Rather rejoice that you go, because out

Gwen has a talent for rubbing the soil between her fingers and looking at the slant of the sun and ciphering the way the land will hold or lose its water.

there are mountain peaks of such grandeur as you have never yet imagined. And be not afraid. The sun is everywhere.

For you still at home, still sprouting: Pause, but not often, in your fish and turtle catching, to listen when the wind whispers. Watch it twirl a leaf, bend a grass blade. See it ripple water and cast down cotton from the cottonwoods. Then think on how there are more things than meet the eye. Think how, though it can sail your kite and push a cloud, you have never really seen the wind.

Doubt not other unseen forces, such power as makes grass grow, flowers bloom, tadpoles hatch, your horses run and the dog wag tail. Think on it, this power, far as stars no man has seen. But never fear it. Be no more disturbed than by the unseen wind. Just be glad and thankful in your hearts, if only for short seconds. Then hurry. Run fast from a fern to where a muskrat feeds. Sit on the hill to watch a hawk and race to the pond to see a dragonfly. Drink it all in. With eyes, ears, fingers, tongue and nose, smell it, taste it, hear it, feel it, see it.

Now you have the time. Then, in a few short years, your wedding June will come and, as with your sisters, such affairs of living as crowd the days will take you who knows where. Then, in your hearts, perhaps the lupine and columbine will bloom even if your house is on the barren moon. Then if you must go down a despairing road, perhaps there will be enough strength in your love of the land to turn you, bring you back.

chapter three

SUMMER

Perfumes of Little Lakes

This day the south wind kept all those promises. As I come down the drive, the air is heavy with the fragrance of lilacs — whites, lavenders and deep, dark, royal purples. As I cross the green lawn, the odor of freshly mowed grass ascends like the freshening smell of perfumed rain.

Sitting where apple blossoms sift down like pink snow is to anticipate bruised fruit warming on the ground where bees swarm to such sweetness. As I go for a drink at the outside faucet, a long, wide blanket of lilies-of-the-valley is such a heady sweetness the taste stays on the tongue, and even the icy water cannot wash it away.

Coming to the creek where there are emerald isles of watercress, I snip enough for salad for five and get the tangy sharpness of the crushed cress in my nostrils. Then, for a special treat, I crush some of the mint that grows wild on the bank. At once the bright, sharp, refreshing smell is stronger than even the taste of spearmint gum on the tongue. I put the sprig in a shirt pocket for carrying around the rest of the day.

Moving out from beneath the weeping willows, I sit on the bank of the creek where a hot sun is bubbling all kinds of odors out of a marsh so fertile the very air seems rich enough to ripen into multicolored layers of algae. Then there is cedar, elusive until I crush a frond, and then the odor is aromatically pungent. Following the path, I go to the pasture where horses have clipped the grass so short there is the smell of dust. But beneath the fence, already there is the first fragrance of clover, threatening to blossom before I have come down into the pungent wood lot of spruce.

Walk anywhere at Little Lakes today and there are wild smells, some rank as skunk cabbage, some indefinable and delicate as violets. Try the hillside where junipers thrive and the understory billows with pink and white honeysuckle, and sometimes the sweetness is so overwhelming I am almost glad to come down where the sun has softened the amber and get a cathartic whiff of resin where a pine lost a bough.

Then, I have only to close my eyes to imagine I am beneath the spreading boughs of a northern woods.

Then lie where the vegetation is eye-high to a duck and roll luxuriously, inhaling fragrances of grasses and flowers you cannot name. Getting up, try a sprig of wild onion, first crushed between fingers and held to the nostrils, then popped into the mouth. After the onion there is no room for other tastes and odors, unless you pull a piece of canary grass to get the pale, tender root to chew.

Make the asparagus run, along the fence, across a little meadow, among the trees, down to a pond shore, along a stone wall, into a grassy ditch, alongside the stable, through the prickly ash, and besides the multitude of odors and the pale panorama of spring colors, there is a tender asparagus bundle for supper.

Many of the fragrances are so subtle and elusive they cannot be sorted. I think the wild, white strawberry blossom really has no odor at all, and I am only dreaming about the little rubies of sweetness that will soon be ripening. The same goes for the wild cherry blossoms, but I would have to go back out to check. Except I think, when I smell the flower, it is really only the promise of the fruit after it has been mashed, sugared and drowned with milk for drinking.

Yet, perhaps I can smell the fragrance of even the dandelion, though maybe I only remember my father's wine — pungent, golden sunshine trapped in a crystal-clear bottle. I think likely it is the same with the grapes, and so as I sit beneath an arbor there is really no odor, yet I am sure I can smell and taste the sweetness of grape jelly.

It is impolite, I suppose, to go around sniffing so as to appreciate all the perfumes of Little Lakes. Except I think we are missing something when we do not. Why, I wonder, is it proper to inhale the fragrance of brandy from a snifter, or to enjoy the bouquet of wine by passing the goblet beneath one's nostrils, and then not polite to hold the salad bowl to one's nose and smell the crisp greens before eating them?

Still this is no day for considering manners or mores, because the south wind has kept those promises, and soon I am going to crush a whole handful of lilac blooms for my pocket, and then sit in the warm sun and watch the birds work.

Eternal reward

Pink and purple lupines, nodding columbines, tiny star lilies, golden rockets. Rainbows of flowers arching color through the rising greenery of next fall's asters and daisies. Universes of wild blooms chipping away from their orbits to flash on mown grass. Galaxies of soft spring shades fading under the quick brilliance of summer's brazen blooms.

Clouds of black bass fry hardly bigger than the moving mists of the yellow daphnia that feed them. Crayfish with babies crusted under curling tails. Young rabbits scooting. Ducklings skittering for flies. Hundreds upon hundreds of hopping, flopping, fledgling birds under hovering cover of colonies of anxious parents.

Child Rebels running from dawn until dusk to see, but never fast enough. For some, life lifts and hovers hardly minutes. Mayfly, miller, for an hour or a day do their dance of death. Then, eggs on the water, they fold their fragile wings. Death, death, death under every stone, always and everywhere so life can come again. Earth's eternal reward.

Prayer of the robin

Prayer has been a consideration of all peoples of all times. Generations of all faiths have tried in many ways to formulate and then define supplication and thanks. I have no qualifications on the subject, but I believe that of all the prayers I have ever heard, the most direct, simple and sincere is that of the robin. I call it the rain song. As clouds of promise come up the sky, and the first drop of rain wets the earth, the robin exults. It requests, praises and gives thanks in one breath for the earth's offering of worms. Listen. Hear it sometime.

Gwen's Corner

Ever feel a season, song, sound or place was especially yours? Ever come to a valley, hill, street or room and know you would be back? There is a special magic for all in sudden things that are instantly familiar. Maybe that is how it is with Gwen and her corner. When she came to take over as the Rebel Queen, she stood on the west dike of New Pool and, looking across into a triangular glen hemmed by Norway pine and spruce, said:

"This is the place. The most beautiful. It is special."

I was surprised, because the earth had black scars where trees had been uprooted for transplanting. All spring, if I would find her, I had only to go to this place. There she would be, salving the earth's wounds with multicolored bandages of tame and wild flowers. So, rightly now, it is Gwen's Corner.

Farewell to Bucko

Bucko died during a starry, silent night. He was the last of all the old gang, a native of Little Lakes. Now there are none who remember how it was when Clear Pool was a marshy mosquito hole, New Pool a tangle of thistle and sticktights and the reaching cedars not even planted. His grave, marked by three bouquets from the three Rebels, is alongside those of his colleagues, Rainey and Ace. His shroud is an afghan, thick and soft, knitted by Rebel Queen 1. She worked on it during our travels when the Rebel children slept and only outside night noises broke the silence.

The big Labrador retriever weakened just at dusk, so we sat with him. He could lift his head, but it was obvious that the feeble thumps of his once wildly excited tail were tolling the final seconds. Even then he was as golden and shiny as the morning he came wriggling into our lives. There was no outward evidence that the old heart had finally worn out. He was sleeping when we went to the house. He was sleeping when the Rebel children checked later. He was sleeping in the morning, but from this sleep there was no awakening.

Bucko, until a few years ago, was always third dog, the pinch hitter of the kennels. When Rainey knocked himself out, Bucko came off the bench to work grouse, woodcock, pheasant and even quail. When Ace was having an off day, Bucko hauled ducks from the icy marshes of Manitoba and the tepid waters of the Louisiana bayous. He was an all-around talented dog, capable of coping with mink or muskrat, raccoon or cottontail, but he was most loved for his gracious acceptance of each child's adulation.

Like a splash of golden sunshine, he followed the Rebels from pond to pond. He ate raw fish they caught and, if they forgot, he dunked his head into their pail and helped himself. When they ate grapes, he ate grapes. Lips curled carefully back from strong, white teeth, he nipped raspberries from the bush. He accepted strawberries, mulberries and cherries, and when the apples were ripe he leaped high to get his share.

But with me he was a no-nonsense dog, a worker. He did not like or readily accept his role as pinch hitter. There were some no-quarter battles and, before Rainey and Ace died, Bucko had established his right to the kennel king's throne. It was not easy. He left one tooth in Rainey's skull and gave Ace a permanent limp. But this is the way of dogs. Never, though, did he show a tooth to me or mine. For his humans, he always carried his heart on his hide. We buried him this morning, and the Rebels have not talked about it yet.

No more pets?

A wash of tears may salve youths' sorrows, but only a quickening of love can heal the mental hurt. Twice now, in three weeks, we have seen

Rebel No. 1 grieve at the passing of a pet. First Scoober, her gluttonous gull, gorged its life away, and now a pink poppy marks its grave in the sunken garden. Rebel No. 2, sensitive to her sister's loss, took seventy-five cents of her allowance and put a white rabbit with pink eyes into her sister's arms. It is ironic that Brig, the dog Rebel No. 2 is charged with disciplining, should kill this gift and again leave a sister, white rabbit wrapped in red scarf, awash with tears.

Every time it happens I am tempted to say: "No more pets!" But, when I analyze that edict, it plainly means: "No more life!" Because as soon as there is life and living, there is sorrow and death. It is all a part of yesterday, today and tomorrow and, if a Rebel will grow, she must grieve. So already there is another gull. Suspicious now, it takes food reluctantly and with an unappreciative snap. It is no cuddly pet, and it may never be. There is the proud look of the hawk in its eye. But perhaps Rebel No. 1 will win its affection. If she does, she is certain to lose it, if not to death, then to a westerly wind that will carry it to its kind.

Thirsty June

Pour one week of rain into the mouth of June, then stand back and watch such an orgy of leaf lifting as can turn the sparse landscape of springtime into a jungle of greenery where every growing thing is fighting for its place in the sun. I was gone two weeks, but when I came back the ferns had grown thirty inches, vines had crawled five feet, spruce had new ten-inch spires, grasses were hip-high and headed out, burdock spread wide tents, and the profusion of flowers, from the cultivated varieties on the hill to the scattered wild ones around the ponds, were all one wild gallop of color.

Not having watched the day-to-day changes, I was overwhelmed. This wanton who was summer embarrassed me. I can get comfortable with the shy maiden, spring, who shows only an ankle-high of white Mayflowers, or perhaps a little greenery in her hair. I can withstand the onslaught of autumn colors because I know they are only red flags of those about to die. And I can even be philosophical about winter.

But flamboyant summer, when stimulated by a week-long drink of rain, is like a whirling gypsy with red lips and flashing skirts, and you cannot look her in the eye or you are a goner. Later along, it will be better. Then the first earthy flush of excitement will have subsided and crickets will stabilize the pulse beat, but now, wow! And to come unsuspecting into such a summertime of lush abandon is like being a boy suddenly and almost sickeningly in love with a woman of experience. So I sat by the window to watch the leaves through the white lace curtains. Then later, toward evening, I sat in a lawn chair close to the house, getting accustomed to the new growth nearby.

Next morning, I made a foray to the nearest pond. In the afternoon, I walked a fence line and a dike. And so, gradually, I became attuned. It will not be many days and summer can flaunt her wiles and I will not weaken, but dance with her instead.

Pomp and remembrance

Tonight, Dear Girl, you smell of perfumed soap and some bottled scent dabbed discreetly behind your ears, but I remember this morning when you brought into the kitchen the odor of well-oiled leather and the good, strong smell of a hard-ridden horse.

Tonight, Dear Girl, in your cap and gown coming down the long aisle that exits on life, you are a picture of sophistication. But I know about your self-doubts, and what is more, I know about the leathery soles of your feet, toughened on the thousand trails you have raced along, barefoot.

Tonight, Dear Girl, I see the silver polish where your toes peek through the lattice of your sandals, but I also know about the sliver beneath your big toenail.

Tonight, Dear Girl, in your cap and gown, you are a grown lady, and soon now we will have to let you go, and then if someday you come back we will not notice the kind of car you drive, because we will be seeing you on your bicycle making the gravel fly and the dust swirl on a fast turn at the top of the drive. And then, no matter to what heights you may rise, and no matter beneath what veneers of sophistication you ultimately hide your sadness and your gladness, we will know about the true heart of you, because we saw it in the helpless bird washed by your tears the day it died in your cupped hands.

So, if tonight, Dear Girl, there is a look of faraway sadness in our eyes, in eyes that should be happy for you, know that it is because not likely, or often again, can we kiss away your pain. So forgive us any gruffness, because we are hiding our feelings. Forgive us, too, if we cannot rise to such an event as your graduation, because as you step from behind the stage curtain to accept your diploma, we are remembering the way you came with a bee sting on your berry-stained face. We are remembering the Christmas you spent in bed because your horse threw you. We are remembering all the many times of crisis because it was when we healed your heart and your little girl hide that we functioned best.

So, if the boy in the front row, looking up, sees a gorgeous girl, it is because he never saw you shoulder a hundred-pound sack of oats and walk away with it, because he never saw you scrub down a dog, never watched you shovel manure, does not know about the scars you have accumulated during eighteen years of a life so full it spilled over into night dreams, which sometimes brought you crying to our bedroom.

Not that you aren't a gorgeous girl, because we know you are. All our girls were gorgeous, especially as each in turn donned the mortarboard and came like a queen down the aisle to the strains of "Pomp and Circumstance."

But, Dear Girl, we know you would rather have run down that aisle, grabbed up your diploma and then whisked on out of the gymnasium to hurl yourself into the arms of the next adventure. We hope you will always have that enthusiasm for life. And then, if your zest leads you, as it surely must, into moments of sadness even your newfound sophistication cannot cope with, then come home, if only for an hour. Then, even if you never mention about how a dream has been shattered, how a hope has guttered, we will know. And, being selfish, and needing to be needed always, you may find, perhaps, some solace because it was here, in the first place, that you learned how love can dry a Dear Girl's tears.

More pitcher plants

Ankle-deep in water, the Rebel Queen and I stood looking at a single flower. It was the deep maroon of the waxy pitcher plant, last bloom of a once-sizable colony.

"I wonder what killed them," the Rebel Queen said. "A few years back, there were scores of plants right here, and the bogs were black-red with their flowers."

We turned away, a little sad that another wild thing was passing from the local scene. Then, something caught my eye, and I called to the Rebel Queen to come. We walked several rods and there, along the water's edge, back of a bank of brush willows, were hundreds of the pitcher plants, more than I had ever seen at one time. So now we come often to the garden of wax flowers that live in a bog where nothing else will grow. And they stand healthy and beautiful, nourished by the insects trapped in the green watery pitchers that surround their blooms.

Lords of Little Lakes

MAY 22

Where a white wood lily flowers at the base of an elm stump, sacrifices are now offered daily to the new rulers of Little Lakes. Offerings placed on the stump include tree swallows killed by the cold, infant grackles caught up in the population war, squirrels and rabbits crushed by traffic and gathered up by the Rebel Queen on shopping trips, still-born ducklings, even porkchops.

Despite this effort to keep the new rulers fully fed, the songbirds of Little Lakes have never been so upset, because a pair of hawks has never nested here before. The red-shouldered hawks, fiercely wild birds, have commandeered a dead tree above the front sweep of lawn. From this high place, they are lords over all they survey, and there is no creature except man to challenge their right to rule.

The hawks came in low on a south wind, planed upward and alighted with a piercing scream in the highest place in the dead elm to survey their domain. Mice scurried deeper into last year's fodder. Cardinals at the bird feeders darted deep into the blue spruce. Cottontails froze. Sparrow flocks blew apart like seeds from a pod.

The hawks sat a while, turning their heads from side to side. Then they flew to the spruce grove above the sunken garden for a meal of grackle eggs. From our vantage point on the sun porch, we could see the yolk running in yellow streaks on their neck feathers. Songbirds set up an indignant din, and now the hawks can never leave the nest tree without being attacked by screaming squads. They shrug off the smaller birds and go about their business, which is mainly nest building and egg laying. The nest building has been a revelation. We had always supposed that hawks merely laid a platform of sticks. This pair used the rawhide-tough wands of weeping willow to weave through and around boughs of spruce.

Some of the willow branches, little leaves bright in the sun, were as long as eight feet and trailed far behind the birds in flight. Some of the spruce boughs, torn from the tree with considerable difficulty, were so large the hawks had trouble gaining enough altitude to reach the nesting limb. Once the nest of willow and spruce was woven, the hawks lined it with dead canary grass from the shores of Fish Pond.

A typical day in the lives of the hawks is an hour of nest building and then time out for courting; another hour of nest building and more time out for courting; another hour of nest building and time out to dive on the gophers or whatever dares cross the clearing below; then more nest building and time to sail to the stump for lunch. When the hawks arrived, a pair of squirrels had been using the tree to raise youngsters. The big birds chased the squirrels around and around the huge limbs. So far, the squirrels are still in residence.

We cannot believe the hawks will bring off a hatch. There is too much traffic in the area. The tree is only a stone's throw from the house. It is on the edge of the bush pantry where the Rebels are wont to roam. But now all traffic is being rerouted. The big birds will be given their chance.

MAY 29

The hawks, Taalon and Teelon, have adjusted to humans, and Teelon, the female, is incubating a clutch of eggs. To keep the pair contented, we have brought fish heads and entrails to their feeding stump to supplement their diet of road-killed squirrels, rabbits and birds. It was not difficult to gain the hawks' confidence. It took less than a week.

In the beginning, we told the Rebels to stay their distance. We put out food at night so the birds would not become frightened. Each day then, we moved closer and closer until they would tolerate us under the elm tree. Then we cranked the lawn mower and gradually drove it closer and closer to the tree. Now, the roaring engine does not frighten the birds.

The only complaint thus far must come from a pair of tree swallows. Though there are plenty of pole-type perches available, Taalon insists on sitting on the swallows' house with his tail fanned out, covering the entrance. Perhaps the female swallow incubating a clutch of eggs inside the house is not afraid. The doorway is too small for the hawk to reach in. Nevertheless, the Rebels have instructions to rout Taalon each time he trespasses on the swallows' property.

JUNE 12

Many birds bathe in Blue Pool, but never until now have we seen hawks take their baths there. In fact, until now, we had never seen a hawk take a bath. Taalon and Teelon come down on especially warm days to the cooling water. They hop from the shore into several inches of water, then wade out until they are three-quarters submerged. After ducking their heads, in the manner of ducks, to permit the water to sluice over their backs, they sit quietly in the water for several minutes. Back on shore again, they shake vigorously, then fly to a perch to primp.

The hawks are late risers. They wait during the gray hour of dawn, motionless as bronze birds. But when the sun lights up their eyes so they shine like flecks of scoured gold, they ruffle their feathers and the day begins. If there are grackles on the feeding stump, the hawks sit there, tearing out feathers and eating a little of the dark red flesh before carrying the carcass to a tree to finish the meal. If a rabbit is on the menu, they stay on the stump and tear it open with talons and beak and eat out the viscera. Subsequently, they eat the flesh.

Taalon leaves the area about mid-morning. At intervals during the day, he returns to circle and look down on his mate. He swoops low over the feeding stump to see if any more goodies have been put out, but nothing tempts him until evening. If the weather is warm, Teelon leaves the nest once during the afternoon to fly down to the stump and feed briefly.

The tremor that passed through the wildlife community when the hawks came has subsided. As people living under the rim of a volcano learn to forget the threat of an eruption, so birds and animals are now mostly concerned with lovemaking and den and nest building. Instead of pursuing and attacking, the hawks are given to sitting for hours just watching for a crayfish, frog, turtle or even insects.

Because there are so many songbirds, and because we have neither the time nor the inclination to keep population statistics, we do not know if the hawks' presence has sent any couples looking for new nesting sites. The hawks were more than a month late in nest building, so most songbird couples already had fledglings and were, therefore, compelled to live in the shadow of sailing death.

JUNE 19

A seven-pound carp speared by Rebel No. 2 in the mill pond went to the feeding stump, but Taalon and Teelon would not eat it, although they will consume a dozen small bluegills during a day. Rabbits seem to be their favorite fare. They relish crayfish. The tempo of feeding has picked up now that the eggs have hatched. Any day, we expect to see two or perhaps three youngsters straining to look over the nest edge.

JUNE 26

Taalon and Teelon are becoming more and more tolerant of the children. Adults, however, have only to show themselves on the front lawn and the birds leave the feeding stump for a tree. Rebel No. 3, the littlest, has come within thirty feet of the feeding birds.

JULY 17

Little Lakes' turtles, scores of them, have disappeared. This spring, on sunny days, every log, stone or low bank in Fish Pond was crowded with painted turtles ranging from the size of a half dollar to a dinner plate. But now, except for those kept as pets behind wire, and some monstrous snappers, turtles are in short supply. We watched the population dwindle, never understanding what was happening. Then the Rebels began bringing in turtle shells neatly cleaned of every speck of meat. The only animal we could think of capable of such an efficient job was the otter, but there certainly are no otters at Little Lakes. Then, one day, a small snapper, size of a saucer, fell from a tall maple. Right! Taalon and Teelon consider turtles a delicacy even more delectable than snake. What is more, turtle catching is as simple for the hawks as pea picking for a child.

JULY 17

Youngsters in the high hawk nest are craning their necks for a look at the world. We still do not know if there are two or three. Perhaps within a week or ten days they will be big enough to get out on a limb and exercise their wings.

JULY 31

Food is increasingly important to Taalon and Teelon now that the two fledgling hawks can sit on the edge of the big nest in the dead elm and practice fluttering. We hear the war cries of the young now, but it is only a thin echo of the shrill parental shriek that freezes gopher or mouse in its tracks so the bird may swoop in for the clutch and the kill.

AUGUST 14

Taalon and Teelon have their kids doing aerial acrobatics. The youngsters have literally been out on a limb for more than a week, jumping up and flapping their wings to get the feel of the wind. Then one day, when there was a ten-mile-an-hour wind from the southwest, both young birds turned into it, spread their wings and glided downward before soaring up and flying. But the birds have not left their home in the huge, dead elm. Now they are as tame, nearly, as chickens, and the youngsters, perched on lower limbs, permit the Rebels to come within ten feet. But the adult birds are still doing the hunting, and when Taalon and Teelon take the kids on their first hunt, we will not be able to watch because they go to fields to the south for mice. I suppose there will be mistakes, and one or another or both the young hawks will pancake with the same kind of belly flops the Rebels made while learning to dive.

AUGUST 21

The hawks have left the big elm where two of the family of four were born. Now, they sit in trees in the pasture to eat their mice, and they scream when the Rebels come to feed the horses.

AUGUST 28

Good-bye, hawks. And what winds will you ride all the days of the year until perhaps you come again in spring to the old nest in the dead elm? Taalon and Teelon have gone now, and so have their youngsters, sure and strong of wing.

Looking back, life among the birds and animals of Little Lakes must have been quite unsettling while Taalon and Teelon raised their youngsters. None — rabbit or mouse, cardinal or turtle, chipmunk or dragonfly — could ever be quite certain when one of the hawks might single it out. We tried to keep enough food on the feeding stump to stay the hawks' predatory habits, but a pair of hawks who have two young gullets to stuff require much meat, and the meat had to be something right off their wild bill of fare and of fairly recent vintage.

Of all, turtles were most plagued. It is a hard fact that the hawks never bothered to kill a turtle before eating it. They just scooped one up, flew to a tree, and began pecking out pieces of flesh from between the shells. It was something of a shock, and a revelation too, because we had never realized the seemingly impregnable turtle had such a vicious enemy. But now the hawks are gone, and turtles once again sun on stumps and logs. There are not many, and where these survivors hid I do not know. But there they are, and once again it is fairly peaceful around Little Lakes.

Little girl

Little Girl? Slender legs on a ladder popping a baby starling back through a knothole in a tree. Charitable fingers giving a rabbit a lick of her Popsicle. Sweet face kissing an aging dog smack on the muzzle. Eager arms carrying an extra cutting of green grass for the horses. Sad eyes gazing at a flower's head hanging from a broken stem. Anxious heart putting corn and water close so an incubating duck can reach it from her nest. Worried brow chasing for the tenth time a baby blue jay from the path where cars come.

Little Girl? Sweetness stung by a bee. Burned by the sun. Bitten by a spider. Stabbed by a fish fin. Bruised by a stone. Cut by sword grass. Pierced by thistles. Little Girl? Delicious as strawberries. Smelling of horse manure. Covered with marsh muck. Scrubbed, combed, starched, grubby, grimy, shining.

Little Girl? Proper person taking small mouthfuls and chewing with her mouth closed when she is ravenous. Cutting her meat when she would prefer to grab and wolf it like a dog. Being polite to people when she wishes they would get lost so she might play. Brushing her teeth while a whole day is a-wasting.

Little Girl? A wet kiss at bedtime. Enormous eyes. A quick hug in passing. Clutching arms in a frightening world. Spilled milk. A bright piece of tomorrow.

Little Girl? Who carries much of my load and weeps only when the door is closed. Hair graying. Hands hardening. Heart holding.

Save the kingfishers

Born in complete darkness at the end of a long tunnel, seven nearly helpless birds struggled on tiny feet until they came to the light. Arranging themselves in a row along the edge of a tiny creek, they chirred for food, but there was no answering chirr, and as the day waned, so did their strength. There they might have died, except that Rebel No. 2 and a Chesapeake retriever named Mike stopped to stand in the cool water. The dog saw the birds first and cocked his head. The thirteen-year-old looked to see what had alerted the dog. Seven young kingfishers stared back.

She took the dog home and went back. The blue-and-white birds were so weak they rested their heads by bracing their long, black bills to the ground. She searched for the parent birds. Except for a flycatcher lifting at intervals to intercept an insect, and except for the worried fluttering of a red-winged blackbird, the airways were empty. Kingfishers are notably noisy. They have a war cry that can be heard from afar, and any intrusion on their domain is met with raucous indignation.

When it was obvious the youngsters had no one to look after them, the Rebel put them into a box and began the trip back to Little Lakes. Then both the youngest Rebels went fishing and shortly had a catch of tiny bluegills and green sunfish. They coaxed the little fish eaters to open their bills and then force-fed them. When all had eaten, they threw a canvas over the cage so it was dark as the tunnel they were born in. But, next morning, two were dead. They were force-fed again; by night two more had died.

Next morning, however, the three survivors did not have to be force-fed. They opened their beaks and grabbed the first thing that came close, even though sometimes it was a child's finger. So now, after ten days, there are three kingfishers growing strong, and when a Rebel comes with fish, they chirr in anticipation. Not born for walking, but to perch and then fly swift and piercing as an arrow, they are clumsy on the ground. So the Rebels wonder and worry if, when the time comes, they will have to teach the trio to sit high on a limb above a pond and then tilt into a lancing dive to catch a swimming fish. And, if this be the case, how do you do it?

City life

Sometimes, though rarely, I come to Milwaukee. I am always glad that I did, because then I can fully appreciate the calm of the country. A day downtown where windowsills are always sooty, where the grinding traffic is never still, where the air always smells as though a bus just went by, this makes the peace and quiet of Little Lakes seem doubly precious.

Out here, I am revived. I can breathe again. My mind can dwell on the things I put it to, and never be jostled by the hundreds of emergencies posed by the proximity of other people. The earth is our heritage. When we deny it, we are in trouble. We must go somewhere to renew ourselves. There must be a place we can run to. As any wild animal first surrounded by four walls goes berserk because there is no avenue of escape, we can lose our perspective when we see there is no way out. The cities cut off all escape routes for many, especially for the young. They close their grimy tentacles, and the horror of being smothered by life brings panic. We may uproot ourselves from the earth. But then, surely as the tree, we will wither.

Ravishing August

Perhaps during some other summer the earth has been so ravishingly bright, but I cannot remember it. Notoriously, August is sere and brown. Long before Labor Day, the valleys have bleached and the hills are baked brown. Most years, color has bled back as if into the earth to await the cooling nights to rise again in aster, gentian and head-high fields of amber daisies. But this year even the gravel hills have color, and you don't have to come to Little Lakes to see it, because every roadside is holding blooms which should have wilted weeks ago.

Ponds brim to overflowing, and Watercress Creek runs with springtime vigor. There has been so much moisture at such propitious intervals that some spruce have three- and four-foot spires, and the lacelike cedars have outgrown even the ivy that races to crest out on their pinnacles.

Reflections in the evening calm of all the ponds are a mosaic of color. The emerald shine of the conifers in the water is a backdrop for the snow-whiteness of Queen Anne's lace, the meltingly bright yellow of butter-and-eggs, the brazen orange of day lilies, the lovely lavender of joe-pye weed, the trailing blue of nightshade, a score or two score flowers that by now should be hanging their heads and wilting in normally arid August.

Grass is still freshly, vividly green. Phlox stand in four-foot banks of white, purple and lavender. In clumps that flank our roads, the day lilies still bloom. The linden trees still hold their little nuts and even the long, narrow tea leaves that by now should be spinning down. The daisies and the black-eyed Susans stand almost head-high, and some of their blooms are a hand-width across. Wild cucumber is still climbing in the cedar and spruce to fringe each green tree with a froth of white blossoms.

Smaller blooms still lift through the tangle of wild grasses so the bottom lands are misty with pastels. No waters have turned that pea green that so characterizes ponds when dog days come. Instead, they sparkle with the vigor of spring and push high on the banks, back into the canary grass, and wet unwary feet. Paths have disappeared in the reckless reach of well-watered willows, and now we do not go to the marsh or along the far dikes unless prepared to cut new trails.

Burgeoning is the word, and it should be reserved for spring and the first few weeks of summer. This year even the conifers, usually done with growing by mid-July, continue to add inches to their spires. It is a great growing year for all wild flora, and if we should forget, there may be reminder some fifty years from now by the growth ring of a felled tree. There this year will be, wider perhaps than any other ring, and perhaps someone tracing it with a forefinger will remember being six or eight or ten that year, and how the rains, among other things, brought such a crop of mosquitoes as put everyone inside for the nights.

Of course, remembering will make it all the more vivid because, just as fifty years can add dimension to even the ordinary, so it will accentuate the extraordinary until the old-timer's story of how it was this year will be received with small smiles hidden behind polite palms.

But that is the way of it, and just as there are no longer any snows like the snows of yesteryear, so in fifty years youngsters will be assured there have been no growing seasons, especially for trees, like this hot, wet summer. But, of course, there will be, just as there will be droughts again and piers will stand naked-legged on mud flats that will crack as they dry in the sun.

These are the days

Blown the blossoms, comes the fruit. Hickory and walnuts, layer upon layer of green, swell now to harden in meaty kernels. Horse chestnuts, a green nutlet for every white flower fallen from the steeple stem. Soon the steeple will collapse into a cluster of spiked sheaths protecting bronze nuts. Multiflora rose petals lie like snow on green grass, growing green berries, which will redden and be relished by waxwings. Many moons of white elderberry blooms slowly green to spheres of fruit. Strawberries, gooseberries, cranberries, mulberries, rich hoard in the bird cafeteria. Wild and tame grapes in tight green sprigs grow toward purpling size.

These are the days, my friend, and daisies parade up the hill to where the yellow flowers of butter-and-eggs look molten in the blazing sun. Phlox are a breath of lilac, linden's yellow flower drips its first sweetness, and on the thistle blooms a purple sun. Rich, pungent algae shades the lazy fish. Cattails have spiked out with brown velvet. Bats dip to sparkling fireflies, and heavy-headed grasses bow in arbors to screen the sparrow's cup of eggs, second clutch, bird's faith unshaken. Yes, these are the days my friend! Days to hoard the golden warmth against such barren times as age and winter bring, when no crickets come to measure the heartbeat of summer.

Real summer

Summer is a river of sweat through the dust on the bronze cheek of a child. It is the strident, insistent cicada, heat bug sawing away to make iron filings of a quiet afternoon. It is dazzling on water. Blinding on glass. Wavering from concrete. Lightning flashes from car chrome. Hot enough to turn a blue sky white.

Taste it: coppery on the tongue. Smell it: tar squeezed from garage roof shingles. Get it in your throat: gray dust puffing upward from bare feet. Feel it on your skin, pressing hot as a knife blade that has lain in the sun.

Summer. Real summer. Hot enough so those birds still with eggs sit not to keep them warm, but so the heat cannot kill the embryo.

Summer. Real summer. Torrid enough to heat up the white stones so a gopher would burn his belly crossing them. You can remember a summer like that even if it lasts but three days. Birds are silent. No robins stalk the lawn. If any living thing uses the airways, it likely is the dragonfly, life juice safe behind metallic, armorlike plating.

Even the mosquitoes stay down in the damp places lest the sun shrivel their wispy wings. Nor do the flies crowd in the glare, but walk around to the underside of the board. Chipmunks? Squirrels? Rabbits? Woodchucks? Foxes? Never, not when there is a cool place underground or in a hollow tree where sap from buried roots provides air-conditioning of a sort.

Horses flat on their sides in the shade. Dogs kenneled and quiet. Ducks, bills wide. Pigeons fluffed at the cote door. Children run from the beaded lemonade pitchers and then back to Blue Pool until, waterlogged, they finally come to a quiet, shadowy corner in the house to read. Day drags. Heat lies on the leaves until they droop. Flowers so brisk on morning stems nod wearily. Pines and spruce bleed a little extra sap to coat cuts. No ants on the sidewalk. They would fry. No butterflies to the windowsill. They would wilt.

Fish? Ganging deep in spring holes. Hunter and hunted, minnow and bass, trout and bluegill, stacked together, down close to the cool mud. Angleworms? Beyond a shovel's reach. Crayfish? Never venturing from under rock or steepled canyon.

Real summer. Down from the hilltop it comes, browning the grass before it. In Wisconsin and at Little Lakes sometimes three days, seldom three weeks. Brazen. Glaring. Simmering until a cloud castle is rent and the rain comes.

Volunteer

More than a check in the mail, the gift of a tree not native to Little Lakes is always cause for celebration. This time it is a mountain ash, already four feet tall upon discovery, gift of some bird, which, having feasted on the red berries of a neighbor's tree, left the seed here.

The lovely linden

These July days there is a perfume in the air above Little Lakes. It comes from the clustering yellow-white blossoms of the linden trees, which crowd around the house and then fan out in all directions to the pasture where one double giant rises a hundred feet into the sky. Add to the perfume — which though delicate is pervasive — the hypnotic humming of hundreds of bronze bees that come to gather nectar, and you have a canopy of sight, sound and smell that can make a shady afternoon in a lawn chair a delicious symphony in living.

Visiting Germans have especially liked our lindens, and more than the ponds or the flowers or the other trees, they point at once to the flowering trees with exclamations of delight. Unter den Linden, Berlin's main thoroughfare, was, of course, named for the lindens that once lined it. Perhaps it is prophetic that Hitler's plans for expansion in that capital city called for cutting all the lindens.

Often called lime trees in Germany, the lindens are best known here as basswoods. Though Europeans sing the praises of this tree, we have not often met Americans who felt impelled to wax poetic over the linden. Perhaps it is because we are a practical people, more inclined toward such solid, commercial woods as walnut and oak. Too bad, because the linden is a tree a man might enjoy even if he is fifty years old when he plants it, because it grows so swiftly that by the time he is seventy, there it stands, ready to hang down flowers for July, shade for the hot sun of August, tea leaves for September and a generous supply of nutlike fruit for chipmunks and squirrels in October.

The leaves used for brewing tea are called bracts. They are not the tree's principal leaves, which are heart-shaped and saw-toothed, but an oblong adjunct to the stem that carries the burden of the flowers and fruit.

The wood of the linden does not have many uses because it is too light. Happily, however, its toughness has made it the favorite of some manufacturers in the fashioning of piano keys. I would like to write that it burns merrily to add good cheer to cold winter nights, but unfortunately it does not. Given a little help, however, from some more combustible woods, it does well enough and then adds a little perfume to the house in memory of summers past.

Of all the Little Lakes trees, surely the linden is the best able to resurrect itself. And this is perhaps as nature intended, because of all the species native to the place, the linden perhaps goes down first in a storm. So it is fitting that almost before the thunder stops rolling and the wind dies down, there, peeking from the stump, are the first of three or six or eight new basswoods clustering to rise to fill the empty space in the sky.

As if this were not enough, think on how the woodpecker and the flicker have an easy time of getting into its hollows to make homes. Unlike more substantial trees that defy apartment dwellers, the linden welcomes occupants and is gracious enough to die out at the top first, so squirrels and raccoons can tunnel down to fashion nurseries for their families.

The age of a linden can be estimated by its bark. As a child's skin is smooth and wonderful to touch, so the young lindens have a gray surface that is smooth as velvet under a finger. As the tree ages, the smooth bark wrinkles until, even as with old people, it becomes deeply furrowed. Then, with numerous slender branches closely spaced, it forms a dense crown from which to drip perfume upon the hot days of July.

Love affairs

Some of Gwen's love affairs are certainly out of the ordinary. Who, for instance, would take time to leave the freeway on her way to Milwaukee to visit a pair of killdeers who have staked a claim to the gravel shoulder of an off-ramp where Moorland Road intersects? Or who would lug a twenty-pound rock a half-mile out of a neighbor's pasture so she might have it by the back door, where she can view its convolutions and colors every time she goes into or out of the house? Or who would battle through a block of brush willow and then wade a marsh of saw grass just to stand and look at a single burst of orange midland lily blooms?

Well, Gwen would, and if you had the energy to follow her, you would see her stoop to examine the intricate, lacelike flower of the crawling wild cucumber, or run a loving finger over the velvet of a shelf fungus on some old stump. Gwen, a woman of some stern disciplines, melts at the sight of an aged piece of wood into which the carpenter ants have tunneled intricate designs, and one ordinary leaf with red veins showing can bring a smile that will last her through an otherwise irksome day.

I do not suppose a flower blooms out here that she does not know about, and if the names of some of the birds escape her, their songs and colors and peculiarities of flight do not. Of course, the word weed is not a part of her vocabulary. You are just as likely to see the purple head of an almost miraculously made thistle lifting from a bud vase as the bloom of a rose.

I suppose visitors are sometimes surprised to see what looks like old, rotting pieces of wood adorning her sunroom table or even hanging from the wall in her living room. Toadstools, mushrooms and puffballs all have their moments in and out of the house. Even when the hickory drops some of its dead branch ends, they might wind up in a wicker basket, and darned if they don't look pretty. Wild grasses of all kinds, cattails, even sticktights, are as likely to adorn the bathroom as the bedroom. Chestnuts, walnuts and hickory nuts are on display in black kettles as much for just looking at as for satisfying the squirrels who come calling.

Every fruit and vegetable in season must be displayed before it is eaten, because there is as much appetite in the mind's eye as there is on the taste buds of a tongue. Then there is her sky. Every sunset is something special. She watches the approach of a storm as intently as she would a stage curtain about to rise on a dramatic play.

I suppose some people might think that a spider web coming down in a silver, spangled canopy from the picture window to a potted plant on the floor is something to be quickly wiped away. But to her it is something to be protected from careless hands so she may watch it catch the changing rays of a traveling sun.

Tribute to a hill

Surely it is absurd to pay a tribute to such a little hill, but men have done it for the purple majesty of mountains, so why shouldn't I, having been as much inspired by this hill, find time to sing its praise?

For comparison, my hill, a hillock, really, is not much bigger in any dimension than the soft lift of a woman's breast. And so its contours, gracefully sloping to join the body of the land, are only gently surprising when breathlessly ascended. Time was when I stood on this little hill and, looking out over Blue Pool and Fish Pond, said that I would build my home so that its front porch would be a stone cliff, abrupt outcropping on its crest. Then I, and these women I live with, would step off such dimensions as would be needed for all the rooms and an underground garage. And then we would see how we might have to cut, for instance, one red cedar, perhaps one oak, and that is maybe all.

But we had a nice house already, and so we only talked about it as children talk about their sandcastles, and if we sat sometimes where the breeze could sweep up from the cold springs and planned windows of enormous width for sweeping vistas, it was only a game we played. And now I am thankful that we never sank foundations, because no house, however contoured, could do otherwise than be a distortion, and that hill had suffered enough indignities already.

To know this hill, you should understand how in the first place it was the gravel dropping of the last glacier, stones carried south from what other northern land no one really knows. Then, if in time during the warming age the hill could accept no seed, there were thousands of years of frost and snow and ice and wind and rain to pulverize the rock so that a thick skin of topsoil covered its gleaming nakedness. Trees followed, trees and blue-stemmed prairie grasses and wildflowers, and all these added gifts of soil, year by year, until the hill became a verdant rise of green.

Regretfully, when the Indians left, the cattle came to graze the hill until sometimes the stones shone through the thin skin and dust devils danced. The cattle left and a mower came to make a lawn of sparse grass, which turned brown in August, and gophers cast up white stones, and so were shot and poisoned for such industry. Then, one spring, a front-end loader stole gravel from an eastern slope to strengthen our road, and still today, though lilacs now hide the wound, a scar remains.

So I apologized for these assaults, and tried to make amends. No more cows or mowers or front-end loaders, and certainly no house, nor even any paths. Then came the resurrection, slow to be sure, but steady as the seasons, which year on year work wonders on any hill. So now the old glory. Jacob's-ladder purple on the slopes. Umbrellas of May apples under a hickory. Trilliums among basswood shoots. A scarf of pale pink and white anemones beneath the curl and curve of an ironwood tree. Butter-and-eggs in the clearings, yellow and white and orange profusion of blooms. A green cast of small junipers from parent trees on the western slope.

Ash trees, tall and pruned slick and straight. In spring, bloodroot like snowflakes and violets like the wash of purple water. Jack-in-the-pulpits, canopies of purple-green in a rain pocket. White pine and red, and such gifts. From us, mountain ash. From the birds, honeysuckle in profusion. Wild strawberry near the spruce, and cucumber and night-shade climbing. Then if there is no bluestem yet, maybe where the brush was burned a patch of prairie will emerge and so complete the cycle on my little hill.

New generation

New life crowds Little Lakes. Tens of thousands of pale, young fish skitter like a wind across the water as bigger bass rise to attack. The warm shallows are pimply with tiny frogs, and shadows of hawks send shivers of movement through schools of polliwogs waiting to leave the water for their time under the sun. Insects hatching turn flat water into a rain of a hundred rings as they rise, and where the marsh stagnates, mosquitoes pause briefly at the surface to dry their delicate wings before joining the whining cloud above. A million insects? Ten million maybe.

A heron gets all the fish fry it can hold in ten stilted steps. And a young coon need never finger for long, because young crayfish are abundant in the mud. Then, if a fox should come, there is such a scat-tering of young cottontails the pups never need wait.

From a hundred, a thousand nests and burrows and dens, homes of birds and beasts and bumblebees, tumble denizens of forest and field, marsh and meadow. Chipmunk's children, blue jay's brats, snake's sib-lings, ten thousand crawling, flying, hopping, slithering, squirming adolescents. Through the trees, across the sky, among the rushes, in the grass, speckle-bellied robins, spotted frogs, hard-backed beetles, up from the water and the earth, out of hollow trees, tumbling from nests of sticks.

Hopeful. Harried. Hurrying. Promise of spring, pride of summer. Frantically hungry. Needing grass and seeds and fruit and meat. Eating to burst a skin, grow legs, strengthen wings, harden predacious teeth. Turtle big as a nickel. Fox fuzzy with pup's fur. Dragonfly with still-wet wings. Fledgling fluffed on a branch. Butterfly, gopher, new as each morning sun.

Challenge for the earth, so brambles arch with weights of berries. Enough clover blossoms to feed whole battalions of woodchucks. Burdened mulberry boughs break. Beneath green husks, the white nut of the hickory hardens. Green berries of bittersweet and multiflora rose drink sunshine for the autumnal blush. The earth lifts and swells and spills over in green billows. Multitudes must now be fed. Fall harvest must grow to ripen for wintertime. And where only since February the lawn was a barren sweep of snow, now cottontails graze and swallows sweep to vacuum insects rising from the grass.

There is this about such lands as are marked by winter: Given a spate of warm, wet days, a miracle overwhelms the earth. Canary grass grows head-high, and timothy is so lush it heads out before a horse can return to the other end of the pasture.

There is that much now, and it is planned. Just as the deer drops her fawn when the grass has come to new green so she can keep an udder always full, so all the world midway between winters becomes a banquet place when there are new mouths to feed by the millions. It is the summertime of living. Miracle of timing. No young are born before the earth is ready for them. Neither do they leave the breast or the nest or the nymph's hard case until the sun's rays are shafting strength to give the plants such succession as is necessary to feed each supplicant in life's chain, microscopic to man. Underfoot and on leaves above and all about, life burgeons. Try to stifle it and it splits rocks to be born and live.

Revel in it, then. Sit on a stone wall, beneath a tree, beside a brook, and see how even the housefly never comes until the heat will rot the meat for its maggot children. No one cares? The earth cares. Its rhythmic drums of resurrection attend even the pine cones, which swell so that by fall the squirrel will have seeds to store for winter's needs. So, too, the maple now hoards energy in its airplane seeds so that autumn winds can deliver them to bird and beast, and so that catfish may also eat when an errant wind casts them across some night's dark water. Fertile womb, my world. Such burgeoning. Pulsing. Opening. Pouring forth miracles, a million right around my feet.

Wind in the trees

Lie down sometime in a grove of trees and, with your eyes closed, try to identify the sound the wind makes as it passes, for instance, through the leaves and branches of such as a poplar, oak, maple, cedar, pine, spruce. You should have no trouble identifying the poplar's sound. Then as you get better at it, you should be able to differentiate between the long sigh of the wind through a red pine as compared to the brisker sound it makes passing over the shorter, more rigid needles of the spruce. It is a slightly maddening pastime, but enthralling too. I am not good at it yet. I can sort out the white oak, common poplar, spruce, pine, chestnut and cedar. But I am having trouble with basswood, the maples, the cherry trees, and most others.

Basement cricket

Moonlight lay a lacy curtain on the deep green rug. It shone faintly on the sun-whitened hair of the smallest Rebel and outlined the sprawling limbs of the other sleeping girls. Leaves of branches near their bedroom windows drooped in the heat. I went back downstairs and listened briefly at our bedroom door. Rebel Queen's breathing was slow and rhythmical. I went through the quiet house and knew which sound had awakened me because suddenly it was missing: the strident cricket on the basement stairs.

Outside, the night was silent. At the dog pen, Brig lifted his head and then put it back down. A brown-and-white rabbit huddled in a shadow. Two ducks turned their heads, but neither made a sound. In the pasture, not even the swish of a horse's tail. Both horses stood, heads drooping. Fish Pond was flat, lifeless. The moon lay like a white platter on its bottom. No fish broke water. No muskrat swam. Even bat alley, where the furry little night fliers patrol from pond to pond, was deserted. Not even a mosquito sang.

In a chair at the edge of Blue Pool, I waited, and it came: a quick burst of silent light from as far as the edge of the world. No roll of thunder. Surely a cat will come, I thought, because there are so many. But there was no rustling in the shadows, nor any squeak of frightened mouse. How could it be? I could not even hear an auto in the distance, no plane murmuring miles high, nothing but the dead, flat heat and the standing statues of trees with lifeless shadows, nothing except, again, the distant flickers of light. Eerie hour. Silent waiting world. Time of in-between. Breathless. Not dead but neither living.

Finally, craggy thunder clouds climbing. Distinct flashes. A vague and muffled rumble. Up the moon-bright sky a boiling front of clouds. Leaping lightning. Thunder closer, crashing. Big drops of rain. A sudden breeze. Clouds across the moon, then darkness. On the way to the house I heard frogs and crickets come alive. In a lightning flash I saw the horses grazing. At the basement steps a cat leapt quick as the shadow of a wind-tossed branch. In the kitchen, I could hear the basement cricket.

Fragrant hay

The pressed summer flowers of new hay are in the stable. No tame variety this, but a wild hay from meadows sown by the winds. How many scents? Lay a cheek to its roughness and find, like delicately

Sacrifices are being offered daily to the new rulers of Little Lakes.

placed spices, this flower and that, a score of crushed fragrances from a field of prairie stems laid while blooming. Lord, what a world of fresh flavors for any horse! Such drippingly green fare sipped out by the sun for keeping! And what hooved friend would trade that ever-changing bill of fare for timothy straight or, if his belly could stand it, alfalfa?

Sometimes I envy the horse its tastes. Would that I could come to the fresh fields and take the juice on my tongue without dressing, pressing, boiling. I have neither the teeth nor the tongue for it, but in my mind's appetite I can relish and savor, and who says nostrils cannot taste? The hay will keep coming until, by fall, the stable is full except for dark caves reached through secret tunnels and perhaps a soft, fragrant nest for lying in when the sleet slants off the roof.

The time is near

An owl last night, quavering from high in the hard maple, prophetic in its trembling, warning that summer is waning, and then there will be no moths for eating, and crusted snow will hide the mice. Teal of the year try the wind this morning. A week and the first will leave until, by the time of frost, most of the blue-winged ones will be beyond freezing waters. Blue heron stilted in the bay. Black-capped night-heron roosting in the bank oak. First to be done with rookery chores, scattering already and drifting, drifting south.

Redwings in feathery whirlwinds, ready for marching orders, celebrate in great congregations where combines have missed nuggets of golden grain. Tree swallows head to the marshes where the first have already gathered until one day they will swarm like colored rain in a last good-bye. The woodchuck feeds more frantically to add an extra inch of fat for the long sleep. The chipmunk, cheeks bulging, comes more often to add seed and nut to wintertime stores. The cottontails graze days as well as nights as if anticipating bleak times on rations of bitter bark.

Now the fox leads pups, and the coon herds kittens anxiously lest they never learn enough before the time of snow to see them through the winter. And one hysterical squirrel is already storing nest leaves in a tree crotch, while the rest of the tribe bury acorns and hickory nuts, regardless of their time of ripening. The gopher digs farther and farther, foolishly, never having learned that, no matter the length of his shallow tunnel, the frost will reach him unless he goes deep.

The methodical bees fly their beelines from whatever flower to add to their hollow-hickory hoard. The eggs of next year's mayflies have long been laid. The ash is already ragging, and the ferns have turned from tender pale to brittle green. And of the leaves, one sumac leaf is red, one birch leaf has tanned, one maple leaf shows pink veins, and a basswood leaf looks old and used.

So you know the time is near, and it will not be long and the nuts of the hickory will be like white stones on the dead grass, the purple grapes will have shriveled on the vine, and the only flowers in the brown marsh will be the fringed gentian, opening and closing sun gauge. I am sure that then, as every year, there will be some days or a week or two during which I will be uncommonly obsessed with death. It always happens, because I cannot help but feel that as autumn measures such time as is left to so many things at Little Lakes, it must also test the texture of our skin.

But then the first snow will come swirling, and I will hurry forth, rejoicing that once more I can meet my adversary, and then, if by February my blood runs thin, who cares, because soon I will celebrate another happy springtime.

chapter four

AUTUMN

Autumn on the wind

Now smell autumn. Taste it. Feel it. Dry and light and heady. Sharp on the wind. Invigorating right up to the last days when moldering brings a heavy odor of ripeness before the sharp freeze again clears the air. Walk your country lane or city street at night. Look up from your dark earth at the sparkling universe. Believe then that your finite mind is no more capable of grappling with the infinite than a just-born babe can fathom physics. So, forget your conceit and let the reasons be. Just see the crisp moon and brittle stars. Hear how a leaf sounds scraping, and how the wind is like water washing, and how the air is sharp to taste and clean to breathe. Just walk with autumn fresh on your face.

The flight is on

Nature is playing her special arrangement of Exodus, and millions, moving to the autumn rhythm of the music, pass in the night. It begins almost as a whisper, only of wings. But then, if you should go out into the night and stand very still and listen intently, you may hear the twitter of sound coming earthward as the migration builds.

All day, the birds feed to gain strength for the long journey. Then, when evening comes, they lift from the meadow, marsh and woodlands to where the moon lights their way south. When the moon is round and high and white, the world pulsates to the wingbeat of passing flocks. Lie in a glade and keep an eye on the moon for the shadows that cross it. These are the migrants, mysteriously moved to desert the homes where they were born and raised and to go to a land they never have seen. Millions are enroute to the land of tropical sunshine. All along the way, there will be dropouts. Robins will scatter through almost every state below the snow area. Some geese will go no farther than southern Illinois; others will travel all the way to the Gulf of Mexico and beyond.

But move most of them will. Some flit from bush to bush. Others fly at treetop level. Still others climb high, where perhaps they can get a lift from the wind and cut by half the time it takes to make the southerly trip. Some of the flyers, notably the trumpeter swan, may climb so high that the flock is not visible and its clarion call comes back to earth only as a thin strand of sound.

Then, when the summer birds have left the land, the migrants from the north move down. Crossbills, grosbeaks, chickadees and nuthatches may move only as far as southern Wisconsin when the weather becomes frigid. Eagles will fly only to where rivers are open so they may fish. Crows will hop back and forth as the weather moderates or stiffens. Some birds move east and others west, though the great general movement is across the continent from northwest to southeast.

The flight is on. It started more than a month ago. It will continue right into winter. How it all began is a mystery that disappeared with the great glaciers. We may speculate, but perhaps we will never know why the birds blow south like swarms of leaves on the wind. But whether we understand or not, it is a spectacle worth viewing. And if, some morning, you awaken to find the trees of your yard swarming with warblers, know that while you slept they blew in. And know, too, that after they have fed and on some night when the wind is right, they will lift once more, and the trees in which they moved like living jewels will be bare again.

One more warm day

Now the turtle seeks the sun, lifts from the clear, cooling waters to ride a log, because during the months ahead there will be oblivion in his mud dungeon at the bottom of the pond. Now the bass swims from beneath the shade of overhanging willows, from under the shelf of weeds, from the dimness of a rock or a log or a web of roots, to swim in the sun before ice comes and diminishes its view of the world above and about.

Even the chipmunk goes to where a slant of sunlight thrusts between two spruce, and here he folds his forepaws to his breast and lets the rays warm him. And the horses come to where the sunny side of the white stable reflects the heat and the night chill may diminish more quickly.

Cottontails forsake the verdant marsh from which mists now rise to hunch in grass on the gravel hill where the white stones cast up from the gopher's hole still get hot at noon. Even flies seek the sunny surfaces, and squirrels rest more often on dead limbs because here there are no leaves to block out the rays of warmth. The birds linger in their dust bath, a pheasant cock stands high on an old snag to be out of the wet grass, and back along the cornfield a raccoon comes from its den to stretch on a limb and luxuriate in the warm sun.

When it was full summer, none so appreciated the sun as now, and even the Rebels seek out paths that are less shaded and sit on such stone walls as have absorbed enough sun to be well heated.

Prelude to winter

The canary grass gallops in golden waves when the wind is up, and the marsh ripples in brown and green currents of color. The tan cattails on rigid stems thrum a sad song, and the billowing green willows are threaded with the gold of dying leaves. There are patches of red along the stands of sumac, and maples that line the old road have sunbursts of crimson among their still-green crowns.

Along pond shores, goldenrod and bootjack flow in buttery yellows to where wild asters are banks of purple. The green berry of nightshade has turned scarlet, and where vines have climbed the cedars, they cluster like ornaments on a living Christmas tree. The grape arbors are dropping leaves and there beneath, in royal blue, sweetness clusters. The apple trees bow with the burden of their fruit, and in a dozen places hawthorns have rained red — tiny fruit, favorite of grouse and children.

Though it is not true, I like to think it all started far north along Lake Superior's shores, and then came south like a forest fire on a wind to this more temperate place. It seems so, anyway, because the color materializes there first and then gallops along on past Minocqua and Winter, past Wausau and Oshkosh, until at last it envelops Little Lakes and all of southern Wisconsin.

Color change is inherent in growing things, and it comes on gradually, starting as early as July when the pinks and pastels harden and whites turn to bronze. The difference is almost unseeable, at least until the maples and sumac fire up. Then, in a week, Wisconsin can be ablaze. But look between, beyond, below and around the startling reds for the softer russets of the oak, the pale drift of poplar leaves, the gold coins showered by the birch. Then, if there is a week of warmth, see how a violet blooms, the dandelions come back and the jewelweed pushes fragile orange blossoms right up between pods, ready to snap and scatter seeds.

Glimpses

Grizzled woodchuck, fine in fall fur, almost filling the live trap set for opossums. Quiet and unafraid when the Rebels come. Almost reluctant to go. Must be prodded. Then down the green path beneath the weeping willows, stopping to look back once before scuttling into the thick spruce. Former pet for sure.

Black Buck at five months terrified of the huge horses. Tail tucked tight as he heads for the kennel. On a leash and back for a more formal introduction. Reluctant. Made to sit on one side of the fence so the horses can smell him and he can smell them. But he won't. Keeps head and eyes averted. What he can't see or smell won't hurt him. Horses are too big for the black Labrador pup. He'd rather chase squirrels.

Turtle, size of a quarter, just hatched and immobile in the morning cold, inert on the earth where cedars edge to the pond. Like dead. Lifted and warmed in a soft hand. Brought to the house and placed in tepid water. Life flows. Head comes out. Legs extend. Ready to face life, it goes to Fish Pond.

Green sunfish hardly longer than an eyelash. Caught up in the mesh of a green gauze net. Popped into a pail and brought to the goldfish bowl on the sun porch to live with a score of snails. Flashing up for food like a sliver of sunshine.

Gray squirrels eat red apples. No nuts this year on nearby walnut and hickory trees, so the squirrels are shadow patches moving through the branches of the apple trees. They are welcome to the fruit. There is more than we and the horses can handle.

One spider in the converted coalbin that is my office. Intricate web just over my head and every time I type it vibrates and the spider comes out of its corner, perhaps thinking a fly has become enmeshed in its trap.

Crayfish scuttle along the muddy bottom of Our Pool, so the Rebels drain it and collect them. Fifty, sometimes a hundred in all sizes. Food for the ducks. They eat the claws and all. Lobster!

Beetles, flies, worms, grasshoppers, half a hundred insects, all in one corner of the kitchen. But they are all dead and waiting to be mounted. Project in biology.

Night-herons just at dusk. A file of black-capped visitors inquiring about lodging, circling in the darkening sky. I call out to them in their own language and they come, first one and then another, until they are all sitting in the oaks along Fish Pond. They never seem to ask about the bird that invited them to stay.

Andora and her ducklings. Tame Andora, mated to a wild drake, has led her youngsters from the little world of Watercress Creek down to the big place that is the mill pond. The youngsters will have to feather fast to be warm when winter comes.

Muskrat on a rock. Sleek and unafraid. Eating roots of the cattail stalk. Waits until the dog is only inches away before diving and swimming like some slippery, mahogany fish for its burrow in the bank.

Cottontail, all eyes, watching from its brown grass form. Seeing me go by, seeing the Rebels pass close, watching the dogs circle, never moving. Ears flat. Fur flat.

Small bass in a small bay. Strikes at a falling seed. Rises to a leaf. Rushes at a twig. Strikes to eat a kicking grasshopper.

Perturbed kingfisher. A fisherman floats on its pond. Around and around, scolding in raucous voice. From lookout to lookout, enraged. No thought to fishing other waters. Futile fury until finally the fisherman docks and ownership of the pond passes back to the bird.

Opossum in shock. Like dead. Lips curled back from long, strong, white teeth. Drooling in its helplessness. Unconscious from fright.

Bubbles from the pond bottom and the clear water clouds as the big snapping turtle digs its winter grave. When the water clears its tail is still visible above the mud. The sun comes out and the water warms. The turtle stirs, digs out and decides to cruise a while longer.

That was Little Lakes last week.

Rock collections

The Rebel Queen delights in rocks. So do the children. So they collect. But there is a distinct difference. The children pick up the pretty stones to add to their hoard. The Rebel Queen only marks them in her mind. Then, during our daily walks, she visits her favorites.

Watercress Creek

Above the Little Lakes road bridge, Watercress Creek is a broad, flat flow of water frosted with the flowers of coontail. Though beautiful, it has few secrets. But below the bridge, where it narrows between rock banks and goes curling from sight beneath dogwood and comes quickly back to light at sparkling intervals, the creek is deeply intriguing.

Here, trout come up from Clear Pool and hold in its current beneath tangled grass arbors. Frogs, safe from the sun, sit on wet rocks. Freshwater shrimp, snails and caddis, like crawling sticks, live along the bottom. In the branch bowers of bush and tree, complete worlds of insects are born, living and dying with birds. Always there is the sound of water, against a plank footbridge, at bends among the rocks, where an errant branch throbs in the current.

Except after a rain, the creek is crystal, and colored pebbles along the bottom take tinting from changing sun and shade. At each bend, water bounces back to form a vortex that deepens holes. The tiny tornado of water detains all manner of edibles for trout too lazy to chase food on the current. Silver by day, softly platinum under a moon, the creek never rests until it loses its identity in Clear Pool.

On leaving Clear Pool and again assuming identity, it roars down a dam and foams across a concrete spillway as though angry at being detained. In a journey of a hundred feet, it spreads into a wide, flat basin, slips smoothly under willows and goes slack in the mill pond. Spilling out of the mill pond, it once more comes alive and, after writhing down a meadow slope, loses itself forever in the Fox River.

As creeks go, it is among the smallest, but even as the Brule, Miramichi and Beaverkill are fascinating waterways, forever changing face, so tiny Watercress Creek is complete, even if in miniature. Except for those of us who live here, the tiny stream attracts but small attention. Visitors step across it never realizing that only minutes ago the water below first came to light after traveling scores of miles in underground darkness.

Reflections on springs

Sometimes we take visitors to the springs and, when we do, they are disappointed. It seems they expect the water to sparkle, but sparkling springs are rare. Mostly, emerging water has little oxygen and does not even properly reflect the sun. It often has a flat taste and, except that it moves, it looks lifeless. But, even as with the least of us, once it has lived a little in wind and sun, it takes on character. Depending on its environment, it is racy or subdued, noisy or silent, glittering and giddy or serenely shiny. Like a child, it reflects its surroundings. An overcast. A sunset. Nodding flowers and the leafy overhang of red-stemmed dogwood or pale yellow willow, they are all there, held as by a mirror. Then, so long as it is busy between banks, its vigor is stimulating. But once it comes upon quieter times, it is quickly and quietly suffocated by all manner of greens until, at last, from all appearances, it is dead under arrowroot and spatterdock, lilies and waupato, pencil reed and sword rush. Like life? Just a little?

Dove-gray days

Sunday, the last day of September. Days and days of gentle rain, falling softly to bead the spruce, streak the windows, rustle on the roof, run like gently breaking glass across the road, glisten where the house lights catch the leaves. Restful days of somber skies made for reflection. Interlude. Time between the brash sun and riotous storms. Days made for touching stone or wood or loved one with tender fingers. Passionless days made for writing quiet poems or baking bread.

Rare time of peace. Horizons wrapped as close around as the nearby hill. Clouds there to touch. Thoughts going nowhere, only hanging like the rain-streaked leaf waiting for some brisker time to make it twirl. Respite, these rainy days. Respite from excitement of color and sound. Respite from rushing around. Slippers on kitchen floor softly.

Doors closing, no banging, quietly over damp sills. Even the clock, cold innards moist, tocks instead of ticks. Even the stairs do not creak as on dry days, and my chair folds softly around my form without the protest that leather makes during days of drought.

We need them, long days and days of gentle rain, surely as does the earth, which must replenish water veins drawn dry by harsh times of growing all too swiftly such multitudes of life as make the hectic summer tire. We need them, the restful days of quiet rain, to gather strength to stand braced against the winter winds, to come to spring with enough reserves to carry us once more to summer.

What would life be without sleep? What tomorrow without the night? What the summer without the spring? What the earth without its dove-gray days, calm as the priest at prayer?

So fret not. The sky has only lowered the shades so the mind may have time to look inward and for once slow the swiftly beating heart that pounds to meet the world's werewolves and windmills. Be thankful, then, for this moistly quiet time, as is the tree that gathers gratefully the strength that may save it when the strong winds blow. Let the rain close your wounds as it does the gaping cracks of drought. Let the quiet days that lay such healing rains upon the earth make your spirit swell again. Then, when the clouds draw back, you may be armored, ready and refreshed, rare gift of the dove-gray rainy days, solace of our souls.

Adventure calls

There is no substitute for adventure. No matter how surrounded by all manner of amusements, the Rebels would rather climb the next hill to see what is on the other side. It is as fundamental as hunger. It is as compelling as love. It is as necessary as air. It is as exciting as Saturday. No matter that the trees here at Little Lakes are as tall or taller, the flowers as bright or brighter, the waters as blue or bluer, the birdsong as sweet or sweeter. No matter, because there is the hill, and who can know without climbing it?

By horse, sometimes, with lunch and canteens, ropes and halters, jackets hanging from the saddles as they ride west toward the river. If they are a long time in getting there, it is because, tempting them at every turn, are trails to follow. And if one leads to a lived-in home, another is sure to lead to an abandoned farm where they can look through the windows of a house that just could be haunted. And if one trail leads only to an adjacent road, the next might lead down into a swamp where the light comes through but dimly, and the horses sink knee-deep in what is easy to imagine as primordial mud. If one trail dead-ends, another is likely to go on and on.

At last, fearful of being lost, they finally turn back, but they have ventured far enough to know about the breathlessness of new and strange places. They finally come to the river, so they unsaddle and put halters with long ropes on the horses, who wander knee-deep in bankside herbage to taste all manner of grasses strange to their gravel pasture.

The Rebels contemplate lunch, but there is a snake and it has caught a frog, which it holds crosswise between its jaws, and the frog is making pitiable mouse sounds. But they do not help the frog, because this is the snake's business, and if, after awhile, they cannot watch, but must walk down to the water to watch a blue heron's lumbering flight, or watch an arrow of ducks spear down into a marsh, or open a black clam, or catch a crayfish, or watch a turtle on a log, they cannot forget the frog.

So they go back, but the snake has gone, and then they can forget, and swallows of water have a special metallic taste of the canteen as they wash down sandwiches. Then they lie back, watching how the sun is like something alive on the water. They are too new to this world, not old enough to let an afternoon be stolen by sleep, so they sort out stones, keeping the smoothest, the shiniest, the most peculiar, the most colorful. And they open a milkweed pod and spread the shimmering silk across the calluses of their palms, and they pick a sumac leaf and trace the veins of red, and they shred leaves from a birch branch and spread the goldlike coins to the current.

And now the horses stand, heads hanging, and they have been surfeited with feeding, and so have the Rebels been surfeited with exploring. So they bring their mounts up out of the marsh, saddle up, and ride east, but with many a backward glance, because across the river there is another hill, and who knows, unless you ride to the top of it, what may be on the other side? Because, when you are new to this world, there is adventure in the butterfly wing, the spider web or one diamond of prismatic dew because it can reflect all the colors anyone might ever hope to see.

Fringed gentian

Thou waitest late and com'st alone
When woods are bare and birds are flown,
And frost and shortening days portend
The aged year is near his end.

Then doth thy sweet and quiet eye
Look through its fringes to the sky,
Blue - blue - as if that sky let fall
A flower from its cerulean wall.

William Cullen Bryant's words took on special meaning as yesterday we came to see how the pitcher plants had survived the summer and, standing there in the moist meadow, saw blooming above the brown, the rare fringed gentian. It was like finding a trace of gold in Watercress Creek, and we could not believe our eyes, so we picked a single bloom and took it to the house to be laid alongside an illustration for verification. It was the fringed gentian, and further exploration showed us a dozen more plants all with unbelievably blue blossoms. We wondered, of course, just how rare the gentian has become. The delicate blossom, which has a way of twisting never quite open and then shut because of its sensitivity to light, has a fringe fine as hair as a protection against insects. Come November, we will collect a few seeds (the flower will not grow from root stock) to see if we can spread its range here at Little Lakes.

At one with the geese

Brule, Wis.
The Rebels
On Little Lakes

Dear Rebels:

The wind comes up the valley today. It races over the river, snatches water from the rapids and sprays it toward the sun. It sighs among the spruce and shakes the poplars until their leaves fall like golden coins to the blue current. Geese ride this wind. They are high and honking, and the sky is penciled with wavering gray lines. Flock follows flock, fleeing south from winter, old birds knowing where the food fields are, young birds making the trip for the first time.

Many an Indian has stood where I am standing to watch. For centuries the great gray birds have passed this way. For centuries men have stood here, envious of the geese. For the big birds, summering in the far, cool north and wintering in milder climes, this is no adventure, but a way of life. Would that we might be so free, needing neither valise, airplane, moving van nor automobile, only wings.

It is a lesson in living. Free of house and a hundred material possessions, we might at last, in spirit, lift like the geese above the obligations that possessions impose. Some have tried being one with the geese, but they have

*always returned. The need to eat. A bed to sleep in. The necessity of children.
These essentials drag them back and then, soon, the whole world of television, clothes and can openers suffocates them. So that is why we came here
— to be, for a time, as free as it is possible to be.*

*Today I will stand in the current and try to catch a steelhead trout, but it
will make no difference if I do or do not. Today the Rebel Queen will stroll
the beaches of Lake Superior, searching for driftwood and worn stones.
Lunch will be a can of beans and a piece of bread. And then we will rest in
the sun, and perhaps a beaver will swim by or a deer will come out into the
glade where a few gnarled apple trees stand. We will not worry about pay-
ing tuition or buying shoes. We will eat when hungry and lie down to sleep
when tired and, insofar as possible, we will be one with the geese, doing only
such things as please us.*

*We have come to a splendid place to be free. Of all the rivers in Wisconsin,
the Brule is still the purest. It still hurries its hundred miles from a swamp
through the red clay hills with the bounce and beauty of yesterday. Let us
hope it keeps its freedom and freshness so that someday when the world is
wearing you down, it will still be shining under the sun, a place for you to
come and be one with the high and honking geese.*

*Love,
Dad*

In shambles

Little Lakes lies in ruins. The leaf canopy has been shredded. The
once-tall grasses lie flat. The green vines have blackened. Husks of nuts
are litter. Pondweed has gone down, back to the black bottom. Once-
flowering stalks are brittle skeletons. End to end, Little Lakes is devas-
tated. No autumn imagery is going to change the truth.

Oh, there are bright trappings. Red berries of the nightshade, clustering like ornaments from the spruce, catch the eye, but they are like
ballroom baubles hanging from a building in a bombed out city.

No. Little Lakes is a shambles. The ferns are flat, and the ooze from
which they sprang is darkly ugly. The banks of once-bright phlox are
ragged rows of brown refuse. The grapevines hang from their arbors in
tatters, wilted and raglike. Look where you will, the blight is on us.
Naked now to the eye, every scar of pick and shovel is as plain as the
cut on a cheek.

Too many years we have looked past the wreckage to find the soul
of Little Lakes still warm and waiting, still alive and vital, still filled
with promise. But, if we know in our minds that the seeds of resurrec-

tion are there, we cannot see them. If we know that spring will come, it is also true that right now all that meets the eye is havoc. Wind and cold have cut down these acres like tornado on a town. The roofs are off and the rooms are empty. Still, we search for our belongings, and if a cardinal flashes in the sun, we try to make it enough. But it is like finding a ring in the rubble while looking for a jewelry box filled with sparkling stones.

Why don't we face it? Where came this eternal optimism? How come we wash the mud from one bright stone? Must we focus on the blue jay's flight to grasp such a shaft of color as will carry us? Do we look beyond the debris to sun shafts on the water to keep our own feelings from freezing? Are we so eternally optimistic lest we ourselves wither?

It goes deep. And if a hundred necessities for living buoy you above it, still, in some unguarded moment, while walking a street, looking through a window, there are the facts. The realization may be but a momentary twinge, but it is there, a piece of dying before your own time. Then, if you live close to the land, the day comes when you cannot deny the destruction. And, if you brood on it, beware. It will take you down. So, pull the shade and pick up a book. Within the book and within yourself is the growing ability to create a separate world. Live in it until the grass is green again.

Winter in waiting

Ten or more years ago there was an October ending of summery mien. Then, during the dark of that night, winter got an icy grip on the land and lakes were not free again until spring. Autumn often has lingered on through a naked, soft-ground Christmas. So, there may be more warm days luminous in the slanting sun. But, once November makes its debut, know that winter is poised to send its shrieking winds. So, hurry. Roof the pet pen. Plant the bulbs. Cover the roses. Hang the door the horse kicked. Store the boats. Hang the storms. Stack more wood. Drain the hose. Hurry now.

Beautiful nights

During the incomparable weather that ushered October into history, the nights were more beautiful than the days. A full hunter's moon, surrounded by sharply glistening stars, brightened even the dim pathways that wind among the clustering spruce. Then, by each midnight, the cold had spread white frosting on the long stretches of lawn, and Little Lakes sparkled. Trees were gaunt shadows against the sky. The ponds were quiet puddles of quicksilver, broken only where muskrats were swimming arrows. Even the ducks remained back in the marsh, where they gabbled sleepily or sometimes sounded a clarion call to a shadow in flight. Then, when the sun routed the moon, the bush pantry and the weed jungles were like deserted battlefields. But you could not see the casualties, because they were down among the grass roots — insects that had not survived the cold. Then, when the days warmed to a golden glow, there were fewer insects in the air. And each day now their numbers will diminish until that day when none will rise to warm their wings in the sun. Then, winter.

Reflecting perfection

Reflections, like memories, are always better than the real thing. In the calm waters of Fish Pond, the cedars along its shores are superbly green and perfectly conical. In the reflection are visible none of the flaws that meet the eye when in the presence of the trees. The branch that has broken and browned or is naked where a horse chewed, the twisted limb, the curved trunk, none of the deformities appear in the reflection, though they are clearly visible on looking directly at the tree.

I know the weeping willow that towers beside Blue Pool is twisted and gnarled and interwoven with many dead branches and yellowing leaves. But when I look into the waters of the pool, I see only a magnificent tree, rising in tier on tier of billowing green leaves. Looking into the waters of New Pool, I see an aster so superb in form and color it takes my breath away. But I know if I examine the flower I will find a frayed and faded leaf and a wilted petal.

Memories are like that. In time, all the little mean and base things that made us less than perfect are gilded over by wishful remembering of the nice things we did. Like reflections, our memories have a way of omitting all the little imperfections, leaving the picture of only a pleasant person. Perhaps this is an act of nature's mercy, because if we had to remember every day of our lives precisely what scoundrels we have been, there would be no living with the memory. Maybe it is good that we forget how we earned the money, but remember only that we gave some of it to charity.

More and more now, I look at reflections. Walking along the shores of Clear Pool, I look to the water to see the white bridge. In the reflection, it shines. As mirrored by the water, it is one of the most picturesque bridges I have ever seen. It is only when I raise my eyes and examine the bridge that I see it is made of odd ends of lumber, crudely fitted together with many a mistake.

Most lives, I suspect, are mainly odds and ends. Examine anyone too closely and it seems that person's character is a happenstance, formed by coincidence and fitted by an accidental whirlwind of events. Not that we do not all mean, with much resolve, to do better. But as the wind twists and the sun burns and the cold freezes the cedar, so fate has its way of intervening in our plans. So we succumb. We recover. We start over. We falter. We fall. We get up. We run, only to trip again. Luckily, on looking back, life loses sharpness, like a reflection. We remember mostly the times we ran strongly against odds. We forget when we stumbled.

Ready for winter

The boats have been pulled up and overturned on the shore. Now they will roof over mouse homes and perhaps even provide a roof for a muskrat. If a muskrat should move in, it will chink with moss any air holes left where the boat's gunwale does not come flush with the ground.

Then, in winter, the harder the snow the warmer becomes the boat made into a home. The snow will pile up over the boat, insulating the city of mice beneath from the rigors of weather. At first, there will be tunnels through the grass, terminating in nests. But after awhile there will not be enough grass to support tunnels and the mice will roam freely.

Eventually the food will have been eaten, and then the mice will have to forage. Any morning there will be dainty, birdlike tracks leaving and returning to the boat home. The foraging mice will go below, through holes slick and round and smooth as though punched into the snow with a broom handle. They will have met the challenge of winter. In spring and well on into summer the mark of the boat will be on the lawn, because the mice and maybe a muskrat will have eaten every vestige of grass from beneath, even on down to and including the roots.

The Rebels, too, must meet winter's challenge. For several weeks now, they have been collecting leaves and heaping them into the pet house. Divided by wire into four compartments so that aggressive pets may be kept away from the more docile, the leafy flooring is almost knee-deep. Even the tallest ducks have to stretch their necks to see. But quickly they will make paths, and then, when winter winds start moaning under the eaves, the animals and birds will be comfortable and warm.

Systematically the Rebels meet the challenge and ready Little Lakes for winter. Bird feeders are brought out and painted. Fishing rods must come up from the shack by the ponds and be hung on hooks in the basement. Dog quarters are given a last scrubbing and fresh bedding is put down. Swimsuits and towels are brought up from the bathhouse and washed and stored for the winter. Open sides on the horse stalls are dropped and secured. Rugs and bedding come out of the shack on Clear Pool. The sprinkling system is drained and antifreeze run down the pipes. The pump is shut off.

Like an army digging in against certain attack, the Rebels go from place to place, making all things secure against the onslaught of winter. Sometimes they complain that summer is too short and winter too long, but I detect a certain swagger, a boldness of eye, an edge to their conversation that was not there during the lazy, warm days. Perhaps they do not like winter, but I am sure it is a challenge. And they rise to meet the threat with more than a little anticipation.

Winter in the country is not nearly as rough as in the days before central heating and indoor plumbing, but it still has its moments. It is a fine feeling for a child to break a path through a head-high snowdrift so she can bring water to a pet.

Adults at Little Lakes are necessarily part of the picture, and the almost daily warning to exercise or diet has no meaning for us. If you live at Little Lakes, there are enough tasks each day to keep the heart healthy. What is more, the Rebels, especially, never have to worry about lethargy of the spirit. There is no time, even in winter, to go about the house complaining that there is nothing to do.

But when evening comes, it is a distinct pleasure instead of a bore, to come into a warm home and watch the fire flicker on the open hearth, knowing that winter has been kept in its place. There is a deep satisfaction in sitting with a book and an apple, knowing you have met the challenge.

Cleansing cold

Closely guarded secrets are revealed now that the leaves have fallen, the grass is flattened by frost and the waters are sparkling clear because algae no longer grows. Throughout the bush pantry, in the forking red fingers of the dogwood and on the woody, gnarled limbs of many flowering bushes, are jewellike nests of tiny birds who raised families there when a shroud of leaves curtained their activity.

Crayfish, their blue armor glinting in the cold sun, are plainly visible as they move slowly among the stones at the bottom of Watercress Creek, and darting fish are naked to the predatory eye of man and bird. Maybe that is why the kingfisher stays right to the time when the last stretch of open water goes under ice. Perhaps now that the moss has gone and the waters are clear, his job of catching fish is so easy it would be folly to go south where warmer weather encourages continued growth of such camouflage as makes fishing difficult.

Visibility is better because dust and pollen, and the moisture that supports both, have been put down by the cold, and the air is so sparkling clear the blue jay's colors come up as vividly as splashed paint. In the brisk air, the blue heron's eyes glint yellow even from a distance, and when the great bird lifts to fly, the watcher can see the crest lie back and the toes come together as the legs straighten to form a rudder.

Spiders are pretty well finished shrouding houses with misty lace, so vinegar water puts a sparkle to the panes, and the washed windows seem to bring the outdoors right inside. The change is so dramatic that for the first few days after the windows have been shined, it seems no glass separates the Rebels from the juncos flirting out among the spruce. Even a rabbit comes to a basement window and is surprised when its twitching nose touches glass. It had planned on hopping right in.

Night lights shine farther, and a flashlight can pick up the glint of a rain puddle away down at the end of the road. Cats' eyes are especially bright in the flashlight's beam, and if you go looking, the rings from where a fish rippled are like little waves of quicksilver. Even the stars seem closer. Since the haze that holds the earth has diminished in density in our area, the heavens are more brilliant, and when the moon comes full, it will glow with such brilliance as was never possible on warm summer nights. It is as though the frost has sterilized our earth and all the shine of polished silver comes to windowpane, star, stone, and owl's eye.

It is as though the creeping growth of things that shroud, like spider's web, moss, algae and mold, has stopped, and the cold has wiped the land, water and sky clean for winter. A child's cheek has a fresh glow, and there is a light in an oldster's eye that was not there during the muddy warmth of a humid summer day. It is most amazing that now we see so many miles away the house on the hill. In summer it was only a little lift in the horizon, but now it has glistening windows and a steep roof with a shining web of antennas atop it.

The air is easier to breathe, as moisture has been wrung from it. It is lighter and fresher now that such additives as come with summer are eliminated. So step out briskly. Breathe deeply. Sweep the sky with your eyes to catch the flash of a sailing hawk's wing.

Digging for gold

Saturday, we searched for gold in diggings I felt certain would hold hardly anything more than a dog's bones, remains of someone's pet brought to that secret place for burial. But I was wrong, because we did find gold, and if it never gets spent that is so much the better because it is the kind for keeping.

It was morning; crows were drifting silent, black flocks across the low, gray sky, so I said it would storm. And then there was rain and wind shortly after breakfast, but no cold, so we went outside anyway, the two youngest Rebels and I, to cover the boats for winter and, when finished with that, to take down the diving board because it has a strip of new carpeting that should be protected against snow. That left us puffing, so we walked in the rain to count muskrat houses in the marsh and, counting droppings, guessed about the number of mink hunting crayfish in Watercress Creek.

Dampened somewhat, we went back to the house, where I had a pipe and a hot cup to chase the chill. Meanwhile, the Rebels brought the dogs, one at a time, to the kitchen for the treat of a cookie, and so that I could say how they were looking, whether too thin or too fat, and tell about the color of their gums and eyes, the texture of their coats and the attitude of their ears and other clues to a dog's well-being.

We went out again to inspect the gate the white mare broke scratching her broad butt, and looked to the wing-wounded pheasant recuperating in a pen with a mallard drake and a buck rabbit. The rain ran us into the kitchen again, and our wet clothes steamed a little, so we warmed ourselves while watching through the window where a cock cardinal at a bird feeder, after each sunflower seed, shook drops of water from his red feathers.

Then, warm if not dry, we went back into the rain and, coming to the creek, crossed over into the spruce. It was dark under the canopy of boughs, so we did not see the diggings right away. Then we stood around the hole speculating while the spruce roof leaked water in on us.

I said I thought someone having no place to bury a dog or a cat had brought it to this place and that was why the carpet of spruce needles was disturbed and there was a mound of fresh earth. The Rebels did not take kindly to the idea that someone had, without asking, buried something on our land, but I said that whatever it was it could not help but enrich the soil and maybe — I laughed a little — "bank robbers have buried their loot here and are only waiting until it is safe to come and get it!"

Even in the dim light I could see their eyes flash, and I felt a tingle myself. Then, all the way back to the house on the hill, the Rebels were mysteriously silent. When they would not come in with me, I sat on the sun porch to watch and shortly saw them hurrying along the old log fence carrying a shovel. So I put my boots back on and went once again out into the rain. By the time I came to the place, they had completed their mission and the soil was all smoothed out again. So I picked up their trail in the soft mud and took it to the road bridge and, coming up the rise, saw them on the road. I gave my little whistle and they turned and came back, and so I asked, "What did you find?"

I would not have had to ask because I could tell by their faces they had found no loot.

"Someone must have been digging worms," the youngest said.

"Yeah," exclaimed No. 2, "and probably using them to catch our trout."

I was sorry I had triggered their hopes with hints about hidden treasure, so I tried to make up for it by building a big fire in the basement fireplace so they could let the heat dry their clothes right on them and they would not have to change before going out to do the chores.

That night I sat in front of the upstairs television, not really watching it, but looking out the big window for the winking lights of airplanes, and I thought about how, when added up, I had pretty much wasted every minute of this Saturday. And I may have gone to bed somewhat disgruntled with myself, except that both Rebels sidled up, one on either side and, cuddling close, talked about what a wonderful day it had been, walking in the rain and standing in the dim light under the spruce probing the diggings for gold. So, it was then I knew that we had found it, the gold I had speculated about.

Images of autumn

My autumn: Walnut tree wearing furry squirrels. Silk sheen of milkweed spilling like frost from bursting pod. Blue blink of gentians in brown bog. Birch, white and almost naked. Wild asters wilted, purple heads hanging.

Across the lawn a wind race of leaves, whispering their excitement. First flame in the fireplace. First signal from the chimney. Stems, the masts of poplar leaves gone sailing. Willow blades still sharply green. Cress in emerald isles. Forlorn ash, shriveled leaves. Fence row of fermenting grapes. Forked sumac bare and bronze as antlers. Single apple bobbing from a bare branch.

Ferns brown and crushed, canary grass matted, vines listless and drooping, reeds broken, rushes bent. Green mist of asparagus dripping with red berries. Oak auburn, hickory tattered, chestnuts shiny as a sorrel horse's hide. Late phlox, lavender diadem. Ivy, red runner, up a green cedar. Acorns bald, fuzzy topknots gone. Fir cone bristling. Pine cone pendant, spruce cones clustering. Scarlet dogwood lancing through dying daisies. Hawthorn fruit lying like black ropes in the grass.

Ponds wearing shawls of mist against morning cold. Clouds like lace for sunbeams to filter through. Spiders sailing from chutes of silken silver. Jealous prickly ash catching thistledown for adornment. Bare sidewalks borrowing leaves to look pretty.

And the squirrels, doves, jays and woodpeckers dining side by side on the acorns dropped by the reaching white oak, but the chipmunk does not come, and now the woodchuck stays below, but the coons quarrel down by the cornfield, and the mink, finding frogs in short supply, paws through the mud for crayfish, and the muskrat piles more rushes on the mound, and the opossum munches on frozen grasshoppers.

Now the horses would rather run than walk, and the dogs pace to be let out. Penned ducks call in the night to the sound of passing flocks, but the bats no longer come to skim the ponds because the frost has cleared the air of insects. Most robins have gathered and gone, but the mourning doves have flocked and trade between fields, water and the spruce where they sleep, and the cardinals edge nearer the house with an eye to where the bird feeders will stand. Juncos flashing the white in their tails, chickadees more voluble, geese going over, glad it seems, but maybe sad.

And there is the odor of earth and burning and of dead grass and the sound of the wind in the west corner and down the chimney, and rain quick and slashing across a window, and the feel of winter beneath the door, and all the ripe things on the red formica counter, and pumpkins by the door, and red cheeks, and excitement of snow, and the feeling of solid security those rows on rows of firewood give.

Now if winter comes, all the seeds will have been sown for springtime, and the trees have taken their precious, life-giving fluid out of the high bare branches down to the safety of their roots. The squirrel's cache is full and he must fight only the blue jay for it. And I will edge my chair closer to the open fire to think on all such amazing preparations as autumn makes.

A pure spring

Snakes were out to sun on the hogsback hill with its oak slopes. There were robins in flocks and, rising from secret places in crumbling logs and from under rocks, insects came for a final fling. A frog sat on a blue rock. Small fish swam over a milky bottom to the warm shallows of a clear pool. Jays left off acorn hoarding to dust on a southern slope.

Hickory nuts were white as rain-washed stones among the tangles of sun-warmed grass and curling brown leaves. At the creek's edge, gentians opened their delicate, fringed chalices, and acres of leatherleaf stretched flat and level as a smooth, brown sea to where the hills began.

You would have thought the spring should make a sound, but there was none. The spring boiled with the force of a small geyser from a white marl bottom, but the waters went silently to the creek, clear except for quick shadows of current. The Rebels had never seen such a beautiful boil of spring water, not even at home, and they asked if it was pure. I looked around. Nowhere, except for one farm a quarter-mile away, were there any houses. So I said it was pure, and they asked: "May we drink?"

When I nodded, they knelt and, rolling their sleeves, put their palms carefully to the bottom, lowered their heads and sucked noisily. Then they immersed their faces and came up pink and smiling and drank and dunked again and again.

When they'd had enough we walked, and Rebel No. 2 asked, "What time is it?"

"Eleven-thirty," I replied.

"And what day is it?"

"November sixth." When she was silent, I asked, "Why did you want to know?"

And she told me, "I want to remember that at 11:30 on Thursday, November sixth, of this year, I drank from an unpolluted spring."

We walked a little way to where the leatherleaf gave way to a sharp slope of thinly grassed rock before I asked why she wanted to remember, and she said, "I want to remember because I may never get the chance to drink from another unpolluted spring, and when I grow up it will be something nice to think about."

It was a memorable day in other ways, because a snake, fat around as a bologna, let itself be picked up, and we discussed how incredibly smooth the center of a sunflower is when the birds have eaten the seeds and the circle softens. We learned that hickory nutting on a slope is easier than on the level, because the nuts roll and collect in windrows behind rocks, branches, tufts of grass or any other thing that will stop them, and there they wait in handfuls.

We discovered, too, that for every hill climbed there is the reward of a vista stretching away across pond and creek and field and woods to where the roads and houses begin. And for every hill climbed, there is the reward of running down it on flying feet, with incredible bounds all the way to the bottom.

Then, when we tired, there was the Indian summer sun, and we three and the dog stretched on a slope so it could wash its warmth across our bodies and we could see such magic as a spider in the oak come earthward on its web. All day it was like that, one small miracle after another, and once we almost forgot that I was carrying a gun in case a pheasant flew, for we almost left it at the base of a hickory tree where we had been gathering nuts.

It seemed even the dog knew that this was a time for things more special than hunting. When two ducks landed far below on a backwater, we did not even go down, but only watched them mark the quiet water with diving circles and swimming vees. So, perhaps it was just as well no pheasant lifted, raucous, to be gunned. Somehow it would have spoiled the day to get blood on my fingers when I picked it up. Because this was one of those days to remember for other things, for snakes and gentians and jays, and how we all went to our knees and bowed our heads to drink the bubbling water of an unpolluted spring.

Telltale trees

A planter of trees, perhaps unwittingly, marks the years of his life, and the inquisitive can point to the seasons he loafed by the size, shape and condition of his plantation. If his trees tell about the spring he sat watching summer come, or the summer he failed to carry enough water to defeat the drought, the trees are also a tribute to the seasons when all his life juices flowed in vigorous abandon and he put down many roots and tended them well. They stand now as a tribute to his burst of enthusiasm.

But more important than the record is the somewhat rare and thoroughly wonderful fact that he was able to live long enough on the same place so he now can see the maples he tended as sprouts billow and cascade in autumnal glory, and finally know that the once-tiny junipers have risen high enough to look down on their own seedlings where the wind cast them marching up the hill.

And if it took sweat, then how much more refreshing was the breeze? Because now in the summing up, that same breeze is abruptly stilled when it comes up against the solid walls of cedars, which rise green and high where once the shores of Fish Pond were a stony waste. And where Clear Pool with mud-streaked shores once lay naked to the sun, now there are willows in solid phalanx to shade the waters. So, no matter what life sometimes brings, I can count myself among the winners when I remember how once a child, now long gone to have children of her own, trimmed the tiny spruce that are so high now no ladder can put rungs up to their spires.

Then if there is a remembered sadness because all the umbrella elms died, there is inspiration in the precipitous thrust of other trees. Basswood, sprout to house-high in fifteen years. Birch, from fragile, speckled wand to white lance against the sky. Oak, three leaves on bending stem to sturdy trunk braced to pass the century mark. Cherry, all kinds, and poplar going wild and higher to top even the eager basswoods.

And sometimes, if I cannot remember, there are pictures to prove that where the bush pantry is now — a jungle of blackberry, dogwood, honeysuckle, mulberry, cedar, spruce, daisy, rose, fern, myriad trees and bushes — a mouse once might have been hard-put to hide.

So I am charitable to myself, and I use it as a balm against the bad days. Then, I look at the pictures, or out the window, and see the whole scene. As heady as the accomplishment may seem, I know that there are areas of regret — a copse with stunted spruce that starved for water, a ragged slash of cedars suffocated in grass, an acre never planted — things of the conscience not even now forgotten.

Listening to the night

Through the white curtains of lace, the moon put a rectangle of light on the green carpet and the edge of our bed. The last Rebel had come in, and we heard the night latch click, heard the yard light switch as she snapped it off. There were no airplanes overhead, nor any trucks grinding along the highway. Not even a dog barked, and the throb of crickets had become so subdued it was likely only an echo in our minds when, up from the ponds, loud and clear and commanding, came the wild quack of a mallard hen.

Gwen raised up in bed and asked, "Did you hear that?"

"Yes," I said, "wild ones going through." The hen quacked again, and then, in a guttural of undertones, drakes added what seemed like assent, and then there must have been a whole flock sounding off with such wild and bold abandon that we both came wide awake, and Gwen decided, "I'm going down. I want to see them."

"They'll never let you get close enough."

"But maybe they will."

"No they won't."

And then the mallards quacked again, and it occurred to me that this was the night before the duck season, and I remembered a night when long ago, for the first time, I had come to Schwantes Point just as the sun was setting. I had come with a little carrying case of five live decoys, and when they felt the lake breeze through the bars of their cage, they exulted, and up from the marshes, which closed on both sides of the hogsback peninsula, twenty or fifty or a hundred wild ones answered them, and then a dozen hunting dogs in waiting cars barked.

I lay back down. "That's how it was," I said, "when I was a boy, and we came the night before with live decoys and a dog, and piled hay in our boat and rowed out in the moonlight to hide in the rushes."

My wife lay back down, too. "It must have been thrilling."

"Yes, it was. Especially the night. Much more thrilling than the next day of shooting. There was something shrouded, mysterious about the night."

"Men and boys don't do it anymore?" She made it a question.

"None that I know of," I said.

The ducks down on the pond quacked again, all together, in an outburst that awakened the dogs in their kennel on the hill, and they caught the excitement of the wild things and added their voices to the clamor.

"What was best about it?" Gwen asked.

"About what?"

"When you were a boy?"

"Best was lying in the boat with the sweet-smelling hay all around, and looking up at the moon to see what shadows were passing. Sometimes you knew it was a blue heron by the span of its wings, and sometimes you knew it was teal by the swiftness of its passing, and sometimes you knew it was only a swirl of blackbirds rousted from their night camp by some hunters."

We did not say anything then, but there were footfalls upstairs, so we surmised one of the children had heard, too, and had gone to a window to look down.

"What is there about the sound of a bird or a duck in the night?" Gwen asked.

"I don't know, but it is like nothing else."

So we did not sleep for a long time, and finally the dogs quieted, and then the mallard hens did not call again, but we could intermittently hear the calmer, quieter quacking of a drake, so we knew they were still there.

Finally, Gwen said, "You lived during a good time."

I thought about that, then said, "Yes, it was a good time. But tonight is a good time, too. We are mystified and thrilled even though we aren't lying in a boat of fragrant hay out in the middle of a marsh."

"Yes, we are. But do you think there are other people having thrills like this?"

"I'm sure of it."

"But how, if they live where there are no ducks?"

"On hearing a goose honking overhead. On hearing the muffled thunder of the nighthawks diving. On hearing the crickets. On seeing a shadow against the moon. On hearing wings."

"Even in cities?"

"Even in cities. If they are listening. If they are looking."

Swirling leaves

If I should come down another thousand rivers, worship at another thousand sunsets, be awed by another thousand raging seas, I will never be so inspired as a during five minutes while, on a high hill, I watched the wind fill the valley below with the ebb and flow of a million swirling leaves.

And if I blush again with spring at the naked beauty of a first white bloodroot, turn miraculously tan under the unabashed sun of still another sultry summer, beat back once more with vigor the winter ice from the threshold of my home, I still will never come quite as close to the universal mysteries as during that autumn moment on the high hill above the swirling swale of color.

Right then I knew that the word brown had so many millions of meanings that it would take more than all the pages of all the books ever written to describe each. Right then I knew that not one single red, now, before or ever, was precisely like any other red, and that the shades of yellow outnumbered the sands, the stones, the stars.

Then as I watched, and the wind quieted and the leaves settled to lacquer the land, I knew I would never again need the word of God or any man to tell me that I was as unique and as grand and as much a part of the purpose as was every beech, butternut, oak or maple leaf a special part of that great cyclone of color.

And I knew then that if I had come only from the Rescue Mission to the Milwaukee River bank, from a Beaver Dam back-country farm to an Ivory Tower, from a birthing beneath a palm to death beneath another palm, I counted, I mattered, and I was as important and unique as each and every leaf was important to that moment when the forest set its summer legions charging down the valley on the winds of death.

And then and there I knew I had come to at least the edge of comprehension. And if I am still not able to describe or fully comprehend, I have felt and touched the mystery of infinity and eternity. And maybe that is something special for a mere mortal, a rare gift to come that close, during the late afternoon of a dying October, to the mystical magic that makes the mouse that steals my corn as much a part of the purpose as an Aristotle or an Einstein.

Finest firewood

Once we were wealthy, rich in firewood, so the sadness we felt in seeing the great elms die was somewhat ameliorated by the dancing fires that brightened our hearths for more than a decade of winters.

But the last elm logs will have been burned before this winter takes its place in Little Lakes history. Then, if more than a hundred trees went up in the smoke of our chimneys and now spread ashes as food for ferns and a multitude of other growing things, when winter again comes sneaking in on some November wind, we will have to lay the sacrificial chunks from some other tree species to warm the tips of our toes and fingers and brighten those bleak corners of which every mind seems to have its share.

We would like it to be oak. But I cannot think of anything more sacrilegious than the wanton destruction of what oaks we have, because they stand in full maturity, rugged symbols of the kind of strength we envy. Then hickory? Walnut? But these are so few, and then how would the squirrels feel? Maple? When it takes a man's allotted three score and ten years to bring their arching branches to where the bright leaves touch a bedroom window?

Well, how about spruce or pine or cedar? But they are not yet middle-aged, and who would, who could, come cutting through their groves, which stand as bulwarks against the snow and cold for every wintering bird? Basswood then? And lose the perfume of their yellow, clustering flowers, which invite every bee from acres around to give a summer hum to almost any lazy afternoon?

Black cherry? When careful hands may turn their talents into such things of rich, velvety beauty as can be carved from the hearts of few other trees? Some wood is just too beautiful to burn. We have some wild black cherry logs drying in the stable, and we wonder if we will ever be able to bring them to the fireplace.

But, what then? Is there no tree for the ultimate sacrifice? No ambitious, easy grower we can cut and dry and light to make our winter home into an oasis of warmth, a corner place of cheer against the night-black cold? Ah yes, but there is one. Two, in fact. And if neither has such sterling qualities for burning as any others of their ilk, then they at least without reluctance, yea, even willingly, put flame fingers high in both our chimneys. Then, if they have a weakness, it is their very eagerness. Touch a match and their pyramid of logs has turned to ash before you are comfortably back into the book you just put down to strike the fire.

No nightlong, reliant, steadfast burners like elm or oak. No desultory log of embers, and hardly a flame, as with cherry. Quick they are, like sunshine briefly between clouds, and then you have to rise from the warmth of the chair whose leather seems to fold like the years around your frame and, sighing, replenish the already dying fire. But, if they burn fast, they grow fast, sprouting from any fallen branch with an overpowering need to thrust so high they are ready for the saw within fifteen years. Our various colonies, both poplar and weeping willow, started from cuttings hardly fifteen years ago and spread today across and into every corner of this place with a determination that has startled and stifled less ambitious trees out of many a year's growth.

So there they stand, thirty and forty and fifty feet high! Arms of one entangled in the arms of another. Welter of branches arching, pushing, crowding, enveloping, preempting. Unmerciful trees, sucking water and every earthy nutrient to come crowding out and above other trees ten times their age. But then the snarling saw for twenty days now, every afternoon, until row upon row of fireplace logs stand like walls of little cabins beneath the spruce where the rain will wet them less, and so in due time they will come light and dry to vanish, except in the once-bleak corners of some mind, where then they will be warm memories.

The hottest fire

The hottest fire? Surely not apple or birch, nor any of the aspens or willows. Oak, hickory? One of the wild or tame cherries? Likely not. Pine knots blaze and spit and sputter, but they do not require the heat level necessary to make an elm log blaze. It may need the services of such demons as allegedly tend hell's fires to get an elm log flaming, but once it does, back away, brother.

Thrill is gone

I shot two Canada geese yesterday. Killed them outright, swiftly and surely out of a flock of fifteen. It was a dramatic moment. I was waist-deep in the muck of a marsh, the rain was coming down hard. My excited dog, hanging on to the side of a new muskrat house, watched them fall. There were two shots, one for each goose, at the so-called moment of truth.

But the old thrill was missing. That feeling the hunter experiences at having bested the hunted was not there. During other yesterdays I would have gathered in the geese, and when my children's eyes widened, I would have experienced the satisfaction my cave dweller ancestors once knew on bringing meat into the family circle. But all I felt now was some relief that I was not too old to wallow in waders through a morass most men were avoiding, and a certain sense of gratification that my reflexes were still good, that I could still shoot quickly and straight.

The high moment of my afternoon afield came when a tiny marsh wren, tail flirting inquisitively, decided to investigate my presence. I was more excited at seeing a whole summer of swallows rise in a great flock to meet the rain drops.

Better than killing the geese was watching their maneuvers as they came over high, thirty in all, and then, dividing their flock, circled warily earthward.

When their query went unanswered, it was I who honked about how safe it was down in the marsh. Then I watched them lose altitude in long, swinging sweeps of flight. When they were at treetop level, I almost forgot I had a gun because I could see their white check patches, and the finger ends of their flying feathers, and I thought about the flat, wild tundra country they had just left and the steaming southern marshes awaiting them.

Maybe I shot because for most of the years of my life I have thrown a gun to my shoulder when a target flies by, and most of the time I have almost instinctively pulled the trigger at the precise moment to make the kill. Not that I felt sorry I had killed the geese. I did not feel sorry. I am still enough of a hunter to take my pound of pride in having seduced the flock with a few plaintive honks, of having picked my birds and caught them dead in the center of my circle of shot. No, there wasn't any remorse. But there was no exhilaration either, and only the dog was beside himself with joy as I shouldered the two birds and began the long, hard pull for high ground.

Of course, what bothers me most is that I always thought maturity would bring answers to all the questions I have always been asking. And now I discover that maturity only brings more questions. I do not know just why it is no longer important that I kill a duck or a goose or a deer or catch a fish. And, what is more, I am suspicious of people who think they have the answers to questions like that.

Artist at work

The Rebel Queen nestles a bulb into the loam as if she is tucking a baby into bed. She fluffs the earth beneath and then runs the covering ground through her fingers so it lies lightly. Crocuses, daffodils and tulips, and I say to her, "But winter will harden the earth."

Still she goes on planting as if each bulb is very special. So I think she mostly likes the feel of soil and the round, fleshy feel of the bulbs. I think, too, she has an instinct in her fingers for painting black earth with riotous or sometimes subdued colors, and I think she has the vision of the true artist who sees the gray canvas already alive, even before the brush lays on the first daub of paint.

The oldest elm

The oldest elm, which had probably one hundred apartments, has finally crashed. Year after year, winds tore branches until finally it stood as a spire reaching above all other trees, a pinnacle of strength. But snow, freezing rain and wind finally weakened fibers. Then, on the day of a punishing storm, the elm tottered, gained momentum and hit the ground, breaking into a thousand pieces.

The tree should have come down ten years ago, but how can you evict starlings, flickers, woodpeckers, raccoons, squirrels and some of the millions of insects that found comfort in the tree's punky interior? The tree had been dead for a decade. It was dangerous standing there, but we could not cut it because of the community of ants and the opossums, bees and screech owls, a hundred, a thousand, tens of thousands of creatures boring the trunk, pecking out their homes, chiseling their burrows.

So we let the tree stand. Sometimes we were worried that it might fall on a horse, a dog, a child, but every time we decided to bring it to earth a sparrow would carry a feather forty feet up to a round hole, and the saw went back to the garage. We knew it was dangerous to let it stand. We knew that some people thought it ugly, rising stark against the sky. But to us, looking up to the hill where it towered over every other living thing, it was of striking beauty.

So we never cut it, though we could have used the wood. We talked about it often, but in the evening we would hear the screech owls in its burrows waiting for night, and we would see the chipmunks crawl beneath the roots for a nap. So we waited and waited. After every windy night, we looked out and there it would be, a monument to all the life that had gone before it. And we would sigh and say, "Well, it looks like it will stand forever."

But of course we knew it would not. We only hoped that when it came down, it would fall clear of the pines that clustered about it, clear of the dogs and children who played on the hill. And it did. It fell clear of all the things we cherish, and it broke into many pieces, and it is good that it fell in autumn, a time there were no young birds in its scores and scores of apartments. And that those who might have been sleeping there, or only resting, managed to fly, jump or scoot to safety.

So now there remain only two dead elms. Although we are going to cut them, we will put up houses of all shapes and sizes on smaller trees so the birds and animals may again come back to Little Lakes and say, "This is our home."

Sequined singer

Hawks scream, but the sky holds no sailing silhouettes. A mallard quacks, but there are no ducks here on the hill. Squirrels chatter, but I have just routed them from the feeder and they are in the safety of a hollow tree. Sitting on the hill watching the ponds below change color, I hear the piercing whistle that the Rebels use to call the horses, but the Rebels are in school. There are snatches of melody, but the windows are closed, and anyway neither television nor radio is being played. Even a faraway crow swerves in flight when it hears a caw like one of its own calling.

All the sounds are made by a flock of small birds grouped in the top branches of twin lindens. When the sun shines, they seem to be feathered in multicolored sequins. In the shade, they are drab and dumpy. This is the bird who steals homes that flickers and woodpeckers have worked so strenuously to round out. It is the bird who routs squirrels from their dens and drives even cats from this range. It is hated by most people, and seemingly despised by all other birds. An outlaw, an outcast, the starling could not care less.

Some people we know are like starlings: they have a different voice for every occasion. The only difference is, starlings know they aren't fooling anyone.

Waning days

Brig, our German shorthaired pointer, never good for much except loving and being loved, is dying. Now, at Little Lakes, poignant as the death of a pet can be, it hardly qualifies as news, since in twenty years there have been hundreds of deaths of pet seagulls, raccoons, woodchucks, opossums, squirrels, horses, dogs, chipmunks, rabbits and you name it.

Except that Brig's death, when it happens, will be the exclamation point to the end of an era, because from here on out, as pets die they will not be replaced. Sitting with Brig sometimes to ease his last weeks with the kind of ear scratching that still delights him, we look back on

Reflections, like memories, are always more perfect than the real thing.

a lifetime of dogs and are surprised that there were so many we often forget the names of some of the lesser lights.

But if the names escape us, the details of each death are still a sharply etched memory, because the death of a pet is one of those things we have never been able to accept with equanimity. Yet it is not the poignancy of their passing with which we are now concerned, but how, accidentally or otherwise, the deaths of many of our dogs have marked the ends of clear-cut segments of our own lives. Though there have been four Bucks, my first was a mongrel arriving about the time of my tenth birthday, and his passing marked the end of adolescence and the beginning of manhood.

Then there was Sad, a diminutive black cocker acquired to fit city living standards, and when she died it marked the end of my apartment living days. The death of Rainey, the dog who accompanied me to happy hunting grounds all across the continent, marked the end of my days as a rod-and-gun writer. After he was buried, rarely did I come to the frosty glades where the partridge lived, trudge the pheasant meadows, or hunker down in a duck blind.

And so now Brig, and when he passes on we will mark the beginning of still one more segment of life and the passing of another. Gradually, now that there is only one child at home full-time, there will arrive unusually quiet times rarely interrupted by the neigh of a hungry horse, the barking of an irate dog, the necessity of looking to the needs of rabbit or duck, tame crow or friend raccoon. From here on out, all animals that cannot fend for themselves will be phased out, and we cannot now decide whether we will welcome the change or if we will sometimes look to the pasture, forgetting there are no horses there.

It will not all happen at once, so perhaps we will gradually become accustomed to it. Inevitably, however, Little Lakes will become a ghost place where only the spirits of a thousand gone-but-not-forgotten pets still live. Then, likely, when they are all gone, we will go, too, perhaps to an apartment in Milwaukee, and then maybe a younger couple will come to Little Lakes to raise their brood, and the horses and dogs will come back, and the days once more will be filled with the necessity of caring for tame raccoons.

Be that as it may, we are now counting down. Already we are down to one rabbit. When Brig dies, there will be only two dogs. They may live another five or six years. The horses are likely to go before them, as some of the children talk about taking them to homes of their own. And that is the way it is out here, now that Brig is dying and we are entering what apparently is the final phase of our Little Lakes idyll.

BOOK THREE

Introduction

In late 1973, "Notes From Little Lakes" appeared for the last time in The Milwaukee Journal. *Three years later, the column resurfaced as a regular feature in the bimonthly magazine* Wisconsin Sportsman. *It continued there through 1982.*

These last columns reached a far smaller audience than those published Sundays in The Journal, *yet they represent some of Ellis' finest writings.*

As Book Three begins, most of the hard work is done at Little Lakes. All the Rebels except Mary, the youngest, have moved on. Most of the animals are gone. The days of pond building are over.

Ellis and Gwen, the Rebel Queen, still nurture the land, even planting trees for wood lots they may never see reach maturity. But now there is time to look around and appreciate "what the land hath wrought."

As Ellis reflects on the fruits of three decades of work, he spells out his vision of human beings and their place in the natural order.

Most entries in Book Three originally appeared in Wisconsin Sportsman. *A few come from writings about Little Lakes that appeared from time to time in "The Good Earth" and "Afield With Ellis," two columns Ellis wrote for* The Milwaukee Journal *from the early 1970s to the early 1980s.*

~ T.J.R.

chapter one

THE LAST GOOD-BYE

From where I sit, I can see the youngest of my five Rebels walking slowly among the trees, shuffling through fallen leaves. She pauses often and sometimes puts a hand to a cheek to flick a finger at what I am sure is a tiny tear.

The last of the clan left at home, this Rebel is no child. Tomorrow, she leaves for her sophomore year at the University of Wisconsin. Today, she is saying good-bye to the dogs, a favorite tree, a watching woodchuck, a redbird cocking a bright eye. There still will be dragon-flies, wings varnished by sunshine. Perhaps a cricket will chirp tentatively. Cottontails will run a short distance and then stop to stare, their wide, brown eyes knowing they have nothing to fear. Turtles will still be testing the noonday sun on a half-submerged log.

I am sure she will stop at the Indian mounds, wondering whether brave, squaw or papoose is buried there. She will pluck a cluster of wild grapes and grimace at the tart, almost sour taste. She may pick several cattail wands or cocoons of milkweed silk. There will be a cray-fish, and it will scuttle backwards when she reaches for it.

All day she will wander slowly from pond to pond, up the creek, through the bush pantry, up the hill among the pines, into the marsh. She will stand often, savoring a scene so that she may flash it back on the mirror of her mind when the snow is deep and that alien place called Madison becomes almost too raucous to be tolerable.

Then, at last, she will come up the hill and walk past the white house to come to the cemetery. Finding a log, a boulder, or perhaps an abandoned ant hummock, she will sit. Here, she will say her last good-byes and, though there are no tombstones, I am sure she can put her palm precisely on the grave of a seagull named Soar, a white duck named Waddle, a dog named Rainey, a hundred, maybe two hundred friends who are woven forever into the fabric of her life. I've tried to teach her that death should be a celebration because only in dying does every living thing ensure the subsequent survival of unnumbered generations.

If, while I am looking, she smiles, I will know her heart is aching to touch once more a banty rooster named Poncho, a white-footed mouse named Ossie. I suppose she is also remembering sunny days when she took the top speedsters from her stable of painted turtles to race them against turtles from the stables of her sisters. Rosy van Etta the mallard, Tattoo the homing pigeon, Copperking the pheasant cock, Whacky the woodchuck, they are all out there feeding a colony of knee-high spruce with such strength as is left in their bones.

Eventually, she will get up and move among the trees. I know also that I will be tempted to go out and put an arm around her, but I will not. As the shadows lengthen, she will come in. Supper will be waiting. She will hurry through the kitchen to feel the soothing cool waters of the bathroom tap. She will regain her composure. Then, by the time we are seated at the table, the talk will be about last-minute packing to ensure an early start for Madison in the morning.

It is a scene that will be repeated next year, the following year, and the year after that, until, one day, just when nobody knows, she will have a home of her own. Then, I am sure, there will be another Poncho, another Copperking, friends of hers and her children.

She already knows that it can happen and only hopes that it will. She knows it can happen because it has already happened to another young woman, her oldest sister, who watches deer from her window and is up to her chin in dogs, cats, snakes and toads.

Then perhaps, just as I have tried, she too will hope to teach her children that death should be a celebration. But she will never forget the day when a tiny dog licked her little girl's hand and then sprawled at her feet, adoration beaming from her amber eyes. It happens. I know, because it happened to me.

chapter two

YEAR OF THE ETERNAL FLAME

Having always kept a surplus of fireplace wood from trees brought down by storms, we decided years ago to install a fireplace in the basement.

Ben Navarre, a stonemason and fireplace builder of local renown, came out of retirement and agreed to do the job if I would help him lift the heavier fieldstones into place. Ben's fireplace, with properly aged wood of reasonably hard fiber, could in the space of half an hour boost the temperature of the rambling, three-room basement from fifty to ninety degrees. While the fireplace burned, members of the family could walk barefoot upstairs no matter how chilly those rooms might otherwise be.

Few were the nights that flames did not flicker in the fireplace. There were snapping, crackling fires of resinous conifers. There were subdued and steady flames of hardwoods. There were glowing ember fires of punky poplars. There were quick, hot fires of many little logs, and the nightlong flames of tremendous logs that hardly fit the grate. The most spectacular fires were those that roared through the hollowed logs of what once was a huge linden. Instead of rolling these logs in, we placed them flat over hot coals. Then the draft raced up through the hollowed-out middle, and there was a roaring volcano of flame.

One winter, we kept the hearth warm by never letting the fire go out, from November to April. We did not plan the marathon fire. Each morning for a week there were live embers, so someone would throw wood on, and presto! A blaze. One of the Rebels remarked one day, "Neat! The fire's been going nonstop for seven days."

That started it. There seemed to be a nonverbal agreement to keep the flames alive. Then, after four or five weeks, another of the Rebels said, "Gee, it's been a month now."

That was when I said, "Let's see how long we can keep it burning."

Well, the basement has places for stacks and stacks of wood, but we were hardly into the new year when we had to press Bumpy, the old truck, into service to haul logs from outside reserves. After a couple of months, keeping the fire alive became a contest. The last person in at night checked it. The first one up in the morning added logs. Anyone making a bathroom visit during the night took a run downstairs to check on what by then we called the eternal flame.

Fieldstones of the fireplace became heated through, and we had the chief of the volunteer fire department check the chimney to make sure we were not setting ourselves up as victims of a barbecue.

"Fine, fine," the chief said. "Good firebricks. No danger."

So, January blazed merrily into February. Once, the fire almost died. On arising, we found a green log hardly half consumed. There was no flame, no smoke, no crackling. Taking the poker, I rolled the log in the grate. A tiny wisp of smoke curled. Then a thread of flame wavered, got a better grip, and grew, and spread. The fire burned on.

When I was bitten by one of those tenacious bugs that doctors, for want of a better name, call a virus, the Rebel Queen took over my job of tending the fireplace. The eternal flame so intrigued her that she also kept a steady fire in the upstairs fireplace, which had been only inter-mittently lighted. Finally, our last chunk of wood had gone to the fire. I would have left it at that, let the fire die, but there were accusing looks because, by that time, nobody wanted the fire to go out. So, I sharpened the chain saw and, as far away as the school, the Rebels could hear it snarl.

With the fire going, windy, wet March did not seem as interminable as it usually does. By April, thousands of dreary hours had been made bright, and many a lofty dream had been given a blazing assist.

Then it happened. On April 8, sap from a green log leaked down on red coals while everyone slept, and the fire died in a sizzle of acrid smoke. It was in its twenty-first week of continuous flame. For rough-ly five months, upwards of three thousand five hundred hours, the fireplace had been the glowing heart of the home.

It was like a death in the family. Nobody said anything. We sat in the kitchen, looking sad. Then, one by one, we followed the sunlight's brief path to our green rug and went outside. There, we were surprised to see that purple violets had crept out onto the lawn, that the creek was gold-plated with marigolds, that the hill was awash with white and pink Mayflowers. Winter was over and, instead of a time of cold agony, it had provided a glowing interlude.

When a Rebel went to the basement to do homework or watch tele-vision, she was never alone. The fire was always there, and it was living, like a friend. All winter, when the Rebels arose long before dawn to do chores, the fire dispelled the shadows and put warm, dancing colors into the most remote corners. Then, when their chores were finished, it quickly warmed their cold toes and fingers.

For the Rebel Queen and me, the fire, changing colors like a sunset, seemed to melt the irritating incidents of the day. Sometimes it was a leaping brightness that cast color to the stones. Sometimes it was a steady, blue flame that spread intense heat. Mornings, it was a glow of dull, red embers, slumbering like everyone else in the house until it was fed afresh.

Its brilliance and warmth soothed aching hearts, laid fears to rest, melted worries. To sit and look into the red heart of it, and at the blue-tipped flames, was to watch today's and tomorrow's problems lift up the chimney with the smoke.

I have been told some people have fireplaces but never start fires in them because they might leave a residue of soot on the firebricks or otherwise smudge the cleanliness of a room. Each to his own, but for me, a fireplace without a fire is like a house without people. Just as it takes warm, beating hearts to make a house a home, so it takes flames to make a fireplace.

chapter three

THE WOOD
LOT WE SHALL
NEVER SEE

Now that the horses have gone, the pasture has become the number one work project at Little Lakes. During the horses' tenure, more than twenty years, they systematically girdled the trees with their persistent nibbling until, except for a growth of burr oak, a scattering of scaly-barked silver maples and two monstrous lindens, they decimated what was once a four-acre wood lot.

The plantings began last year, and already two swales are putting up some one hundred white cedar spires, and there is a colony of black spruce tightly grouped as a bird fortress against any wind. There is a tight community of honey locust, and aspen with quaking leaves are putting roots through the topsoil into old Indian graves. A scattering of box elders and silver maples rising from seed are being thinned, a few select trees being spared and given special attention.

Our plan calls for an orchard — apple, cherry and plum — never to be sprayed because the fruits are intended for the wild ones. All plantings will be grouped according to species. We hope for a nice grove of fifty to a hundred mountain ash. There are plans for a sugar maple settlement. There will be a southern border of black walnut, several rows of white pine, and intermittent exclamation marks of tightly grouped junipers.

There will be others, all except the fruit trees coming from an over-abundance of seedlings already establishing thick undergrowth on other Little Lakes acres. Many were transplanted last fall. With all our slave labor gone off to homes of their own, it will not be a one-season crash program, but an ongoing chore of digging holes, setting seedlings, tamping soil around roots. It would be somewhat heroic to say it does not matter that we live long enough to see the trees come to such maturity as guarantees reproduction. Of course, we think about that. And, of course, we sometimes feel a little sad and even perhaps depressed that we will not be there when the walnut trees bear.

But it is a transient mood, rarely interfering in this partnership we have with nature to accommodate our small talents as best we know how to her own special talents for knowing about where things should grow. Not that we haven't wanted to smack her pretty face when she plays tricks and sometimes goes on a rampage. Then we sit back and say, "Damn, why did you go and do that?"

Of course, we already know how the pasture will look in ten or twenty or fifty years. That is the trick, the secret of carrying through with a plan from which we will never directly benefit. That is our reward, this mind picture we keep before us of how the wood lot will someday look. Oh, sure, sometimes we try to sound noble by saying we are doing it for future generations and to make the earth a better place. And there is some truth in that, but what really motivates us is that we already can see how it will look. We already know how cool and sweet-smelling and green it will be. And what is more beautiful than that?

So, as we sweat from one planting hole to another, as my old bones protest and my leaky lungs wheeze, we keep the picture bright. We even know, when we permit ourselves to think about it, that the wood lot in our minds is probably much prettier than the real one will be after insects, wind, frost and sun and other natural hazards take their toll. So, as we plant in the springtime of this wood lot and the autumn of our years, we cannot even blame the horses for what they did to the original grove of trees, because, did you ever see such well-manured soil?

It is rich, rich with the droppings of two decades of overfed horses. Where in some places there once was hardly six inches of topsoil, now there is twelve, and it has real horsepower for growing tall trees quickly. So, perhaps our mind picture is not so far removed from reality after all. Maybe our new little forest will be as beautiful and sweet-smelling as the one we picture in our minds.

That gives us a fresh shot of adrenaline, and we put old Bumpy, the truck, into reverse, swing him about, and go racing back for another load of seedlings, because there are clouds on the western horizon, and we want to get more seedlings into their planting holes so the approaching storm may water them down.

chapter four

PEG LEG PETE

Imagine awakening and coming to the kitchen for coffee, only to find the table covered with the remnants of surgery: medicine bottles and such surgical tools as a razor-sharp knife, scissors, rubber bands, tiny splints and a tweezers. It happened to the Rebel Queen one morning years ago. Rebel No. 2, always first up and outside, came to the house shortly after daybreak with a wild mallard drake who had been caught in a muskrat trap. I was at the kitchen table and, having viewed the mangled leg, set my coffee aside to give first aid. I applied a tourniquet, fashioned splints from a wooden ice cream spoon and tried to set the leg. But it was broken beyond repair, and amputation was the only proper surgical procedure. Snip! Off came the leg. Then I loosened the tourniquet to let a fresh supply of blood down.

By then, Rebel No. 3, still in her long red nightgown, took over the job of cleanup nurse. While she sponged, Rebel No. 2 held the duck upside down so I could work on him. Since there is no muscle, only tendons, in a duck's leg, I left the tourniquet on and applied compresses, and then a big bandage held in place with rubber bands to cushion the sore stump. The drake had no sooner come off the operating table than the Rebel Queen came into the kitchen and, even before coffee and still with a morning stomach, had to look down on the grisly scene.

The drake had lost so much blood we doubted he would live. But, live he did. Three days after the operation, he was doing fine in a box in the basement, gobbling corn we put down, angrily pecking the Rebels' hands. The stump healed, and the duck could stand erect and maneuver well. He could take off and come to a perfect one-point landing with hardly a wobble. We decided to make him a peg leg. After considering and rejecting many materials, I settled on cork and, using the butt section of an old spinning rod, hollowed it out so it fit over the stump. I strapped it in place with leather laces from an old boot. But the duck, accustomed to skittering around on one leg, just tucked the peg leg up under his feathers and refused to use it.

Peg Leg Pete become one of the residents of Little Lakes. Eventually, he went from his box in the basement out to the poultry pen where we kept, at that time, an assortment of ducks, rabbits and other pets. Each day during that winter, it became increasingly apparent that Peg Leg would not survive on land. So, one cold day, we took him down to where the springs keep Watercress Creek from freezing. With considerable misgivings, we set him free. He floated well for awhile, but then, because he had been out of the water for so long, his oil glands failed and he gradually began to sink.

We waded into the creek thinking to rescue him but, by propelling himself with his wings, he stayed beyond our grasp. Finally, wet and half frozen, we gave up and went back up to the house to thaw out. We did not see the drake until two days later. We were crossing the bridge in a car on our way to church, and there, standing on his one good leg, firmly planted on a submerged rock, stood Peg Leg.

All that winter we scattered corn in the shallows. There were days when the thermometer went below zero, and always Peg Leg looked disconsolate, miserable. Several times we regretted having let him go and tried to recapture him, but he always eluded us, and by spring he was swimming so well that his one good leg was not putting him into a continuous circle. Still, he had not tried his wings, and when the thaw came and the other ducks who grouped in the creek moved down into Clear Pool and on across to the mill pond, Peg Leg did not follow.

Each day, on crossing the bridge, we saw him alone on the surface of the creek, and then the Rebels tried to herd him south to where the motley collection of ducks was foraging on tendrils. But he would not pass the bridge, and it was not until a May day when all three dogs suddenly converged on his sanctuary that he pushed himself aloft with his one good leg and a powerful downbeat of wings. Then there he was, flying high over the billowy willows all dressed out in new green leaves, over the marsh, to angle down and glide to a crooked halt where the other ducks were grouped near the shore of the mill pond.

In the ensuing years, he had a lot of narrow escapes that we know of — from hawks, from dogs, from boys with pellet guns or slingshots. We suppose he also had his share of escapes we did not know of — from mink and fox and some of the big boar opossums who patrolled these shores. But he survived, learned to swim straight, became stronger than most ducks on the wing, and even dared to make lawn landings to get in on some of the corn and bread that were always being spread. Perhaps his greatest triumph came one spring when there was only one hen for an assortment of nine drakes, and he bested the bunch by getting her and siring a brood of ducklings.

Sometimes, however, he would disappear, and then we would ask our neighbor, Mrs. Sybil Yug, when we met her at the post office, if she had seen him. Usually she would say "Yes," and explain that he was on the mill pond with her ducks. But sometimes she would say, "No," and then we would wonder if something had finally caught him, or if he had died of disease or old age, or if he had flown as far as the Fox River and some hunter was wondering about the one-legged duck he had shot.

Yet always, for years, he turned up. And if we did not see him most of one autumn, then in winter he would gravitate back to Clear Pool or Watercress Creek with the other ducks on their way to the last of the open water. Of course, he could not go on forever, but then neither can you or I. But to have lived all those years completely on his own, in somewhat severe surroundings, with but one good leg to help him over the hurdles — that is an accomplishment of which many might feel proud.

chapter five

THE MOST BOUNTIFUL SUMMER

If Bernice, the first Rebel Queen, could come back to see what the land hath wrought, she might be reluctant to return to whichever heaven death whisked her. Especially since, in more than twenty-five years, Little Lakes has never had such a lush summer as the one now being preempted by autumn. When Bernice died sixteen years ago, the future of Little Lakes was at a critical crossroads. The three clumps of ferns brought from Door County had spread to just nine. Only a single, sickly bittersweet clung to a rotting stump, producing no blooms or berries, since it had no mate, and bittersweet, like men and women, must travel in pairs to reproduce.

The six-hundred-fifty-foot-long regiment of white cedar was but a pallid, sparse and not very promising windbreak along the eastern bank of Fish Pond. Wild asparagus was as rare as Indian arrowheads. The now-towering spruce were all but suffocated each summer by such ruffians as burdock, prickly ash, quack and sword grass, not to mention stinging nettles. Most of the elms, some as big around as hippopotamuses, were dying from Dutch elm disease. Ninebark, wild plum, wauputo, water lilies, wild cherries, thousands of plantings had either been ravaged by rodents or insects or had just disappeared, victims of drought or frost or unsuitable habitat.

Luckily, however, instead of mourning the passing of the elms, we celebrated such triumphs as the surprising growth of a single birch clump, sole survivor from a planting of two hundred and fifty. Instead of weeping over our failures, we discovered amazement in canary grass, which in some places topped eight feet. If Fish Pond froze out at about three-year intervals, we were gratified that Blue, Clear and New Pools always had water and oxygen to spare. If we did not have enough money to buy a truck for hauling rocks for riprapping, we were grateful to spread a tarpaulin in the family station wagon and settle for one meager load at the end of each working day.

Lord, I do not know how Bernice put up with it, having a passel of kids and a husband always tired from trying to make one more buck to add to the dragline and bulldozer fund. That is why I wish she could meet Gwen, the tiny fireball who came to pick up the pieces of a fragmented family and a small oasis on the verge of going back to desert habitat. If she could see those ferns now! Hundreds of clumps, faithfully tended by Gwen, spread to half-a-dozen areas, all standing straight and tall as hoe handles and green as emerald seas.

And that regiment of cedar! A nigh impenetrable barrier rising taller than any ladder on the place, filling the air with a fragrance that can turn a man's head more quickly than the perfume of any woman. There is no room to write it all or, for that matter, even a miniscule portion of what this land hath wrought. Though all the elms have disappeared in smoke up the fireplace chimney, there are already second generation trees a foot in diameter. And the ninebark has taken over pockets and filled them with such dense growth that there are seeds enough for any wintertime army of bird occupation.

The brambles, held in check, bow low to the ground, laden with berries. Limbs of the mulberries, when the fruit was ripe, threatened to break. Fish Pond's aerator not only prevents freezeouts but keeps the water open for visiting ducks. Asparagus? You could never eat it all. Wauputo, cherries, lilies, a hundred wildflower species, and red and white pine and many species of spruce, balsam, maple, you name it, are having youngsters of their own.

I have no adequate words for this year's abundance, nor could I have any appreciation for what has happened to this little piece of land if I did not have photographs Bernice took before she died. In the midst of abundance, it is difficult to remember the sparse years, just as it is difficult to remember the smashed fingers, dislocated joints, weary muscles, bruises, all the aches and pains, all the heartaches.

But even more difficult is the apportioning of praise for Bernice, Gwen and the children: Sharon, Suzanne, Debbie, Diane and Mary. Even now, the last of the Rebels, Mary, home from the university for the summer, is cutting away new growth instead of planting, so the more tender, shy and fragile flowers may have their day in the sun.

It has been an experience. I am not talented enough to describe it so all might fully understand. But Bruce Hutchison, a Canadian, in his essay, "The Land, Always the Land," came pretty close when he wrote, "Real ownership of land has to be established by man's own labors, by the immersion, almost premature burial, of his body in the earth."

chapter six

IMMORTALITY

For a quarter-century, the burial ground of Little Lakes' wild and not-so-wild ones has remained unmarked except for wild roses, wild geraniums, gone-wild hollyhocks, violets, wild climbing cucumbers, Queen Anne's lace, and chicory. But, at last, on a redwood board, hand-lettered in white acrylic by Suzanne, sometimes known as Rebel No. 2, this:

Home. Home at last.

Rich is this soil in memories, some joyful, some sad, many tragic, but all of consequence. Beside the bones of such dogs as were family are those of uncounted, nameless robins, victims of DDT. Buried here also are ducks who thought they were people, and fierce-eyed hawks who resisted all our efforts to repair their injuries. There are banty roosters and pheasant cocks, and squirrels who thought our house was theirs. There are foxes, mice, raccoons, turtles, opossums, snakes, and even pet fish.

So you know there must have been children, because who except the young are capable of such compassion as insists flowers belong on the grave even of a crayfish? Hundreds of creatures have been buried here. Some were friends for many years, others acquaintances of but hours. Some, most perhaps, were just neighbors minding their own business in homes high in trees, or far below in burrows, or screened by bushes. If they accepted the children's food, water and protection, they paid with songs, paw prints decorating the snow, or perhaps a delicious, thrilling, mysterious sound in the night.

Even as humankind, they are an important part of this place, this country, this world, this universe. Just ask any child. The roll call:

Dogs: Rainey, Bucko, Ace, Captain, Eekim, Sergeant.

Bullfrogs: Boom, Bong.

Mice: Cynthia, Ossie.

Ducks: Aristotle, Goldie, Peg Leg Pete, Greta, Rosy van Etta, Waddle, Silver, Gerty, Daisy, Dinky.

Geese: Duke, Duchess, assorted goslings.

Woodchucks: Pee Wee, Gussie.

Raccoon: Rickey.
Chickens: Poncho, Maude, Mabel, Marge, Millie, Big Red.
Blue jay: Mickey.
Crows: Caw Caw, Blackie.
Pigeons: Jackie, Fireflash, Tattoo, Jet, Apache, Mercury, Dawn, Falling Star.
Seagulls: Swoop, Swirl, Sail, Soar.
Pheasants: Copperking, harem.
Squirrels: Eric, Henry.
Chipmunks: Half-a-Tail, Squeaky.
Guinea pigs: Donnie, Ralphine.
Rabbits: Charcoal, Gram, Scamper, Snowflake, Licorice, Beanie, Boscoe, Skippy.
Hawks: Taalon, Teelon.
Horses: Joker, Tequila, Devil Dancer, Taffy.

Devastating is the priestly admonition that the dog a child petted will not be waiting to wag (when she dies) her way into heaven. Heaven without dogs? Or gerbils? Or sparrows? Or toads? If the gates are closed to the likes of these, then heaven is a hoax.

Immortality is for all. Eternity passes on by those interred to grasses, flowers and fruits, which in turn nourish cottontails and crows, opossums and woodchucks, chickadees and mice, which in turn are eaten by foxes and mink. It goes on and on, to the end of time.

Egotistical people, given to sorting blacks from whites, Lutherans from Catholics, Buddhists from Jews, rich from poor, setting aside burial grounds that segregate, even in death, one human from another, reserve the garbage can for those feathered and furred whom they consider inarticulate.

Of course, they never learned the language of a wagging tail, a plaintive meow, bird songs that celebrate in litanies the wonders of the world. These people are not welcome here. We do not want them walking among such innocents who quarreled and killed only as a necessity to survival. Intent is the essence of innocence.

(P.S. Mortal remains of some of the above-named, because of their size or the circumstances of their death, necessarily rest in other places. They are here but in spirit.)

chapter seven

THE PHANTOM
OF LITTLE LAKES

Since the engine that formerly kicked this old, tattered carcass smoothly along on eight cylinders now chugs like an old one-lunger outboard motor, it has become necessary to find a supplemental source of energy. For several years, it was a gasoline-powered lawn tractor named Jeremiah, and anyone within a quarter-mile, including ducks, woodchucks, foxes, crows and other birds and animals learned to know precisely when I was traveling.

They also learned how long it would take me to get from Point A to Point B, which made it easy for poachers, feathered, furred and almost human, to make an adjustment in their itinerary. Of course, a man riding a vehicle, whether bicycle, car or even a horse or tank, can approach, if not his own kind, then any of the wild ones without taking the precautions necessary to make a similar stalk on foot.

Why? I do not know. But, I have ridden a horse right among Canada geese, and an auto alongside deer, neither of which would have tolerated me on foot at such close quarters. So, the wild ones here at Little Lakes grew so accustomed to the chugging and chattering tractor that they accepted it with as much equanimity as they did the wind, and would move only so far as necessary to be in a lee when the tractor or the wind went by. In many ways, it was a pleasant plus. Except for my therapeutic mile on foot each sunrise, my days were (and are) spent on the tractor and surprisingly, we, the tractor and I, have been accepted by permanent members of the fur and feather fraternity, and tolerated by their migrant cousins.

Still, the tractor, I felt, was sinful in such a silent place. The engine fumes were an insult to every flower. Though powerful, it was a clumsy bull of a vehicle that jangled nerves, jolted joints, strained muscles, and tenderized a bottom sadly lacking in padding. Electricity, of course, was one answer. But golf carts had to be written off for a number of reasons. And every other electrical conveyance, even with modifications, lacked power, stability, maneuverability, something.

Then, while running down still another lead, I came upon a four-speed, six-battery tractor that General Electric took off the market, for whatever reason, about five or six years ago. Though I had misgivings, I wrote a check. Now, I go buzzing around Little Lakes, up and down hills, through brush, marsh and meadow, sounding like an electric razor. Now, if human poachers can no longer be sure in which pond it is safe to wet a line, the biggest bonus is the complete acceptance of the new vehicle by the wild ones. They actually seem to refuse to acknowledge its existence.

For example, a gray fox coming home from a night of hunting continued on a collision course until the new tractor and I were so close I could see the fox's whiskers before it popped off the trail. After we passed, the fox popped back out of the brush to watch as if in disbelief. The cottontails, thick almost as fuzz on a peach, do not zigzag to get out of the way. We, the tractor and I, have to zigzag to keep from hitting them. As we ride the dike of Fish Pond, wild ducks swim over to turn first one bright eye, then the other, on us. Muskrats pause momentarily before resuming feeding, and fish, spooky enough to dive from the shadow of a cruising swallow, fin idly within spitting distance.

It is incredible! Strange dogs on the prowl, charging along the trails, wait until the last moment to veer as if avoiding a stump. The neighbor's cat, which has always been careful to stay a long stone's throw away, sits beside the vehicle to look up and meow. Birds perch on it. Squirrels steal corn from the box mounted behind the seat. Chipmunks, spotting a hawk, dart up into the tractor's frame to safety next to the power unit. And raccoons stop fingering creek shores for crayfish only long enough to sniff a few times before nonchalantly waddling on.

Gradually now, the tractor is beginning to take on the appearance of an old-time peddler's cart. There are hooks for two five-gallon pails in which to carry apples, corn for the ducks, freshly caught fish, cold beer, or whatever. There are hooks for a bow saw, wrenches, pruners, pliers, filet knife and sundry tools. Depending on the project in progress, there may be a caulking gun, power saw, sledge, hacksaw, nails and screws, hammer and screwdriver, and usually binoculars. It is a great convenience, though as I have noted, it is spooky to stop within two feet of a cottontail and have the rabbit keep right on grazing while I say, "Hey, look you. Aren't you afraid of winding up as hasenpfeffer?"

Naturally, I have named my steed. And since it seems I am the only one who admits its existence, what other name than Phantom?

chapter eight

COMING OF AGE

To watch a piece of land, and all the flora and fauna thereon, literally lift from a sea of mud to the threshold of ecological maturity is as rewarding as fathering a passel of human sprouts and sending them off into the world to raise sprouts of their own. It is difficult to convince friends, as they look out over the lush land that is Little Lakes, that little more than a quarter-century ago, it was, simply put, a muddy mess.

But it was. We wallowed in mud. Everything from draglines, backhoes and bulldozers to garden tractors got stuck in the mud. The dry grit of it was between our teeth all summer, and kept boot bottoms slippery all winter. We tracked it into the house. We carried globs of it into the car and down into the office in Milwaukee.

Spoil from the four ponds we were digging sometimes was mounded twenty feet, and even in August — the digging was done in winter — the bulldozer would hit blocks of ice and, with a great sucking and sighing, sink into the ooze. When the digging was done and the spoil distributed as evenly as possible, the greening was so gradual that at first it seemed it would take forever. Then, no matter what we planted, the newly turned soil insisted on following a natural plant progression from bootjack to thistles to quack to box elders and burdock.

Gradually, of course, the pines, cedars, spruce, walnuts, oaks and birch, and ground cover ranging from lichens and creeping vines to Solomon's-seal and shoulder-high ferns, began to change the face of the place. The evolution was slow, but once started, it was steady. Still, unless you were alert, you hardly noticed. Sometimes it was necessary to dig out old photographs to remember that where waters now grow fish and lily pads, where trees wear birds and flowers wear bees, all was nothing but a muddy mess.

But do not take my word for it. Reckon instead on the testimony of the wild ones who, year after year, decided in increasing numbers that Little Lakes was finally becoming a fit place to call home. I thought about it last week while seated on the sun porch watching three wood duck drakes perched in the still-leafless crown of a shagbark hickory less than fifty feet from the window. All three drakes had nesting hens.

Yet, it is less than twenty years ago that the first wood duck couple decided that these acres might be fitting to live on.

Actually, for the record, I was watching a reflection of the three drakes in the glass top of the sunroom table. Not wanting to show a silhouette at the window and take a chance of frightening them, I sat back, and there, bright as could be, the ducks were mirrored by the glass. The drakes, enemies during mating, had decided to tolerate each other now that their hens were safely on eggs. One hen is in a basswood thirty feet from the house. Another is in an oak at the far southern end of the property, and the third is in a man-made house-nest bordering Watercress Creek on the far north end of the place. Since the first wood duck pair nested here, the species nested only at rare intervals in our trees. Now, they do so regularly.

Other wild ones, plant and animal, give testimony to the approaching maturity of a piece of habitat which once, having been pastured, was virtually sterile. In the beginning, after the mud, chickadees sometimes wintered here. Now that the conifers are tall and strong and seeding themselves, at least eight or ten pairs are in residence year round.

Muskrats, of course, came in hordes. Mink denned along pond dikes. Great blue herons and black-crowned night-herons visited sometimes, but now they come regularly before and after the rookery interval. Green herons and bitterns stay and nest. Even crossbills visit since spruce cones now yield a bountiful harvest of seeds. Rose-breasted grosbeaks have decided the acres are woodsy enough to nest in. Doves are everywhere. Tanagers flirt with the idea of homesteading and probably will become regular residents within the next few years.

We have brought thousands upon thousands of plants in from all over the state. Some found the place not to their liking. Others flourished until now it is impossible to catalog them, since just about the time it seems the list is complete, another stranger joins the throng. Now, planting tame flowers seems a little like gilding the lily. We are gradually phasing out formal flowers so that, in a few years, except for the iris, columbine and phlox — maybe twelve or fifteen perennials — only the wild ones will bloom.

This morning, I saw the first clutch of mallard ducklings come up the creek with the hen. Three other mallard hens will likely see youngsters pop from their eggs before the spring is over. In addition to the wood ducks and mallards, there are two teal incubating eggs, and another teal who lost her clutch of eggs to a predator was the object of a fight between drakes on Watercress Creek this morning.

Before summer is over, the gray fox kits will have left the den on the side of the hill to go hunting, and the hawks and owls will have easy pickings, since the cottontail crop is proof positive that rabbits really do make love rapidly. And so it has come to pass that Little Lakes is a thriving wildlife community. And if we feel a little proud sometimes, we keep our fingers crossed, lest wind and water in the robes of a tornado or flood churn our green acres and, once again, we have to start over with a muddy mess.

chapter nine

THE VALUE
OF PROPERTY

I am constantly amazed at the facility exhibited by real estate dealers in pricing big and little pieces of the good earth. They buy and sell by the frontage inch, frontage foot, lot, acre or estate as if they were butchers cutting up a cow and reckoning the going price of steak, prime rib, pot roast, liver and neck bones.

Luckily for the commerce of this country, neither the butcher nor the real estate agent is deterred by the drivel of dreamers. Otherwise, our truly remarkable and efficient marketplace would become hopelessly bogged down in the quicksands of sentimentality. Which explains why some of us are not buyers or sellers. If not always content, at least we have become resigned to going through life with a patch on our pants. In time, some of us even flaunt the patch and, making like modern-day Thoreaus, look down our sunburned noses at the money-makers with an outward gesture of disdain that does not always hide the envy.

But, to get back to the real estate dealers and the good earth, there have been a couple of times during the tenancy of the Ellis clan when it seemed provident to sell. Once we even went so far as to give a real estate agent sixty days to accomplish the transaction. At once, we knew we were in trouble. He swooped across the place as fast as a hunting hawk, which likewise plays percentages because fields have mice, too.

"But this place," we tried to slow him down by stopping to point, "in spring is a purple carpet of violets." Never batting an eye, he swept on with a measuring rule, notebook and pencil. He did not even estimate the worth of all the pond diamonds set to sparkling when a breeze scuffed the water. Nor did he make any note of the value of columbine, fern, day lily, Queen Anne's lace or vetch; flicker, teal, green heron, oriole or cardinal; dogwood, elderberry, blackberry, hawthorn or honeysuckle; spruce, maple, hickory or oak; bluegill, pollywog, bass, mud minnow or sunfish; canary grass, cattail, pencil reed or knotweed.

He measured all the buildings, counted the rooms, noted insulation thickness, appraised heating units. He added the going rate of houses as aged as ours, and the going rate of stable and garage. Then he said, "But being it's a pretty place, I think we can up the price a little."

By then, we had long stopped listening, but when he named a price, we tuned back in to add so many thousands of dollars that he turned pale and killed his car engine three times on the way down the drive. But, despite the outlandish price, a figure we thought would be a certain deterrent, customers came.

Then, when one lady, pointing to a place, said, "This might make a nice garden," we did not tell her it would not grow anything because it was a pet dog burial ground and the earth was too salty from tears. Then, when a man figured he would bulldoze the pasture flat, since it would be an ideal location for a tennis court, we figured if he could not recognize an Indian burial ground, it would not matter anyway if we told him.

Of course, most of the people who came were only curious. But there was one who, with practiced eye, measured how the thousands of man-hours had been meshed with the years nature had put in. He knew better than any real estate agent that earth is no swatch of cloth to be priced by the yard, but a living, growing, changing thing whose price must be gauged like beauty that can be measured only in the eye of the beholder.

This man frightened us as he upped his bid closer and closer to the asking price — so close, in fact, that we invited an accountant out to talk about deducting the cost of white water lily plants from our profit on the place. Then, when he said, "What white water lilies?" we remembered and said, "Oh, yeah, the muskrats ate them."

"But what about the bur reed root purchased at six dollars for thirty-five, the redhead grass roots bought for twenty-seven dollars for three hundred, the wild celery root bought for twenty-four dollars per three hundred, the sago pond tubers for twenty-four dollars for three hundred?" And after each query, he shook his head.

"But surely the thousands upon thousands of trees we planted?"

Again a head shake. "Not unless you're in the tree business."

"But surely the endless hours of toil of two parents and five children. After all..."

"No. No. No."

And so the days of the option to sell dwindled, and on the last day the man who wanted the place named his final figure.

"I can't raise a penny more," he said, and I felt truly sorry for him because he was buying pond diamonds, too, and such things as orioles and kingfishers, and even bur reed and Queen Anne's lace, the kind of trash most people burn. And besides that, he, too, had a patch on his pants.

chapter ten

THE ANNUAL ENIGMA

Why, at my age, am I providing tender, loving care to a three-year-old sapling Gwen planted early in spring to add to the considerable tree colony already at Little Lakes? Certainly, we do not need more trees. And most certainly, I will not live to see them mature, nor is it likely that Gwen will, either.

Yet, in our mind's eye, as we move from sapling to sapling, we have visions of red berries that will hang in clusters on the mountain ash, see the tiny apples that will decorate the hawthorns, and marvel at the candles that in spring will put a pale halo of fire to the pines. Is it because we choose to forget what a time-consuming and laborious job it is to plant, and then, for years, to fight off the rodents and maverick plants that crowd around determined to destroy our colonies?

Do we do it because someday a great-great-great-grandson or daughter will come this way and on a summery day look up and say, "Mel and Gwen planted these trees many, many years ago"? I do not think so. Because, even though both of us are dreamers, we know that Little Lakes is not likely to survive urban sprawl, and that one day the trees will be cut down, and houses will rise to replace them. Neither do I believe that either of us is altruistic enough to take on such muscle-aching, hand-blistering tasks so that we may "make our contribution to this beautiful world."

After a glass of currant wine, we may try telling ourselves, and any willing to listen, that our motives are ennobling. But, being only ordinary people, there is little that is noble about either of us. So why, coming from somewhere deep down within us, is there the need to come to spring with a spade and an infant tree, knowing that for years we must be slaves to its well-being if it is to rise and decorate these acres?

Looking back, it seems it has been as ordinary a part of life as eating, as ordinary as getting up or going to bed. And so, through the years, as I have moved from house to house (before coming to Little Lakes), I have left a trail of trees behind. Some already have been overlaid with concrete. A few still provide oases of green.

Some are sure to say it is the plan of whichever God they declare allegiance to. But the atheist who also plants trees is likely to say that it is a perversion of the survival instinct — trees for beauty and shade instead of maize for each morning's breakfast. Whichever, there seems to be in most of us a drive as primeval and forceful as the one that brought us together as couples to plant the seeds that produced our children.

Whether it is a forest in the sand country or but a window box of geraniums in a ghetto, given the chance most of us will, at some time, be mysteriously impelled to plant a seed or a sapling. Looking back, I have tried to remember a spring when we did not plant something — something, that is, other than a garden when that was a necessary part of providing a living. I cannot think of one. If it was not trees, it was ninebark. If it was not a bush, we added to the daffodil colony. If it was not tame flowers, we ran out ahead of freeway construction, trucking home trilliums, jack-in-the-pulpits, wild geraniums, shooting stars.

There have been water lilies, and then a time to plant duck potato. There has been sago, bur reed, wild celery, sweet flag, wampee (duck corn), elodea, nutgrass. Sometimes, nothing survived. Sometimes, we got a fifteen percent survival. And then, on occasion, a plant grew so profusely it became a pest and we had to eradicate it. Of course, there were bonuses. Songbirds flocked in until the territorial battles were a thing to behold each spring. Ducks wintering over in open spring holes climbed above the fifty mark and then scattered each spring to add to their colonies.

All the time, of course, muskrats seemed intent on destroying everything we planted, and on destroying the ponds, too, by drilling through the dikes. We had to declare war.

But where do we draw the line? On chipmunks and squirrels? On diving ducks who visited to pull water plants out by the roots? Well, mostly, we just waited and hoped there would be enough of everything left for seeding. Mostly, it has worked that way: one for us, fifty for the wild ones, and even something for posterity.

chapter eleven

IF EVER
I WOULD LEAVE ...

Sometimes we can forget, but then, often in the middle of a dark, quiet night, the nagging idea of departure from Little Lakes comes to sit in a grim corner of the mind like a patient vulture. If I send it winging by picking up a book, or rising and going to my writing chair, I know this bird will be back to continue the countdown, heartbeat by heartbeat.

Really, I suppose we should go now. Time has caught up with us, and saw and ax and hoe and rake are already rusting because projects rarely get beyond the planning stage, and the long walks, for the most part, have dwindled until some weeks we only window watch. Of course, we talk about it, about how life would be less complicated in a fully automatic apartment overlooking Lake Michigan. Except we know that while watching a storm building lake waves, we would be wondering if the ancient maple by the road, the great-great-great-grandfather linden on the hill, and the military rigid and creamy-colored poplars along the dike were withstanding the onslaught.

During each downpour, we would worry that the new occupants of Little Lakes may have forgotten to pull some boards from the Clear Pool dam so that the rush of water might stay in the Watercress Creek channel instead of rampaging overland to dig escape routes clear down to the gravel beneath the black loam.

And, are the birds being fed? The muskrats routed from vulnerable pond dikes? The tree-swallow houses in good repair? Blue Pool being flushed regularly to keep surface debris from sinking to decay into odoriferous muck? Are the annual invasions of bush honeysuckle and prickly ash being met and turned back? Has the burdock marched right into the shade and killed the May apple? Are enough dead trees left standing to provide homes for flickers, squirrels, raccoons and wood duck couples?

No, a Milwaukee apartment would never do. We would not resist the temptation to visit, to offer advice. We would be phoning until our calls became a nuisance, even an invasion. We might even so anger the new owners as to cause them to prevent our intrusion with a court order. When you have worked hand in hand with nature for nearly thirty years, a parcel of land becomes as precious as a wife, as much loved as your children. All its blemishes, all its beauty, are as familiar to you as the contours of the old leather chair that has learned to accommodate every bend of your body.

But how far away is far enough? Well, memories are forever, and it is one thing to accommodate to a new mistress, and yet another to forsake a wife who knows what you want even before you do.

"When I grow too old to dream, I'll have you to remember..." are words to a fine old song, even though it is a melody of surrender. Never to dream? Whether eight or eighty, dreaming is the main ingredient of life. Stop dreaming and your last breath will be quick in coming.

There is something about home, especially a home built with enough joy to make the blood, sweat and tears inconsequential. More than the writing of an epic poem or the successful struggle to the top of the financial pyramid, a home, whether built of sod or magnificent marble, is an accomplishment beyond calculating if the hands that cut the sod or shaped the marble belong to you. Then, if the house you built gives you continuing contentment, it is the earth around it that presents the never-ending challenge, a challenge that you can meet only by getting into double harness with nature as your running mate.

Nevertheless, I talk about leaving Little Lakes. Doctors have said I should. Friends hear about such things as falling out of a tree during a heart attack, and being mired in the swamp, and they say the land will kill me if I do not leave. Perhaps. Yet I cannot conceive of a spring during which I cannot walk the trails of Little Lakes anticipating the rebirth of thousands of flowers brought here many years ago. I cannot imagine a summer not being able to enjoy the coolness of the springs that air-condition a certain spruce grove.

I would miss counting the birds and counting the years a certain house sparrow with vivid white markings comes around. I would miss the winter and could not tolerate a land where the sun always shone, or a winter in the city, where the snow turns quickly to sooty slush.

So, even though common sense prompts me to go, I resist. Someday, of course, having no alternative, I will leave. But when that day comes, rest assured, I'll be leaving feet first.

Heaven without animals?
If the gates are closed to such as these, then heaven is a hoax.

AFTERWORD

Few in this mobile age have had the rare privilege of living in one place long enough to lie in the shade looking up through the leaves of a tree they planted as a spindly sapling.

Today, now that we have sprouted wings and wheels, distance does not impede us. Though our ancestors had good reason to climb the mountain to see what was on the other side, we know the pastures are seldom greener than right here at home. Still, amazingly, we move, impelled perhaps by residual curiosity such as goaded our pioneering forebears.

I have been the route, strange places, strange faces, but then I came home. And thirty years spent right here have convinced me that no dollars or offspring, no faraway mountain or valley, can provide as much satisfaction as the sun shining on a clear pool that I have dug where grass once stood ragged guard around a morass.

I know how lucky I am to come down a cool, dim trail through an aisle of high cedar spears and remember when, on hands and knees, we planted six-inch seedlings among white stones, careful not to crush the speckled white eggs of a killdeer couple.

It is wondrous to flick a popper to water and boat a bluegill, knowing it is descended multiple generations from a pair I brought from a nearby lake many, many years ago. It is rewarding, too, sometimes at evening, to survey the many tons of stones that gird the streams and ponds, knowing that each and every single rock was once wet in the handling by a little of our sweat.

And there is the secret: The only way to form a true partnership with nature is if we invest sweat, blisters and aching backs. Then, most stones have felt our touch, and most blooms, seeds and fruits are the harvest of our efforts. So, like a loving mother, we care. And the tears are very personal when the tail end of a tornado uproots trees, and lightning smites a burr oak. And we know the frustration until the fifth planting of tubers finally produces floating green pads to frame the white blooms of the water lily. We worry, too, because the snakes we imported do not show, and because the pollywogs we brought in were eaten by bass.

But no disappointments can permanently tarnish our love affair. We celebrate anniversary after anniversary as acolytes at spring's priestly ritual of re-creation. And we ask forgiveness if we sometimes experience feelings akin to godliness.

Mel Ellis, 1912-1984

If you liked *Notes from Little Lakes*,
you'll want to keep up with new offerings
from The Cabin Bookshelf.

FOR INFORMATION:

WRITE . . . . 1234 Hickory Drive
Waukesha, WI 53186

CALL 414/542-1540

FAX 414/542-1740

TOLL FREE 888/40-CABIN (22246)

E-MAIL . . . . cabinbks@execpc.com

The
Cabin Bookshelf

BOOKS TO READ BY THE FIRE